Navigating Mental Health Complexities in Clinical Practice

12 Weeks of Intense Training for
Mental Health Professionals

Harrison S. Mungal, Ph.D, Psy.D

2 | P a g e

Navigating Mental Health Complexities in **Clinical Practice**

Copyright © 2024 Harrison S. Mungal

Contact author via email: info@harrisonmungal.com

info@agetoage.ca

www.agetoage.ca

www.harrisonmungal.com

www.harrisonmungalbooks.com

Facebook: Harrison Mungal

Twitter: AgeToAgeInc1

LinkedIn: Harrison Mungal, Ph.D., PsyD

YouTube: Harrison Mungal

Phone: 905-533-1334

ABOUT *the*
AUTHOR

Harrison Sharma Mungal, BTh, MCC, MSW, PhD, PsyD

Harrison Sharma Mungal, possessing dual doctoral distinctions in Clinical Psychology and Philosophy in Social Work, demonstrates an unwavering commitment to ameliorating the well-being of his clients. Renowned internationally for his profound insights into cognitive therapy, his expertise spans mental health, addiction, relationships, and family dynamics.

In his role as a highly sought-after workshop presenter, Dr. Mungal extends his practical approach to assisting individuals, couples, families, and corporations. His global influence is evident through engaging presentations at conferences, seminars, and media platforms, where he adeptly integrates humor and enthusiasm into nuanced discussions on mental health, addiction, relationships, and parenting.

Dr. Mungal's innovative and scientifically grounded methodology has garnered acclaim, earning him accolades from diverse institutions. He extends his influence through offering training and consultations to a wide array of community partners, including esteemed professionals in the medical, social work, first responder, law enforcement, and senior management domains.

Actively involved in pioneering cognitive research, Dr. Mungal leads ground-breaking studies addressing mental health challenges such as addiction, psychosis, anxiety, and depression. His work includes the exploration of practical applications, exemplified by initiatives like music therapy for schizophrenia, substance abuse and addictions in the food service industry, and vaccination protocols for young children.

Boasting over two decades of professional acumen, Dr. Mungal has left an indelible mark on the fields of mental health and psychiatry, providing services to diverse communities impacted by brain injuries, refugees, victims of warfare, and individuals in crisis. His pragmatic therapeutic repertoire encompasses evidence-based treatments like Cognitive Behavioural Therapy (CBT), Cognitive Processing Therapy (CPT), Dialectical Behavioural Therapy (DBT), and Acceptance and Commitment Therapy (ACT).

TABLE *Of* CONTENT

INTRODUCTION

Welcome to this comprehensive mental health workbook *"Navigating The Complexities of Mental Health in Clinical Practice!"* Our primary aim is to enhance your understanding of various mental health topics, equipping you with knowledge and skills that are crucial in today's fast-paced world. Mental health is a vital aspect of overall well-being, yet it often remains under-discussed and misunderstood. This workbook is designed to bridge that gap, providing clear, accurate, and useful information about a range of mental health issues.

This workbook is structured into a twelve-week program, each week dedicated to a specific aspect of mental health. Starting with an exploration of mental health versus mental illnesses, we progress through topics such as anxiety, mood disorders, psychosis, personality disorders, and more. Each chapter is crafted to build upon the previous, culminating in a comprehensive understanding of mental health assessment and intervention techniques.

To get the most out of this workbook, we encourage you to actively engage with the material. Read through each section thoughtfully and take time to reflect on the discussion questions and exercises provided. This is not just a reading exercise; it's an interactive tool designed for your active participation. Whether you're a mental health professional, a student, or simply someone interested in understanding more about mental health, this workbook is for you.

It's important to understand what this workbook can and cannot do. While it offers a comprehensive overview of various mental health topics, it is not a substitute for professional medical advice, diagnosis, or treatment. If you're dealing with a serious mental health issue, or if you're in crisis, it's crucial to seek help from qualified mental health professionals. This workbook is designed to enhance your knowledge and understanding, which can be especially beneficial for those in the mental health field, Social Workers, Psychotherapists, Therapists, Counsellors,

Spiritual Leaders, Care Givers, Mental Health Professionals, Students, or anyone interested in the topic. However, it's not intended to be a standalone tool for diagnosing or treating mental health conditions.

We encourage you to approach this workbook with an open mind and a willingness to explore not only the material but also your own reactions and thoughts about the topics covered. Mental health is a deeply personal subject, and you may find that some sections resonate more strongly with you than others. Use these moments as opportunities for self-reflection and growth. Remember, learning about mental health is not just an academic exercise; it's a journey towards greater self-awareness and understanding, both of which are essential for personal well-being and effective interaction with others. Be patient with yourself and remember that understanding and managing mental health is a lifelong process.

Week 1

MENTAL HEALTH

and MENTAL ILLNESSES

Mental health, fundamentally, encompasses our emotional, psychological, and social well-being. It significantly influences how we think, feel, and act, especially in handling stress, making choices, and interacting with others. According to the Public Health Agency of Canada (2016), mental health is not merely the absence of mental illness but a state of overall well-being.

Firstly, it's crucial to understand that mental health is a vital part of our lives. It affects our thoughts, emotions, and behaviours, and it also plays a significant role in our relationships with others. Mental health is essential at every stage of life, from childhood and adolescence through adulthood.

Moreover, mental health is deeply intertwined with physical health. The World Health Organization (2018) emphasizes that there is no health without mental health, highlighting its importance in overall well-being and quality of life. Mental health disorders can significantly impact physical health, leading to increased risk of chronic physical conditions.

Several factors contribute to mental health. These include biological factors, such as genes or brain chemistry, life experiences like trauma or abuse, and family history of mental health problems. Mental health is also influenced by lifestyle choices, social connections, and environmental factors.

It's important to note that mental health is a dynamic and fluid state. It can change over time and across circumstances. For example, someone may experience good mental health generally but face mental health challenges during periods of intense stress or change.

Good mental health is characterized by a person's ability to fulfill several key functions and activities. These include the ability to learn, the ability to feel, express and manage a range of positive and negative emotions, and the ability to form and maintain good relationships with others.

Additionally, maintaining good mental health involves achieving a balance in all aspects of life: social, physical, spiritual, economic, and mental. This balance is different for each person and can change over time and in different situations.

Resilience plays a critical role in mental health. It refers to the ability to cope with adversity and bounce back from difficulties. Resilient individuals can deal with stress and function well even in the face of challenges, trauma, or tragedy.

It's important to address common misconceptions about mental health. For instance, having a mental health issue doesn't mean a person is weak or flawed. Mental health challenges can affect anyone, regardless of age, gender, social status, or ethnicity.

The stigma associated with mental health problems can be a significant barrier to seeking help. It's crucial to promote an understanding that mental health issues are common and treatable. Societal acceptance and support can make a substantial difference in the lives of people dealing with mental health challenges.

Early intervention is key in managing mental health issues. Recognizing early signs and seeking professional help can significantly improve outcomes. Mental health issues, like physical health issues, can be managed or treated.

Mental health awareness and education are vital. Public health initiatives and education can play a significant role in demystifying mental health issues and promoting mental wellness.

Support systems, including family, friends, and community resources, are crucial for maintaining mental health. Social support can provide emotional support, practical help, and a sense of belonging, which are all beneficial for mental well-being.

Lifestyle choices also impact mental health. Activities such as regular physical exercise, healthy eating, getting enough sleep, and managing stress can significantly contribute to mental well-being.

It's also important to understand the role of mental health professionals. Psychiatrists, psychologists, therapists, and counsellors can provide valuable support and treatment for mental health issues.

Mental health is a crucial aspect of overall well-being. It encompasses our emotional, psychological, and social functioning and affects how we handle stress, relate to others, and make choices. Understanding mental health, acknowledging its importance, and promoting mental well-being are essential steps in achieving a healthier, more balanced life.

Mental illnesses on the other hand are commonly misunderstood and stigmatized, yet they are widespread and can affect anyone. They are significant health conditions involving changes in emotion, thinking, or behaviour, or a combination of these. Mental illnesses are associated with distress and/or problems functioning in social, work, or family activities.

Mental illness can be more accurately understood as a spectrum, ranging from mild to severe conditions, and can vary in duration, from transient to long-lasting. It's essential to recognize that mental illness is not a result of personal weakness, lack of character, or poor upbringing.

The prevalence of mental illness is significant. According to the Canadian Mental Health Association (2021), in any given year, 1 in 5 Canadians experiences a mental illness or addiction problem. This statistic demonstrates the widespread impact of these conditions.

There are various types of mental illnesses, each with its unique symptoms and impacts on an individual's life. These include mood disorders, anxiety disorders, psychosis/schizophrenia, eating disorders, personality disorders and addictive behaviours.

Mood disorders, such as depression and bipolar disorder, primarily affect a person's emotional state. They are characterized by persistent feelings of sadness or periods of feeling overly happy, or fluctuations from extreme happiness to extreme sadness.

Anxiety disorders, the most common form of mental illness, involve more than temporary worry or fear. For a person with an anxiety disorder, the anxiety does not go away and can get worse over time. Symptoms can interfere with daily activities such as job performance, schoolwork, and relationships.

Psychosis/Schizophrenia is a severe mental health disorder characterized by distortions in thinking, perception, emotions, language, sense of self, and behaviour. Common experiences include hallucinations (hearing voices or seeing things that are not there), delusions (fixed, false beliefs) and paranoias.

Eating disorders, including anorexia nervosa, bulimia nervosa, and binge-eating disorder, involve preoccupation with food, body weight, and shape. They can have serious physical and emotional consequences.

Addictive behaviours involve engagement in rewarding stimuli, despite adverse consequences. These behaviours can include the use of substances like alcohol, nicotine, illicit drugs, prescription medications, gambling, as well as activities like gaming, pornography, eating and shopping.

The causes of mental illnesses are varied and complex. They can include genetic factors, biochemical imbalances, environmental stresses, psychosocial stressors or a combination of these. For instance, certain mental illnesses, such as schizophrenia, have a strong genetic component.

Trauma, abuse, dysfunctional upbringing, and stressful life events, such as the death of a loved one, divorce, or neglect, can also contribute to the onset of mental illnesses. Chronic stress, especially when not managed well, can lead to conditions like depression and anxiety disorders.

The treatment of mental illness varies depending on the type and severity of the condition. It often includes a combination of medication, psychotherapy and psychological treatment. Medications can help manage symptoms, while psychotherapy (or "talk therapy") helps individuals understand their illness and cope with everyday challenges.

Early diagnosis and treatment are critical for effectively managing mental illness. Unfortunately, stigma and lack of understanding often lead to significant delays in seeking treatment.

Mental health professionals, including psychiatrists, psychologists, social workers, therapists and counsellors, play a vital role in diagnosing and treating mental illnesses. They use a variety of tools and techniques to help individuals manage their conditions.

It's important to note that recovery from mental illness is possible. With appropriate treatment, many individuals with mental illness achieve significant improvement in their symptoms and quality of life.

Promoting mental health awareness and understanding mental illness is crucial in reducing stigma. Education and open conversations about mental health can lead to greater acceptance and empathy for those affected by mental illnesses.

The diagnostic process for mental health conditions involves a comprehensive assessment by a qualified mental health professional. This process typically includes a detailed interview, a review of the patient's/client's medical, psychiatric, and social history, and may also involve physical examinations and lab tests.

Diagnosis is often made based on the criteria outlined in the Diagnostic and Statistical Manual of Mental Disorders (DSM), published by the American Psychiatric Association. This manual provides standardized criteria to help professionals diagnose mental health conditions. Psychological testing also assist with formal diagnoses.

It's crucial to approach diagnosis with cultural sensitivity and awareness, as cultural factors can influence how symptoms are experienced and expressed. Mental health professionals are trained to consider these factors when diagnosing and treating patients/clients.

A proper diagnosis often requires time and may involve multiple sessions. It's an evolving process that may change as more information becomes available or as the patient's/client's symptoms change over time.

Co-morbidity, the presence of more than one disorder in the same person, is common in mental health. This complexity can make the diagnostic process more challenging and requires a comprehensive approach.

Mood Disorders (e.g., Depression, Bipolar Disorder)

1. **Depression**: Diagnosing depression involves identifying key symptoms such as persistent sadness, loss of interest in enjoyable activities, changes in weight or appetite, sleep disturbances, fatigue, feelings of worthlessness, and recurrent thoughts of death or suicide. The DSM-5 provides specific criteria, including the duration and severity of symptoms.

2. **Bipolar Disorder**: This disorder is characterized by episodes of mood elevation (mania or hypomania) and depression. Diagnosis involves identifying these episodes and differentiating them from other mood disorders. A thorough patient/client history and sometimes input from family members are crucial in diagnosing bipolar disorder.

Addictive Behaviours and Substance Use Disorders

Diagnosis of substance use disorders involves assessing the pattern of substance use and its impact on functioning. Criteria include increased tolerance, withdrawal symptoms, unsuccessful efforts to cut down use, and significant time spent obtaining or using the substance. The DSM-5 provides a detailed framework for diagnosing these disorders.

Obsessive-Compulsive Disorder (OCD)

OCD is diagnosed based on the presence of obsessions (repeated, persistent, and unwanted thoughts) and compulsions (repetitive behaviours or mental acts that an individual feels compelled to perform). The DSM-5 outlines specific criteria, including the impact of these symptoms on daily functioning and their duration.

Phobias and Panic Attacks

1. **Phobias**: Diagnosing a phobia involves identifying an excessive and persistent fear of a specific object, situation, or activity. This fear typically leads to avoidance behaviour and causes significant distress or impairment in social, occupational, or other important areas of functioning.

2. **Panic Attacks**: Diagnosis includes identifying recurrent, unexpected panic attacks and persistent concern or behaviour changes related to the attacks. Panic attacks are characterized by an intense period of fear or discomfort, accompanied by physical symptoms such as heart palpitations, sweating, trembling, shortness of breath, or dizziness.

The diagnostic process is a critical step in the management of mental health conditions. Accurate diagnosis is key to developing an effective treatment plan, which may include medication, psychotherapy, lifestyle changes, better eating habits, exercising, hobbies or a combination of these approaches. It's important for patients/clients to work closely with their healthcare providers throughout this process.

Anxiety disorders are characterized by excessive fear or anxiety that is difficult to control and causes significant distress or impairment. This type of mental health condition is more than just temporary worry or fear; if the anxiety does not go away and may even worsen over time. People with anxiety disorders may avoid certain situations out of worry. They may also have physiological or physical symptoms like heart palpitations, sweating, trembling, or dizziness. The impact of anxiety disorders on a daily life can be profound, affecting work, school, and personal relationships.

Depression is a common but serious mood disorder that negatively affects how a person feels, thinks, and handles daily activities. Symptoms of depression can include a persistent feeling of sadness, loss of interest or pleasure in activities, changes in appetite or weight, sleep disturbances, loss of energy, feelings of worthlessness or excessive guilt, difficulty thinking or concentrating, and recurrent thoughts of death or suicide. The effects of depression can be debilitating, impacting all areas of a person's life, from their personal and social relationships to their performance at work or school.

Psychosis is a mental health condition characterized by a disconnect from reality. Symptoms can include delusions — false beliefs that are not based in reality, such as paranoia — and hallucinations, which involve seeing or hearing things that do not exist. Psychosis can also include disorganized thinking, exhibited through speech that makes little sense, and extremely disorganized or abnormal motor behaviour, including catatonia. The impact of psychosis can be severe, significantly affecting an individual's ability to function in daily life and maintain reality-based perceptions and interactions.

Personality disorders are characterized by enduring patterns of behaviour, cognition, and inner experience that deviate markedly from the expectations of the individual's culture. These patterns are inflexible and pervasive across a broad range of personal and social situations, leading to significant distress or impairment in social, occupational, or other important areas of functioning.

Types of personality disorders include, borderline personality disorder, characterized by instability in interpersonal relationships, self-image, and emotions; antisocial personality disorder, marked by a lack of regard for the moral or legal standards in the local culture; and narcissistic personality disorder, characterized by a pattern of grandiosity, need for admiration, and a lack of empathy.

Diagnosing personality disorders can be challenging. Symptoms often overlap with other mental health disorders, and there is a high degree of variability in how these disorders present themselves. Moreover, there are common misconceptions about personality disorders, often perpetuated by stereotypes and stigma. For instance, not all individuals with antisocial personality disorder are violent, as commonly portrayed in media. Understanding these disorders requires a nuanced approach that considers the individual's life history, personality traits, and the impact of their behaviour on their functioning and relationships.

Anxiety, depression, psychosis, and personality disorders are key mental health conditions, each with distinct characteristics and impacts on individuals' lives. Understanding these conditions is crucial for effective diagnosis, treatment, and support, as well as for reducing stigma and misconceptions associated with mental health challenges.

Diagnosis vs. Behaviour

Understanding the difference between clinical diagnoses and behavioural symptoms is fundamental in mental health. A clinical diagnosis is a formal identification of a disorder, condition, or disease based on established criteria and often involves a thorough assessment, including a medical examination, psychological evaluation, and consideration of a person's history. Behavioural symptoms, on the other hand, are observable actions or reactions of an individual, which may or may not indicate an underlying disorder.

Context plays a crucial role in behavioural assessment. The same behaviour may be interpreted differently depending on factors like the individual's age, cultural background, and the situation in which the behaviour occurs. For example, a child's temper tantrum could be a normal part of development, a reaction to stress, or a sign of a behavioural disorder, depending on various factors.

Recognizing this distinction is key to avoiding misdiagnosis and ensuring that individuals receive appropriate care. It also helps in understanding that behaviour is a complex interplay of many factors, and not all behaviours, even if they seem unusual or problematic, are indicative of a mental health disorder.

Mental Illness vs. Organic Issues

Distinguishing between mental illness and organic brain conditions is important in the field of mental health. Mental illnesses are typically considered to be primarily the result of psychological, social, and environmental factors, although they can also have a biological basis. Organic brain conditions, on the other hand are caused by physical changes in the brain structure or function, often due to diseases or injuries.

Conditions like delirium, dementia, Alzheimer's disease, and amnesia are examples of organic brain conditions. Delirium is characterized by a sudden change in attention and cognition, often due to an underlying medical condition. Dementia encompasses a range of symptoms associated with a decline in memory and other thinking skills severe enough to reduce a person's ability to perform everyday activities, with Alzheimer's disease being the most common cause of dementia. Amnesia refers to the loss of memories, such as facts, information, and experiences.

While there is some overlap in symptoms between mental illnesses and organic brain conditions, the approach to diagnosis and treatment often differs. Organic brain conditions often require medical interventions and management of the underlying physical health condition, whereas mental illnesses typically respond to a combination of psychotherapy, lifestyle changes, and medication.

The impact of organic brain conditions on mental health can be profound. These conditions not only affect cognitive functions but can also lead to changes in personality, emotional well-being, and behaviour. Understanding and managing these changes is a critical part of treatment and care for individuals with these conditions.

Mental Illness and Pervasive Developmental Disorders (PDD)

Differentiating between mental illness and Pervasive Developmental Disorders (PDD) is essential in the realm of mental health. While both can affect psychological functioning, they are distinct in their origins, characteristics, and treatment approaches. Mental illnesses encompass a wide range of mental health conditions that affect mood, thinking, and behaviour, such as depression, anxiety disorders, and schizophrenia. Pervasive Developmental Disorders, on the other hand, are a group of conditions characterized by delays in the development of socialization and communication skills.

Understanding Autism Spectrum Disorder (ASD), Asperger's Syndrome, and Childhood Disintegrative Disorder is crucial within this context. Autism Spectrum Disorder is a developmental disorder that affects communication and behaviour, and its symptoms can range from mild to severe. Asperger's Syndrome, once considered a separate condition, is now part of the broader autism spectrum. Individuals with Asperger's typically exhibit difficulties in social interaction and nonverbal communication, along with repetitive behaviours and highly focused interests. Childhood Disintegrative Disorder is a rare condition characterized by late onset (usually after at least 2 years of normal development) of developmental delays in language, social function, and motor skills.

The unique challenges and characteristics of PDDs include difficulties in social interaction, communication, and repetitive behaviours. Unlike some mental illnesses, PDDs typically become evident during early childhood and continue throughout life. The severity and combination of symptoms can vary greatly among individuals, making personalized care and intervention essential.

While there is no cure for PDDs, early intervention and therapies can improve function and reduce symptoms. Interventions may include behavioural therapy, speech therapy, occupational therapy, and specialized educational programs. The focus is often on improving social skills, communication, and behaviour management.

Moreover, it's important to recognize that individuals with PDD often have co-occurring mental health conditions such as anxiety or depression. Addressing these co-occurring conditions is critical for improving overall well-being and quality of life.

Understanding the differences and intersections between mental illness and Pervasive Developmental Disorders is vital for accurate diagnosis, intervention, and support. It also underscores the importance of a nuanced approach to mental health that accommodates the diverse needs of individuals with these conditions.

Professional Perspectives on Mental Health and Illness

Healthcare professionals play a critical role in the diagnosis, treatment, and management of mental health and illnesses. It is essential for them to have a comprehensive understanding of the various mental health conditions, their symptoms, and the best practices in treatment and care. This knowledge allows for accurate diagnosis and effective intervention, which are crucial in managing mental health issues.

Professionals need to be aware of the latest research and developments in the field of mental health. Staying informed about new treatments, therapies, and diagnostic tools ensures that patients/clients receive the most current and effective care. Understanding the biological, psychological, and social aspects of mental health is also key, as this holistic view can inform more effective treatment strategies.

The importance of a multidisciplinary approach cannot be overstated. Mental health care often requires the collaboration of various professionals, including psychiatrists, psychologists, psychotherapists, social workers, and nurses. Each professional brings a unique set of skills and perspectives to the treatment plan, enhancing the quality of care. This collaborative approach ensures that all aspects of a patient's/client's health, including physical and mental well-being, are addressed.

Ethical considerations are paramount in the field of mental health. This includes respecting patient/client confidentiality, obtaining informed consent, and practicing non-discrimination. Healthcare professionals must be committed to ethical principles and ensure that their practices align with these values.

Patient/client-centered care is another critical aspect. This approach involves respecting patients'/clients' values, preferences, and needs, and involving them in decision-making about their treatment. It's about treating the person, not just the illness, and requires a compassionate and empathetic approach to care.

Conclusion

This chapter has provided an in-depth overview of mental health versus mental illnesses, covering various aspects from general principles of mental health and illnesses, diagnostic processes, and key mental health conditions, to the differentiation between mental illness and organic issues, as well as pervasive developmental disorders. It has also touched on the professional perspectives necessary in the field of mental health, emphasizing the importance of a multidisciplinary approach, ethical considerations, and patient/client-centered care.

The key takeaways from this chapter include the understanding that mental health is a complex and multifaceted aspect of human life, involving emotional, psychological, and social well-being. Mental illnesses, while challenging, are treatable conditions that require a compassionate, informed approach. The importance of early diagnosis, the role of a supportive environment, and the need for a comprehensive, multidisciplinary treatment approach are also crucial elements.

As we prepare for the next steps in this training, it's important to build upon the foundational knowledge provided in this chapter. The upcoming weeks will delve deeper into specific aspects of mental health and treatment strategies, equipping participants with the skills and understanding necessary to effectively manage and support mental health, both for themselves and others.

Week 1

The Workbook

Week One

MENTAL HEALTH

and MENTAL ILLNESSES

Welcome to Week One of our comprehensive program focusing on the intricate landscape of mental health and mental illnesses. This week is designed to provide a foundational understanding of these crucial concepts, crucial for any mental health professional. We will explore the distinctions and intersections between mental well-being and various mental disorders, a fundamental aspect of effective mental healthcare.

Our journey begins with mental health, acknowledging its multifaceted nature and impact on overall well-being. We then delve into the realm of mental illnesses, aiming to demystify and understand their complexities. This week's focus covers a range of topics, including the nuances of mood disorders, addictions, OCD, phobias, and panic attacks, providing an in-depth view of their diagnostic criteria and manifestations.

Additionally, we examined the often-challenging task of differentiating between mental health disorders and behaviours, as well as distinguishing psychiatric conditions from organic mental disorders and pervasive developmental disorders (PDD). In this workbook, each day is structured to enhance your understanding through reflective exercises and guided activities, encouraging a deep and practical engagement with the material.

This week is not just about gaining knowledge; it's about refining your skills and perspective as a mental health professional. Through thoughtful reflection and engaging activities, you will enhance your diagnostic acumen, deepen your empathetic understanding, and sharpen your ability to respond effectively to the diverse needs of those you serve.

Prepare to immerse yourself in a week of learning that promises to be both enlightening and transformative, setting the stage for advanced professional development in the field of mental health.

Day 1: What is Mental Health?

1. Reflective Exercise 1: Describe your understanding of mental health and how it's evolved over your career.

_____

_____

_____

_____

_____

2. Reflective Exercise 2: Recall a positive example of mental health in your professional experience and analyze the contributing factors.

_____

_____

_____

_____

_____

3. Guided Activity: Identify and discuss three strategies that can promote good mental health in the workplace.

_____

_____

_____

_____

_____

_____

Day 2: What are Mental Illnesses?

1. Reflective Exercise 1: Reflect on how mental illness is portrayed in media versus your real-life professional experiences.

_____

_____

_____

_____

_____

_____

2. Reflective Exercise 2: Consider a difficult case involving mental illness. What were the key challenges and learnings?

_____

_____

_____

_____

_____

_____

3. Guided Activity: Research and summarize the current criteria for diagnosing a common mental illness in your practice.

_____

_____

_____

_____

_____

_____

Day 3: Diagnoses of Mood, Addictions, OCD, Phobias, and Panic Attacks

1. Reflective Exercise 1: Reflect on a patient/client or case study that challenged your understanding of these conditions.

_____

_____

_____

_____

_____

2. Reflective Exercise 2: Discuss the complexities involved in diagnosing these conditions.

_____

_____

_____

_____

_____

3. Guided Activity: Create a diagram showing the overlap and differences in symptoms of these disorders.

_____

_____

_____

_____

_____

_____

Day 4: Overview of Anxiety, Depression, Psychosis

1. Reflective Exercise 1: Reflect on a challenging case involving anxiety, depression, or psychosis.

_____

_____

_____

_____

_____

2. Reflective Exercise 2: Analyze the effectiveness of different treatment approaches for these conditions based on your experience.

_____

_____

_____

_____

_____

3. Guided Activity: Develop a case study or role-play scenario involving a patient/client with one of these conditions.

_____

_____

_____

_____

_____

_____

Day 5: Personality Disorders

1. Reflective Exercise 1: Consider your experiences with patients/clients with personality disorders and the impact on treatment plans.

_____

_____

_____

_____

_____

_____

2. Reflective Exercise 2: Reflect on the challenges in managing long-term care for personality disorders.

_____

_____

_____

_____

_____

_____

3. Guided Activity: Write a brief guide on strategies for effectively communicating with patients/clients with personality disorders.

_____

_____

_____

_____

_____

_____

Day 6: Differentiating Diagnosis from Behaviour

1. Reflective Exercise 1: Recall an instance where behaviour was misconstrued as a symptom of mental illness.

_____

_____

_____

_____

_____

_____

2. Reflective Exercise 2: Discuss the importance of context in understanding patient/client behaviours.

_____

_____

_____

_____

_____

3. Guided Activity: Analyze a hypothetical case to differentiate between behavioural issues and mental health symptoms.

_____

_____

_____

_____

_____

_____

Day 7: Mental Illness vs Organic Issues & PDD

1. Reflective Exercise 1: Reflect on the diagnostic challenges of differentiating mental illness from conditions like dementia or PDD.

_____

_____

_____

_____

_____

2. Reflective Exercise 2: Consider the consequences of misdiagnosis in cases involving organic brain disorders.

_____

_____

_____

_____

_____

3. Guided Activity: Create a decision-making flowchart to aid in differentiating between mental illnesses, organic issues, and PDD.

_____

Week 2

ANXIETY

Anxiety, a prevalent mental health concern, affects a significant portion of the population worldwide. In Canada, anxiety disorders are among the most common mental health issues, impacting individuals across various ages and backgrounds. Anxiety, by definition, is a natural human response to stress. It's characterized by feelings of fear, apprehension, and nervousness. While normal anxiety is a typical reaction to stressors, it becomes a disorder when it is excessive, persistent, and interferes with daily functioning.

The essence of anxiety lies in its role as a survival mechanism. Historically, anxiety has served as an adaptive response to threats, preparing individuals to face or flee danger. However, in modern contexts, this response can become maladaptive when triggered inappropriately. Anxiety disorders encompass a range of conditions, each with unique features, yet all share the core characteristic of excessive, irrational fear or worry.

It's crucial to distinguish between everyday anxiety and an anxiety disorder. Normal anxiety is temporary and linked to specific situations, whereas an anxiety disorder persists, often without a clear or proportional trigger. The impact of anxiety disorders on an individual's life can be profound, affecting personal, social, and professional domains. People with anxiety disorders often experience a reduced quality of life and may struggle with daily tasks, relationships, and work responsibilities.

The prevalence of anxiety disorders varies, but they are widely recognized as a significant public health issue. According to a study, anxiety disorders affect approximately 10% of the population globally, indicating their widespread impact (Bandelow & Michaelis, 2015). In Canada, anxiety disorders are reported to be the most common mental health disorder, affecting a significant portion of the population (Remes et al., 2016).

Anxiety disorders are categorized into several types, including Generalized Anxiety Disorder (GAD), Panic Disorder, Social Anxiety Disorder, and specific phobias, among others. Each type has distinct characteristics but shares the commonality of excessive and persistent anxiety and fear. Generalized Anxiety Disorder, for instance, is characterized by chronic, exaggerated worry about everyday life, often to the point where it is disproportionate to the actual source of worry.

Understanding the etiology of anxiety disorders is complex, as they arise from a combination of genetic, environmental, psychological, and developmental factors. Genetics play a role, with studies indicating a hereditary component to anxiety disorders. Environmental factors, such as stressful life events, trauma, and early childhood experiences, also significantly contribute to the development of these conditions.

The brain's chemistry and functioning are integral to understanding anxiety disorders. Neurotransmitters, chemical messengers in the brain, are involved in the regulation of mood and anxiety. Imbalances or dysfunctions in neurotransmitter systems, such as serotonin, dopamine, and norepinephrine, are associated with anxiety disorders (Bandelow & Michaelis, 2015).

Treatment for anxiety disorders is multifaceted and often includes a combination of psychotherapy, medication, and lifestyle modifications. Thought Developmental Practice (TDP) by Harrison Mungal, PhD, PsyD and other evidence-based therapies are a widely used and effective treatment approach. It focuses on identifying and challenging negative thought patterns and behaviours associated with anxiety. Medications, such as antianxiety, antidepressants and anxiolytics, can also be beneficial in managing symptoms. Medications, including selective serotonin reuptake inhibitors (SSRIs) and serotonin-norepinephrine reuptake inhibitors (SNRIs), are also commonly used to manage symptoms.

In addition to professional treatment, self-help strategies play a crucial role in managing anxiety. These include stress management techniques, regular exercise, the development of the frontal lobe, adequate sleep, and a healthy diet. Mindfulness and relaxation techniques, such as meditation and deep breathing exercises, have also been shown to be effective in reducing anxiety symptoms.

Public awareness and understanding of anxiety disorders are essential for promoting early identification and intervention. Reducing stigma and increasing knowledge about these conditions can encourage individuals to seek help and support. Healthcare professionals play a critical role in diagnosing and treating anxiety disorders. Their understanding of the complexity and impact of these disorders is crucial in providing effective care.

Anxiety disorders represent a significant mental health concern with a substantial impact on individuals and society. Understanding the nature, causes, and treatments of anxiety is vital for effective management and support of those affected. Ongoing research and public education are essential in advancing our understanding and approach to these complex conditions.

Major Anxiety Disorders (MAD)

Major Anxiety Disorders (MAD) represent a group of mental health conditions characterized by significant anxiety and fear that are persistent and often debilitating. These disorders go beyond the normal anxiety experienced in daily life, leading to substantial distress and impairment in social, occupational, or other important areas of functioning. Understanding MAD is crucial for effective diagnosis and treatment.

MAD encompasses several specific disorders, each defined by unique symptoms and patterns of anxiety. These include Generalized Anxiety Disorder (GAD), Panic Disorder, Social Anxiety Disorder (Social Phobia), Specific Phobias, and Agoraphobia. Each of these disorders shares the commonality of excessive fear and anxiety but differs in triggers and manifestations.

Generalized Anxiety Disorder is marked by chronic, excessive worry about a variety of topics, events, or activities. This worry is difficult to control and often disproportionate to the actual likelihood or impact of the feared event. Individuals with GAD may experience restlessness, fatigue, difficulty concentrating, irritability, muscle tension, and sleep disturbances.

Panic Disorder is characterized by recurrent, unexpected panic attacks – sudden periods of intense fear or discomfort that peak within minutes. Symptoms during a panic attack can include heart palpitations, sweating, trembling, shortness of breath, feelings of impending doom, and fear of losing control. Panic Disorder may also involve ongoing worry about having additional attacks and avoiding situations where attacks have occurred.

Social Anxiety Disorder involves a significant fear of social or performance situations in which embarrassment or negative evaluation by others may occur. This fear can lead to avoidance of such situations or enduring them with intense anxiety. The disorder can severely impact an individual's ability to engage in social, academic, or occupational activities.

Specific Phobias are characterized by marked fear or anxiety about a specific object or situation (e.g., flying, heights, animals, receiving an injection). The phobic object or situation almost always provokes immediate fear or anxiety and is actively avoided or endured with intense fear or anxiety. This fear or anxiety is out of proportion to the actual danger posed.

Agoraphobia involves intense fear or anxiety about two or more of the following situations: using public transportation, being in open spaces, being in enclosed places, standing in line or being in a crowd, or being outside of the home alone. Individuals with Agoraphobia fear these situations due to thoughts that escape might be difficult or help might not be available in the event of developing panic-like symptoms or other incapacitating or embarrassing symptoms.

The classification of MAD in the DSM-V is based on specific criteria that outline the nature, duration, and severity of symptoms for each disorder. These criteria are designed to help mental health professionals accurately diagnose and treat these disorders. It's important for clinicians to carefully assess symptoms and their impact on an individual's functioning to differentiate between normal anxiety and a diagnosable anxiety disorder.

DSM-V Criteria for Major Anxiety Disorders

The Diagnostic and Statistical Manual of Mental Disorders, Fifth Edition (DSM-V), is a critical tool used by mental health professionals for the diagnosis of mental health conditions, including Major Anxiety Disorders (MAD). The DSM-V provides standardized criteria to ensure consistency and accuracy in diagnosis, which is vital for effective treatment and understanding of these disorders.

For each type of MAD, the DSM-V outlines specific diagnostic criteria. These criteria include the nature, duration, and severity of symptoms, as well as the impact on the individual's daily functioning. The manual also includes differential diagnoses to distinguish these disorders from other mental health conditions with similar symptoms.

Generalized Anxiety Disorder (GAD) in the DSM-V is characterized by persistent and excessive worry about various activities or events. The individual finds it difficult to control the worry, which is associated with three or more of the following symptoms: restlessness, being easily fatigued, difficulty concentrating, irritability, muscle tension, and sleep disturbance. These symptoms must be present for more days than not over at least six months.

Panic Disorder is defined by recurrent unexpected panic attacks. A panic attack is an abrupt surge of intense fear or intense discomfort that reaches a peak within minutes. During this time, four or more symptoms (such as heart palpitations, sweating, trembling, sensations of shortness of breath, feelings of choking, chest pain, nausea, dizziness, chills or heat sensations, numbness or tingling sensations, derealization or depersonalization, fear of losing control, and fear of dying) must occur.

Social Anxiety Disorder (Social Phobia) is characterized by significant anxiety and discomfort about being embarrassed, humiliated, rejected, or looked down on in social interactions. This leads to avoidance of social situations or enduring them with intense fear or anxiety. The fear or anxiety is out of proportion to the actual threat posed by the social situation.

Specific Phobias involve marked fear or anxiety about a specific object or situation. The phobic object or situation almost always provokes immediate fear or anxiety and is actively avoided or endured with intense fear or anxiety. The fear or anxiety is disproportionate to the actual danger posed by the specific object or situation and is persistent, typically lasting for six months or more.

Agoraphobia involves marked fear or anxiety about two or more of the following five situations: using public transportation, being in open spaces, being in enclosed places, standing in line or being in a crowd, or being outside of the home alone. The individual fears or avoids these situations due to thoughts that escape might be difficult or help might not be available in the event of developing panic-like symptoms or other incapacitating or embarrassing symptoms.

The diagnostic process as outlined in the DSM-V is significant as it guides clinicians in identifying the specific type of anxiety disorder, which is crucial for selecting the most effective treatment approach. Accurate diagnosis also helps in understanding the prognosis and informing the patient/client about their condition.

Signs and Symptoms of Anxiety

The signs and symptoms of anxiety disorders can be physical, emotional, and behavioural, and they can vary significantly among individuals. Recognizing these symptoms is key to seeking timely and effective treatment.

Physical symptoms of anxiety as mentioned before can often include increased heart rate, rapid breathing, restlessness, or feeling tense. Some individuals might experience sweating, trembling, gastrointestinal issues, or fatigue. These physical manifestations are often the body's response to perceived stress or danger, part of the 'fight or flight' response.

Emotional symptoms include feelings of apprehension or dread, trouble concentrating, feeling tense or jumpy, anticipating the worst, and restlessness. Anxiety can also lead to feelings of irritability and a sense of impending doom or danger.

Behavioural symptoms can include avoidance of feared situations, excessive checking or reassurance seeking, and changes in normal routine due to anxiety. People with anxiety disorders may also demonstrate nervous behaviours, such as pacing, nail-biting, or increased need for reassurance from others.

These symptoms manifest in daily life in various ways, such as impacting social interactions, work performance, or daily routines. For instance, someone with social anxiety might avoid social gatherings or public speaking engagements, while a person with panic disorder might avoid places where they previously experienced a panic attack (Craske et al., 2017).

The signs and symptoms of anxiety disorders are multifaceted and can significantly impact an individual's life. Understanding these symptoms, guided by the DSM-V criteria, is essential for recognizing anxiety disorders and seeking appropriate help and treatment.

Differentiating Behaviour from Illness

Distinguishing between normal anxious behaviours and an anxiety disorder is a critical aspect of mental health assessment. Anxious behaviours are common and often a normal part of life, but when these behaviours become excessive, persistent, and impact daily functioning, they may indicate an anxiety disorder.

One technique to differentiate between the two is to evaluate the intensity and frequency of the anxiety-related behaviours. While it's normal to experience anxiety in stressful situations, such behaviours are considered part of a disorder when they are overly intense compared to the situation and occur frequently or even without an obvious trigger.

Context is crucial in assessing anxiety. Normal anxiety has a clear and understandable cause, such as an upcoming exam or a job interview. However, in an anxiety disorder, the anxiety may appear disproportionate to the situation or may arise without any identifiable cause. Understanding the context in which anxiety occurs can help in distinguishing whether it's a symptom of a disorder or a normal reaction.

Duration is another important factor. Normal anxious feelings are typically short-lived and resolve once the stressful situation is over. However, in anxiety disorders, the anxiety is long-lasting, and the worry or fear is constant or recurrent, often lasting for several months or more.

Assessing the impact of anxiety on daily functioning is also essential. An anxiety disorder is likely if anxiety significantly interferes with daily activities, such as work, school, or social relationships. In contrast, normal anxiety does not typically impede everyday functioning to a significant degree.

Causes of Anxiety

The causes of anxiety disorders are multifaceted, involving a complex interplay of biological, psychological, and environmental factors. Understanding these factors is essential for effective treatment and management of anxiety disorders.

Biological factors play a significant role in the development of anxiety disorders. Genetics contribute to the risk, as having a family member with an anxiety disorder increases the likelihood of developing such disorders. However, genetics alone does not determine the development of anxiety disorders; it only increases susceptibility.

Brain chemistry is another biological factor. Neurotransmitters, the brain's chemical messengers, are involved in regulating mood and emotions. Imbalances or dysfunctions in neurotransmitter systems, especially those involving serotonin, norepinephrine, and gamma-aminobutyric acid (GABA), are linked to anxiety disorders (Maron & Nutt, 2017).

Psychological factors, including personality traits and early life experiences, also contribute to anxiety disorders. Individuals with certain personality traits, such as perfectionism or a tendency to be easily overwhelmed by stress, may be more prone to developing anxiety disorders. Childhood experiences, such as trauma or a history of abuse, can increase the risk as well.

Environmental factors encompass life events and current stressors. Traumatic events, such as accidents or natural disasters, can trigger anxiety disorders. Ongoing stress from work, relationships, financial concerns, or other life situations can also contribute to the development of anxiety.

Anxiety disorders arise from a combination of biological, psychological, and environmental factors. Understanding these causes is crucial for recognizing the complexity of anxiety disorders and for providing comprehensive and effective treatment.

Evidence-Based Therapies for Anxiety

Evidence-based therapies for anxiety disorders are critical in managing and treating these conditions. These therapies have been scientifically tested and proven effective, offering individuals with anxiety disorders a chance for relief and improved quality of life.

Thought Developmental Practice (TDP) developed by Dr. Harrison Mungal has been proven to recondition the mind and restructure thoughts. It creates a diversion to develop new neuropathway in the brain, like teaching the less dominant writing hand to become dominant. Changing negative thinking to become positive, implementing several strategies to help individuals cope.

Medications as mentioned before with selective serotonin reuptake inhibitors (SSRIs) and serotonin-norepinephrine reuptake inhibitors (SNRIs) are commonly prescribed due to their efficacy and relatively favourable side-effect profiles. Benzodiazepines may also be used, particularly for short-term relief of anxiety symptoms, though they are generally avoided for long-term use due to the risk of dependence.

Psychotherapy, including psychodynamic therapy and supportive therapy, can be beneficial for some individuals with anxiety disorders. These therapies focus on understanding the underlying psychological factors contributing to anxiety and helping individuals develop coping mechanisms. Psychotherapy can be particularly effective when combined with other treatments, such as CBT and medication (Carpenter et al., 2018).

Emerging treatments for anxiety disorders include mindfulness-based therapies and acceptance and commitment therapy (ACT). Mindfulness-based therapies focus on developing awareness and acceptance of thoughts and feelings without judgment. ACT combines mindfulness skills with the practice of self-acceptance, encouraging individuals to embrace their thoughts and feelings rather than fighting or feeling guilty for them.

Another emerging treatment is the use of digital interventions, including online CBT and mobile applications. These digital tools can increase accessibility to treatment, especially for those who may have barriers to accessing traditional in-person therapy.

The efficacy of these treatments varies among individuals, and what works for one person may not work for another. Therefore, a personalized approach, often involving a combination of different therapies, is typically the most effective. It's also important for treatment to be continuous and adaptive, as anxiety disorders can change over time.

Coping Strategies for Anxiety

Coping strategies are essential tools for individuals dealing with anxiety, providing practical ways to manage and reduce symptoms. These techniques can be used alongside professional treatments to enhance overall well-being and resilience.

Time management techniques can help reduce anxiety related to workload or deadlines. Prioritizing tasks, setting realistic goals, and breaking tasks into smaller, manageable steps can help reduce feelings of overwhelm.

One effective coping strategy is practicing relaxation techniques, such as deep breathing exercises, progressive muscle relaxation, and guided imagery. These methods help reduce the physical symptoms of anxiety by calming the nervous system and promoting a sense of relaxation.

Mindfulness and meditation are also beneficial for managing anxiety. These practices involve focusing on the present moment and accepting thoughts and feelings without judgment. Mindfulness can help break the cycle of constant worry and rumination that often accompanies anxiety.

Regular physical exercise is another valuable coping strategy. Exercise can alleviate anxiety symptoms by releasing endorphins, natural mood lifters, and by providing a healthy outlet for stress and tension. Activities like walking, jogging, yoga, or swimming can be particularly effective.

Maintaining a healthy lifestyle is also crucial in managing anxiety. This includes getting adequate sleep, eating a balanced diet, and avoiding excessive caffeine and alcohol. Good sleep hygiene can significantly impact anxiety levels, as poor sleep can exacerbate symptoms.

Journaling can be a therapeutic way to cope with anxiety. Writing down thoughts and feelings can provide a release and can also help in identifying patterns and triggers of anxiety. Journaling can be a form of self-expression and self-discovery, offering insights into personal coping mechanisms and stressors.

Developing a support network is vital. Talking with friends, family, or a support group can provide emotional support and reduce feelings of isolation. Sharing experiences with others who understand can be comforting and reassuring.

Ruling Out Self-Harm, Suicide Ideations and Homicidal Ideations (SI/HI)

In the context of anxiety disorders, assessing the risk of self-harm, suicide ideations (SI) and homicidal ideation (HI) is crucial. Anxiety, particularly when severe, can be associated with an increased risk of self-harm and, in rare cases, aggression towards others.

Healthcare professionals should conduct thorough risk assessments for self-harm, SI/HI as part of the diagnostic and treatment process. This involves asking direct questions about thoughts of self-harm or harming others, intentions, and any previous history of such behaviours.

It's important to create a safe and non-judgmental environment when discussing these sensitive topics. Patient/Clients should feel understood and supported, not judged, or stigmatized. Effective communication is key to encouraging openness and honesty during these discussions.

If a risk of SI/HI is identified, immediate action is required. This may involve developing a safety plan, which includes removing access to means of self-harm or harm to others and providing resources for immediate support during crisis situations.

In cases where there is a significant risk of harm, referral to specialized mental health services or emergency intervention may be necessary. Collaboration with other healthcare providers, including mental health specialists and, if needed, law enforcement, is important to ensure the safety of the individual and others.

Ongoing monitoring and support are essential for individuals at risk of SI/HI. This includes regular follow-up appointments, psychoeducation for the individual and their family, and ensuring access to emergency mental health services when needed.

Coping strategies for anxiety are diverse and can significantly improve the quality of life for individuals suffering from anxiety disorders. Ruling out self-injury and homicidal ideation is a critical component of the treatment and management of anxiety disorders, ensuring the safety and well-being of the patient/client and those around them.

Professional Insights on Anxiety

Healthcare and mental health professionals play a crucial role in the identification, treatment, and management of anxiety disorders. A deep understanding of these disorders is essential for providing effective care.

Professionals should recognize the multifaceted nature of anxiety disorders. Anxiety can manifest differently in each individual, with a wide range of symptoms and severity levels. This requires a personalized approach to diagnosis and treatment, considering the unique circumstances and needs of each patient/client.

Staying informed about the latest research and developments in the field of anxiety disorders is important. This includes understanding the most effective therapeutic interventions, medications and emerging treatments. Continuous education ensures that professionals are equipped with the most current knowledge and skills to assist their patients/clients effectively.

Effective communication is a cornerstone of treatment for anxiety disorders. This involves actively listening to patients/clients, validating their experiences, and providing clear and concise information about their condition and treatment options. Empathy and a non-judgmental attitude are vital in building trust and rapport with patients/clients.

Best practices in care for individuals with anxiety disorders include a holistic approach that addresses both the psychological and physiological aspects of the disorder. Integrating psychotherapy, medication management, and lifestyle interventions can offer a comprehensive treatment plan that caters to the individual needs of the patient/client.

Collaborative care is also key. This involves working with other healthcare providers, such as psychiatrists, psychologists, primary care physicians, and social workers, to ensure a coordinated and effective approach to treatment.

Professionals should also be aware of the stigma associated with mental health disorders, including anxiety, and work towards reducing this stigma in both clinical settings and the broader community.

Conclusion

This overview of anxiety has highlighted key insights into the nature, causes, and treatment of anxiety disorders. Understanding the complexity and impact of these disorders is essential for effective management and support of those affected.

Key takeaways include recognizing the difference between normal anxiety and anxiety disorders, the importance of accurate diagnosis using criteria such as those in the DSM-V, and the effectiveness of evidence-based treatments and medication.

The role of coping strategies in managing anxiety cannot be overstated. Techniques like mindfulness, relaxation, and lifestyle changes are invaluable tools for individuals dealing with anxiety.

Professionals play a critical role in the care of individuals with anxiety disorders. Their understanding of the disorder, continuous education, effective communication, and empathetic approach are fundamental in providing the best possible care.

Anxiety disorders are complex and require a comprehensive and empathetic approach to treatment. Continued learning and understanding are crucial for both professionals and the public in supporting those with anxiety disorders. Empathy towards those experiencing anxiety, reducing stigma, and promoting awareness are essential steps towards a more informed and supportive society.

Week 2

The Workbook

Week Two

ANXIETY

Building on our foundational learning from Week One, where we explored the multifaceted landscape of mental health and mental illnesses, this week we shift our focus to a specific and prevalent topic: Anxiety. In the previous week, we dissected the complex interplay between mental health and mental illnesses, gaining insights into various conditions, their diagnosis, and management strategies. Our journey illuminated the nuances distinguishing mental health challenges from pathological conditions and provided a robust framework for understanding various mental disorders.

As we have transition to Week Two, our objective was to delve deeply into the realm of Anxiety, a condition that manifests in myriad forms and impacts a significant portion of the population. As we have unravelled the intricacies of Anxiety, including its clinical presentation, causes, and effective management strategies, we will start by examining Mixed Anxiety-Depressive Disorder (MAD), a condition that often presents a diagnostic challenge due to its overlapping symptoms with other mood disorders.

Our exploration not only involved understanding the clinical criteria and symptoms of Anxiety as outlined in the DSM-V but also the practical aspects of distinguishing between anxious behaviours and an anxiety disorder. This distinction has been crucial in clinical practice for accurate diagnosis and effective treatment planning.

Moreover, we have investigated the etiology of Anxiety, considering the biological, psychological, and social factors that contributes to its development. Understanding these factors has been essential for a holistic approach to treatment and care.

A significant part of this week has also been devoted to discussing evidence-based therapies and coping strategies for Anxiety. This has equipped us with practical tools and techniques to manage this condition effectively in clinical settings.

Furthermore, we emphasized the importance of ruling out suicidal and homicidal ideations (SI/HI) in patients/clients presenting with Anxiety, critical steps in ensuring patient/client safety and well-being.

Finally, we concluded the week by reflecting on what professionals need to know about Anxiety. This not only reinforced our learning but also highlighted areas that require further attention in professional practice and training.

Day 1: What is MAD (Mixed Anxiety-Depressive Disorder) and Anxiety?

1. Reflective Exercise 1: Describe your understanding of MAD and its distinction from other mood disorders.

_____

_____

_____

_____

_____

2. Reflective Exercise 2: Consider a patient/client who presented with anxiety. How did their experience inform your understanding?

_____

_____

_____

_____

_____

3. Guided Activity: Create a mind map to explore the different types and causes of anxiety.

Day 2: DSM-V Criteria for MAD

1. **Reflective Exercise 1**: Compare the DSM-V criteria for MAD with a real case study.

2. **Reflective Exercise 2**: Reflect on the challenges of using DSM-V criteria in diagnosing MAD.

3. **Guided Activity**: Develop a checklist based on DSM-V criteria for MAD for use in a clinical setting.

_____

_____

_____

_____

_____

_____

_____

Day 3: Common Signs and Symptoms of Anxiety

1. **Reflective Exercise 1**: Recall a patient/client showing classic signs of anxiety. How did these symptoms present?

_____

_____

_____

_____

_____

2. **Reflective Exercise 2**: Think about a case where anxiety symptoms were atypical. What did you learn?

_____

_____

_____

_____

_____

_____

3. **Guided Activity**: Create an infographic illustrating the common signs and symptoms of anxiety.

_____

_____

_____

_____

_____

_____

Day 4: Distinguishing Between Behaviour and Illness

1. **Reflective Exercise 1**: Reflect on a scenario where it was difficult to distinguish between a behaviour and an anxiety disorder.

_____

_____

_____

_____

_____

_____

2. **Reflective Exercise 2**: Discuss the importance of context in differentiating behaviour from illness.

_____

_____

_____

_____

_____

_____

3. **Guided Activity**: Analyze a hypothetical case to determine if the behaviours are symptomatic of an anxiety disorder or not.

_____

_____

_____

_____

_____

_____

Day 5: Causes of Anxiety

1. **Reflective Exercise 1**: Consider the various causes of anxiety you have encountered in practice. How do they differ?

_____

_____

_____

_____

_____

_____

2. **Reflective Exercise 2**: Reflect on a case where the cause of anxiety was not immediately apparent.

_____

_____

_____

_____

_____

_____

3. **Guided Activity**: Research and summarize the biological, psychological, and social factors contributing to anxiety.

_____

_____

_____

_____

_____

Day 6: Therapies and Coping Strategies for Anxiety

1. **Reflective Exercise 1**: Discuss your experience with evidence-based therapies for anxiety.

_____

_____

_____

_____

_____

_____

2. **Reflective Exercise 2**: Reflect on coping strategies you've recommended to patients/clients and their effectiveness.

_____

_____

_____

_____

_____

_____

3. **Reflective Exercise 3**: Reflect on the importance of assessing for suicidal ideation/homicidal ideation (SI/HI) in patients/clients with anxiety.

_____

_____

_____

_____

_____

_____

4. **Reflective Exercise 4**: Recall a case where ruling out SI/HI was crucial in managing a patient/client with anxiety.

_____

_____

_____

_____

_____

5. **Guided Activity 1**: Create a protocol or checklist for assessing SI/HI in patients/clients presenting with anxiety.

_____

_____

_____

_____

_____

6. **Guided Activity 2**: Develop a resource list or guide of effective therapies and coping strategies for anxiety.

_____

_____

_____

_____

_____

_____

_____

Day 7: What Professionals Need to Know About Anxiety

1. **Reflective Exercise 1**: Summarize the key insights you have gained about anxiety this week.

_____

_____

_____

_____

_____

_____

2. **Reflective Exercise 2**: Reflect on areas of anxiety management you feel need more attention in professional training.

_____

_____

_____

_____

_____

_____

3. **Guided Activity**: Develop a brief presentation or educational material for colleagues on critical aspects of understanding and managing anxiety.

_____

_____

_____

_____

_____

_____

_____

Week 3

MOOD **DISORDER**

Major Depressive Disorder (MDD) is a significant mental health condition characterized by persistent sadness and a lack of interest or pleasure in previously enjoyed activities. It is more than just feeling down or experiencing temporary emotional responses to daily stresses and challenges. MDD affects an individual's thoughts, feelings, behaviour, and overall health. The understanding of MDD has evolved over time, as researchers have delved deeper into its complexities.

One of the core aspects of MDD is its duration and intensity. The feelings of depression in MDD are long-lasting and can significantly impair an individual's ability to function in daily life (American Psychiatric Association, 2013). This distinguishes MDD from normal fluctuations in mood. It's important to recognize that MDD is not a sign of personal weakness or a condition that can be willed away. People with MDD cannot simply "pull themselves together" and get better.

Depression, as a broader term, includes various types of depressive disorders, of which MDD is the most common. Other types of depressive disorders include persistent depressive disorder (dysthymia), postpartum depression, and seasonal affective disorder, each with unique characteristics and symptoms.

The exact cause of MDD is not fully understood but is believed to be a complex combination of genetic, biological, environmental, and psychological factors. Research indicates that changes in brain chemistry, particularly in neurotransmitter levels, play a critical role in the onset and course of MDD (Belmaker & Agam, 2008). Neurotransmitters like serotonin, norepinephrine, and dopamine are involved in regulating mood, emotions, and other key functions in the brain.

Environmental factors, including life events such as trauma, loss of a loved one, a difficult relationship, or any stressful situation, can trigger MDD in people who have an inherent susceptibility to the disorder. Furthermore, psychological factors like low self-esteem and being overly dependent, self-critical, or pessimistic also contribute to the development of MDD.

The symptoms of MDD are varied and can affect each individual differently. Common symptoms include a persistent feeling of sadness, hopelessness, and helplessness. People with MDD may lose interest in activities they once enjoyed and may experience changes in appetite and sleep patterns. Physical symptoms such as aches, pains, headaches, or digestive problems that do not ease even with treatment can also be present.

Cognitive symptoms are equally significant in MDD. This includes difficulty concentrating, making decisions, or remembering details. Individuals might experience feelings of worthlessness or guilt and have recurrent thoughts of death or suicide. The intensity of these symptoms can vary from mild to severe and can lead to significant impairments in an individual's daily life.

Diagnosing MDD requires a thorough evaluation by a healthcare professional. The Diagnostic and Statistical Manual of Mental Disorders, Fifth Edition (DSM-5), provides criteria for diagnosing MDD, which includes experiencing five or more depressive symptoms over a two-week period, with at least one of the symptoms being either a depressed mood or loss of interest or pleasure (American Psychiatric Association, 2013).

Treatment for MDD often involves a combination of medications and psychotherapy. Antidepressants, particularly selective serotonin reuptake inhibitors (SSRIs) and serotonin and norepinephrine reuptake inhibitors (SNRIs), are commonly used to treat MDD. These medications work by altering the brain chemicals involved in mood regulation.

TDP can be effective in treating MDD by helping individuals change negative patterns of thinking and behaviour and develop better coping skills. Other treatments, such as electroconvulsive therapy (ECT) and newer modalities like repetitive transcranial magnetic stimulation (rTMS), may be considered in severe cases or when other treatments have not been effective.

The management of MDD also includes lifestyle modifications, such as regular physical activity, a healthy diet, adequate sleep, and avoiding alcohol and drugs. These lifestyle changes can help reduce the symptoms of depression and improve overall well-being.

It is crucial to understand the impact of MDD on an individual's life. It can affect personal relationships, job performance, and the ability to handle daily activities and responsibilities. The stigma associated with mental illness can also make it difficult for individuals to seek help.

Raising awareness about MDD, its symptoms, and treatment options is essential. Education can help reduce stigma and encourage individuals suffering from depression to seek help. It is also important for friends, family members, and caregivers to be supportive and understanding.

Healthcare professionals play a critical role in the diagnosis and management of MDD. They need to be aware of the latest research and treatment options to provide the best care for their patients/clients. This includes understanding the importance of a comprehensive treatment plan tailored to each individual's unique needs.

Major Depressive Disorder is a complex and debilitating condition that requires a multifaceted approach to treatment and management. Understanding the nature of the disorder, its symptoms, causes, and treatment options is vital for those affected, as well as for healthcare providers.

Depression: An Overview

Depression, in its broader sense, encompasses a range of emotional states and disorders characterized by feelings of sadness, emptiness, or irritable mood. It is accompanied by bodily and cognitive changes that significantly affect an individual's capacity to function. This concept of depression goes beyond Major Depressive Disorder (MDD) and includes various types, each with its unique features and challenges.

Understanding depression in its entirety requires recognizing that it is not just a singular condition but a spectrum of disorders with diverse presentations and severities. This spectrum includes conditions like Persistent Depressive Disorder (dysthymia), Postpartum Depression, Seasonal Affective Disorder (SAD), and bipolar disorder, among others.

Persistent Depressive Disorder, also known as dysthymia, is a type of depression characterized by a chronic, albeit less severe, depressed mood. Individuals with dysthymia may experience symptoms for years, significantly impacting their life and functioning, although the symptoms are typically not as severe as those of MDD.

Postpartum Depression is a specific type of depression that can occur in the weeks and months following childbirth. This condition is noteworthy due to its timing and potential impact on both the mother and child. Postpartum Depression goes beyond the "baby blues," which is a more common and less severe form of emotional distress following childbirth.

Seasonal Affective Disorder (SAD) is a type of depression related to changes in seasons. Typically, it begins and ends at about the same times every year. Most people with SAD experience symptoms starting in the fall and continuing into the winter months, sapping their energy and making them feel moody.

Bipolar Disorder, previously known as manic-depressive illness, is a disorder that causes unusual shifts in mood, energy, activity levels, concentration, and the ability to carry out day-today tasks. It is characterized by episodes of mood elevation (mania or hypomania) and depression, making it distinct from other depressive disorders, which do not feature manic episodes.

Understanding the different types of depressive disorders is crucial for accurate diagnosis and treatment. Each type requires a tailored approach to treatment and management. For instance, treatment for SAD might include light therapy, while treatment for Postpartum Depression might involve a combination of therapy and support for the unique challenges of motherhood.

The causes of these various types of depression are as diverse as the disorders themselves. They can include a combination of genetic, biological, environmental, and psychological factors. For instance, SAD is closely related to the lack of sunlight in the winter months, affecting the body's internal clock and leading to feelings of depression.

The symptoms of these depressive disorders can overlap with those of MDD but also have distinct features. For example, in Bipolar Disorder, the depressive episodes may resemble MDD, but the presence of manic or hypomanic episodes provides a clear differentiation.

It is important for healthcare providers to be aware of these different types of depressive disorders to provide appropriate care. Misdiagnosis can lead to ineffective treatment and unnecessary suffering for the patient/client. As such, a thorough clinical assessment, which may include patient/client history, physical examination, and sometimes, psychiatric evaluation, is essential.

In addition to professional treatment, self-care and support from family and friends play a crucial role in managing all forms of depression. Understanding and compassion from loved ones can provide significant emotional support to individuals dealing with these challenging conditions.

The broader concept of depression encompasses a range of disorders, each with unique characteristics, causes, and treatment requirements. Recognizing the diversity within depressive disorders is key to providing effective and compassionate care to those affected by these conditions. Understanding the full spectrum of depression is vital for healthcare professionals, patients/clients, and their support networks.

DSM-V Criteria for Major Depressive Disorder (MDD)

The Diagnostic and Statistical Manual of Mental Disorders, Fifth Edition (DSM-5), published by the American Psychiatric Association, provides standardized criteria for diagnosing Major Depressive Disorder (MDD). These criteria are fundamental in guiding clinicians in the accurate identification and treatment of MDD. The detailed examination of these criteria is critical for understanding the complexity and nuances of this mental health condition.

According to the DSM-5, the diagnosis of MDD requires the presence of five or more of the following symptoms during the same 2-week period, with at least one of the symptoms being either a depressed mood or loss of interest or pleasure in almost all activities:

1. **Depressed Mood**: Most of the day, nearly every day, as indicated by subjective report or observation by others. This may manifest as feelings of sadness, emptiness, or hopelessness.

2. **Markedly Diminished Interest or Pleasure**: A significant decrease in interest or pleasure in all, or almost all, activities most of the day, nearly every day.

3. **Significant Weight Loss or Gain**: A change in weight when not dieting or weight gain (e.g., a change of more than 5% of body weight in a month), or a decrease or increase in appetite nearly every day.

4. **Insomnia or Hypersomnia**: A pattern of disrupted sleep that can include difficulty in falling asleep, staying asleep, or sleeping more than usual.

5. **Psychomotor Agitation or Retardation**: Observable by others, and not merely subjective feelings of restlessness or being slowed down.

6. **Fatigue or Loss of Energy**: Nearly every day, individuals may experience a profound lack of energy or feel excessively tired.

7. **Feelings of Worthlessness or Excessive Guilt**: This can be a disproportionate or inappropriate feeling of guilt, often about things that would not normally cause such a reaction.

8. **Diminished Ability to Think or Concentrate**: This includes indecisiveness and may be noted by the individual or observed by others.

9. **Recurrent Thoughts of Death**: This can include suicidal ideation with or without a specific plan, or a suicide attempt.

These symptoms must cause clinically significant distress or impairment in social, occupational, or other important areas of functioning. Additionally, the episode must not be attributable to the physiological effects of a substance or another medical condition.

It's important to note that these criteria represent more than just a checklist. The diagnosis of MDD requires a comprehensive clinical assessment by a qualified mental health professional. This assessment includes understanding the context, severity, and duration of symptoms.

While the DSM-5 criteria are essential for standardizing the diagnosis of MDD, there are limitations to consider. One limitation is the potential for over-diagnosis, as the criteria can sometimes capture normal responses to significant life stressors. Another issue is the possibility of under-diagnosis in cases where individuals may not fully articulate their symptoms or when symptoms are atypical.

Furthermore, the DSM-5 criteria are based on a categorical approach to diagnosis, which may not capture the full spectrum and complexity of depressive disorders. Some critics argue for a more dimensional approach that considers symptoms on a continuum rather than as discrete categories.

Despite these limitations, the DSM-5 criteria for MDD are a critical tool in clinical practice. They provide a structured framework for identifying and understanding depression, guiding treatment decisions, and facilitating communication among healthcare providers.

The DSM-5 criteria for diagnosing Major Depressive Disorder are an integral part of clinical practice, providing a standardized approach to identifying this serious mental health condition. While they are not without limitations, these criteria are essential for guiding the assessment, diagnosis, and treatment of MDD. Understanding these criteria is crucial for mental health professionals, ensuring accurate diagnosis and effective treatment for individuals suffering from depression.

Signs and Symptoms of Depression

Depression is a multifaceted disorder that affects individuals in various ways. Recognizing the signs and symptoms of depression is crucial for early intervention and effective treatment. These symptoms can be broadly categorized into emotional, physical, and cognitive domains, each impacting an individual's daily life and functioning in significant ways.

Emotional Symptoms

1. **Persistent Sadness or Low Mood**: This is often the most noticeable symptom. It's a deep, overwhelming sense of melancholy that doesn't go away.

2. **Loss of Interest or Pleasure**: Individuals may lose interest in activities or hobbies they once enjoyed, leading to a reduction in engaging in social activities or hobbies.

3. **Feelings of Hopelessness and Helplessness**: A pervasive sense of despair and the belief that things will never get better.

4. **Irritability and Frustration**: Even minor issues may provoke intense irritation or anger, more than what would be expected.

5. **Feelings of Worthlessness or Guilt**: Excessive self-criticism or feelings of guilt over perceived failures and responsibilities.

6. **Suicidal Thoughts or Behaviours**: Thoughts of death, suicidal ideation, or suicide attempts are severe emotional symptoms that require immediate attention.

Physical Symptoms

1. **Changes in Appetite and Weight**: Significant weight loss or gain due to a decrease or increase in appetite.

2. **Sleep Disturbances**: This includes insomnia (difficulty falling or staying asleep) or hypersomnia (oversleeping).

3. **Physical Aches and Pains**: Unexplained physical symptoms such as headaches, back pain, or muscle aches.

4. **Fatigue and Loss of Energy**: Persistent tiredness and a lack of energy to perform daily tasks, even those that are routine.

5. **Psychomotor Agitation or Retardation**: Restlessness, an inability to sit still, or conversely, a slowing of physical movements and speech.

Cognitive Symptoms

1. **Trouble Concentrating and Making Decisions**: Difficulty focusing, making choices, or remembering things.

2. **Negative Thinking**: Pessimistic views of oneself, the world, and the future.

3. **Cognitive Distortions**: Patterns of negative or distorted thinking, such as overgeneralizing or catastrophizing situations.

The impact of these symptoms on everyday life and functioning can be profound. Emotionally, depression can lead to a withdrawal from social interactions and a loss of interest in maintaining personal relationships. This social isolation can further exacerbate feelings of loneliness and worthlessness.

Physically, the symptoms of depression can lead to a decline in overall health. Sleep disturbances can affect cognitive function and physical health. Changes in appetite and weight can lead to nutritional deficiencies or contribute to obesity-related issues. The fatigue associated with depression can make it challenging to maintain employment or fulfill household responsibilities.

Cognitively, depression can significantly impair an individual's ability to function effectively in work or academic settings. The decreased ability to concentrate and make decisions can affect job performance and academic achievement. Negative thinking patterns can lead to a diminished ability to cope with stressors and challenges, creating a vicious cycle that perpetuates the depressive state.

It's important to recognize that these symptoms can vary greatly in intensity and duration from person to person. In some cases, symptoms may be relatively mild but persistent, while in others, they may be severe and debilitating.

The wide-ranging effects of these symptoms underscore the importance of early detection and treatment of depression. Without proper treatment, the symptoms can persist and lead to a significant decline in quality of life. It's also crucial for individuals suffering from depression to receive support and understanding from family, friends, and healthcare providers.

The signs and symptoms of depression encompass emotional, physical, and cognitive aspects, all of which can significantly impair an individual's daily life and functioning. Understanding these symptoms is essential for the identification and treatment of depression, as well as for providing the necessary support to those affected by this condition. Recognizing the multifaceted nature of depression is key to addressing it effectively and compassionately.

Distinguishing Behaviour from Illness

Differentiating between depressive behaviours and an actual depressive disorder is a crucial aspect of mental health assessment and diagnosis. This distinction is vital because not every manifestation of depressive behaviour indicates the presence of a clinical depressive disorder like Major Depressive Disorder (MDD). Understanding and applying techniques to distinguish these can lead to more accurate diagnoses and effective treatment plans. Here are some of the techniques for differentiation:

1. **Clinical Assessment**: A comprehensive clinical evaluation is essential. This typically involves a detailed interview where a mental health professional assesses the individual's symptoms, history, and current functioning.

2. **Observation of Symptom Patterns**: Clinicians look for patterns in symptoms, such as their persistence, severity, and impact on daily life. Depressive behaviours that are transient or situational might not indicate a depressive disorder.

3. **Use of Standardized Diagnostic Tools**: Tools like the DSM-5 provide criteria for diagnosing depressive disorders. These criteria are based on symptom type, duration, and impact on functioning.

4. **Screening for Physical Health Conditions**: Sometimes, physical health conditions can mimic depression. A thorough medical examination can rule out physical causes of depressive symptoms.

5. **Assessment of Psychosocial Factors**: Understanding the individual's environment, life stressors, and support systems can provide context for depressive behaviours and help in differentiating them from clinical depression.

The Role of Duration, Intensity, and Functional Impairment

1. **Duration**: One of the key factors in diagnosing a depressive disorder is the duration of symptoms. According to the DSM-5, symptoms must persist for at least two weeks to consider a diagnosis of MDD (American Psychiatric Association, 2013).

2. **Intensity**: The severity of symptoms is also critical. While everyone feels sad or down at times, the intensity of these emotions in depressive disorders is usually greater, often overwhelming, and can feel insurmountable.

3. **Functional Impairment**: Perhaps the most telling sign of a depressive disorder is the level of functional impairment. This refers to the degree to which symptoms interfere with daily activities, such as work, school, social activities, and relationships. In depressive disorders, there is a noticeable decline in one's ability to function normally.

Importance of Accurate Differentiation

Misdiagnosing depressive behaviours as a clinical disorder can lead to unnecessary treatment, including medication, which may not be appropriate or beneficial. Conversely, failing to identify a depressive disorder can lead to a lack of treatment and worsening of symptoms. Therefore, accurate differentiation is crucial.

Moreover, understanding the nature and context of depressive behaviours can lead to more targeted and effective interventions. For example, if depressive behaviours are linked to a specific stressor, addressing that stressor might be more effective than treating for a depressive disorder.

Mental health professionals must adhere to ethical guidelines and use evidence-based practices in diagnosis and treatment. This ensures that patients/clients receive the most appropriate and effective care based on their specific needs and circumstances.

Distinguishing between depressive behaviours and a depressive disorder is a nuanced process that requires careful consideration of various factors, including symptom duration, intensity, and functional impairment. Accurate differentiation is crucial for effective treatment and management of depressive symptoms and disorders. Mental health professionals must rely on comprehensive assessments, evidence-based tools, and ethical practices to make these determinations.

Causes of Major Depressive Disorder (MDD)

Major Depressive Disorder (MDD) is a complex condition with no single cause. Its development is influenced by a confluence of genetic, biological, environmental, and psychological factors. Understanding the interplay of these factors is crucial in comprehending the etiology of MDD and in formulating effective treatment strategies.

Genetic Factors

1. **Heritability**: Studies have shown that MDD can run in families, suggesting a genetic component. Research estimates that approximately 37% of the variability in risk for MDD is due to genetic factors (Sullivan, Neale, & Kendler, 2000).

2. **Genetic Variants**: Specific genetic variants have been associated with an increased risk of developing MDD. However, no single gene is responsible; rather, it is the interaction of multiple genes that increases susceptibility.

3. **Family Studies**: Research on families with a history of MDD has provided valuable insights into the genetic aspects of this disorder. These studies have shown that first-degree relatives of individuals with MDD are at a higher risk (Sullivan, Neale, & Kendler, 2000).

4. **Twin Studies**: Monozygotic twin studies have further reinforced the genetic links to MDD. If one twin has MDD, the likelihood of the other twin developing it is significantly higher than in dizygotic twins (Sullivan, Neale, & Kendler, 2000).

Biological Factors

1. **Brain Chemistry and Neurotransmitters**: Imbalances in brain chemicals, particularly neurotransmitters like serotonin, norepinephrine, and dopamine, play a significant role in MDD (Belmaker & Agam, 2008). These chemicals are crucial in regulating mood, emotions, and stress response.

2. **Hormonal Imbalances**: Changes in hormonal levels, especially during periods such as puberty, pregnancy, and menopause, can trigger MDD. Stress hormones like cortisol are also implicated in the development of depression (Belmaker & Agam, 2008).

3. **Brain Structure and Function**: Imaging studies have shown differences in the brain structure and function of people with MDD. Areas like the hippocampus, amygdala, and prefrontal cortex, which are involved in mood regulation and cognitive functions, often show abnormalities in depressed individuals (Lebow, H. I. 2021, July 2).

4. **Inflammation**: Recent research indicates a link between inflammation and depression. Chronic inflammation, which can result from lifestyle factors and medical conditions, might contribute to the onset of MDD (Lebow, H. I. 2021, July 2).

Environmental Factors

1. **Stressful Life Events**: Traumatic or stressful life events, such as the loss of a loved one, financial problems, or a breakup, can trigger MDD, especially in individuals genetically predisposed to depression.

2. **Childhood Trauma**: Experiences of abuse, neglect, or trauma during childhood are strongly linked to the development of MDD later in life. These experiences can have long-lasting effects on an individual's psychological well-being.

3. **Social Environment**: Factors such as social isolation, lack of support, and unhealthy relationships can contribute to the onset of MDD. The quality of one's social and family relationships plays a significant role in mental health.

4. **Socioeconomic Status**: Lower socioeconomic status, which can lead to chronic stress, insecurity, and reduced access to resources, is a risk factor for MDD.

Psychological Factors

1. **Personality Traits**: Certain personality traits, such as neuroticism, pessimism, or low self-esteem, can predispose individuals to MDD. These traits can affect how a person copes with stress and adversity.

2. **Cognitive Factors**: Negative thinking patterns, such as rumination and cognitive distortions, play a critical role in the development and maintenance of MDD. These patterns can affect how individuals perceive and interact with the world around them.

3. **Coping Styles**: Ineffective coping mechanisms, such as avoidance or substance abuse, can increase the risk of developing MDD. Adaptive coping strategies are crucial in managing life's challenges and stressors.

4. **Psychological Theories**: Various psychological theories, including the psychodynamic theory and cognitive-behavioural theory, provide different perspectives on the psychological underpinnings of MDD.

The development of MDD is best understood as the result of the complex interaction of these genetic, biological, environmental, and psychological factors. No single factor can fully explain the onset of MDD, and the combination and weighting of these factors can vary greatly among individuals.

Moreover, the interplay between these factors can create a feedback loop. For example, a genetic predisposition to MDD may be triggered by environmental stressors, which in turn may lead to changes in brain chemistry and function, further exacerbating the condition.

It is important for healthcare providers and researchers to consider the multifactorial nature of MDD when diagnosing and treating this disorder. A comprehensive approach that addresses the wide range of contributing factors is crucial in effectively managing MDD.

The Role of Neurochemistry in Major Depressive Disorder (MDD)

The neurochemistry of the brain plays a pivotal role in the development and experience of Major Depressive Disorder (MDD). This role is primarily centered around neurotransmitters, which are chemical messengers that transmit signals between nerve cells in the brain. The most significant neurotransmitters implicated in MDD are serotonin, dopamine, and norepinephrine. Understanding the function and imbalance of these neurotransmitters provides insight into the complexity of brain chemistry in mood regulation and the pathophysiology of MDD.

Serotonin

1. **Function**: Serotonin is often referred to as the "feel-good" neurotransmitter. It helps regulate mood, appetite, sleep, memory, and sexual desire. It's also involved in cognitive functions such as learning and processing information.

2. **Imbalance in MDD**: Lower levels of serotonin are commonly associated with depression. This imbalance can affect mood and emotional responses, leading to the classic symptoms of MDD, such as sadness, loss of interest in activities, and sleep disturbances (Cowen & Browning, 2015).

3. **Treatment Implications**: Many antidepressants, particularly selective serotonin reuptake inhibitors (SSRIs), work by increasing the levels of serotonin in the brain. These medications can alleviate the symptoms of depression by restoring the balance of serotonin.

Dopamine

1. **Function**: Dopamine plays a crucial role in the brain's reward system. It influences motivation, pleasure, and euphoria. It's also important for motor control and cognitive functions.

2. **Imbalance in MDD**: Decreased dopamine levels are linked to a lack of pleasure and motivation in MDD, a symptom known as anhedonia. Dopamine dysregulation can lead to reduced engagement in pleasurable activities and a general sense of dissatisfaction.

3. **Treatment Implications**: Some treatments for MDD, especially those targeting anhedonia, focus on enhancing dopamine neurotransmission. This approach can help restore the reward system's functioning and improve mood and motivation.

Norepinephrine

1. **Function**: Norepinephrine, also known as noradrenaline, is integral to the body's stress response. It affects attention, perception, and responding to new or challenging situations.

2. **Imbalance in MDD**: Imbalances in norepinephrine levels are associated with symptoms of depression, such as fatigue, apathy, and impaired alertness. Altered norepinephrine levels can affect stress response and arousal, contributing to the symptomatic presentation of MDD.

3. **Treatment Implications**: Some antidepressants, like serotonin-norepinephrine reuptake inhibitors (SNRIs), work by increasing both serotonin and norepinephrine levels, addressing a broader range of depressive symptoms.

Complexity of Brain Chemistry in Mood Regulation

1. **Interconnectedness**: The neurotransmitters in the brain do not operate in isolation. There is a complex interplay between serotonin, dopamine, norepinephrine, and other neurotransmitters in regulating mood and emotional responses.

2. **Individual Variability**: The neurochemical basis of MDD can vary significantly among individuals. This variability is one reason why some people respond well to certain antidepressants while others do not.

3. **Beyond Neurotransmitters**: While neurotransmitters play a crucial role, they are only one part of the equation. Other factors, such as receptor sensitivity, neural circuitry, and genetic influences, also contribute to the complexity of brain chemistry in MDD.

4. **Ongoing Research**: The understanding of neurochemistry in MDD is continually evolving. Ongoing research is exploring other aspects of brain function, including neuroplasticity, neuroinflammation, and the role of other neurochemical systems in the pathophysiology of depression.

The role of neurochemistry in Major Depressive Disorder is both significant and complex. The balance and interaction of key neurotransmitters like serotonin, dopamine, and norepinephrine are crucial in the regulation of mood and the manifestation of depressive symptoms. Understanding this neurochemical landscape is essential for the development of effective treatments and the management of MDD. Continued research in this field is vital to unravel the complexities of brain chemistry and its impact on mood disorders.

Evidence-Based Therapies for Depression

The treatment of depression is a multifaceted process, with a range of evidence-based therapies available. Effective treatment often requires a combination of psychotherapy, medication, and in some cases, alternative therapies. The choice of treatment depends on the severity of the depression, the individual patient's/client's preferences, and their response to previous treatments.

The goal for support should be to focus on identifying and changing negative thinking and behaviour patterns. Individuals suffering with depression need to develop healthier ways of thinking and behaving, including improving interpersonal skills. This is particularly useful for individuals whose depression is closely linked to their relationships and social environment.

Addressing unresolved past conflicts and feelings which is affecting current behaviours. There need to be an increase of self-awareness and understanding on influences and behaviours, which can be particularly beneficial for individuals with a history of trauma or childhood issues.

Group therapy offers an opportunity for individuals to share experiences and learn from others in a supportive environment. It can provide a sense of community and reduce the isolation often felt by people with depression.

Medication

Antidepressant medication as mentioned before is another cornerstone of depression treatment. Selective serotonin reuptake inhibitors (SSRIs) are commonly prescribed due to their effectiveness and relatively favourable side-effect profile. SSRIs work by increasing the levels of serotonin in the brain.

Serotonin and norepinephrine reuptake inhibitors (SNRIs) are another class of antidepressants. They act on both serotonin and norepinephrine neurotransmitters and can be particularly effective in cases where SSRIs are not suitable or ineffective.

For some individuals, other types of antidepressants such as tricyclic antidepressants (TCAs) or monoamine oxidase inhibitors (MAOIs) might be prescribed. These are generally considered when newer medications are not effective, but they often have more side effects.

The choice of medication is highly individualized, based on the patient's/client's symptoms, medical history, and response to previous treatments. It's not uncommon for patients/clients to try several different medications before finding the one that works best for them with the least side effects.

Alternative Therapies

Exercise has been shown to have a therapeutic effect on depression. Regular physical activity can help alleviate symptoms by releasing endorphins and improving overall health. Other alternative therapies include acupuncture, dietary supplements (like omega-3 fatty acids and St. John's Wort), and light therapy, particularly for Seasonal Affective Disorder (SAD).

Individualization of Treatment Plans

The most crucial aspect of depression treatment is the individualization of the treatment plan. What works for one person might not work for another. Factors like the severity of symptoms, patient/client history, comorbid conditions, and personal preferences play a significant role in determining the best treatment approach.

Ongoing assessment and adjustment are often needed. Treatment plans should be flexible, adapting to changes in the patient's/client's condition and circumstances. A collaborative approach, involving the patient/client in decision-making about their treatment, can lead to more effective and satisfying outcomes.

Moreover, considering the potential side effects of treatments, especially medication, and weighing them against the benefits is essential. Open communication between the patient/client and healthcare provider about side effects, concerns, and expectations is vital for successful treatment.

In short, treating depression effectively requires a comprehensive, individualized approach. A combination of psychotherapy, medication, and sometimes alternative therapies, tailored to the patient's/client's specific needs and preferences, is often the key to successful treatment. This personalized approach, combined with ongoing assessment and adjustment, ensures that the treatment plan remains effective and responsive to the individual's changing needs.

Coping Strategies for Depression

Managing depression involves more than just medical treatment; it also encompasses a range of coping strategies that individuals can employ to alleviate symptoms and improve their overall well-being. These strategies include practical advice on lifestyle changes, mindfulness practices, and self-care routines, all of which play a crucial role in the holistic management of depression.

Making changes to one's lifestyle can have a profound impact on managing depression. Regular physical activity is one of the most effective lifestyle changes. Exercise releases endorphins, known as 'feel-good' hormones, which can improve mood and reduce symptoms of depression. Even moderate activities like walking or gardening can be beneficial.

Adequate and quality sleep is essential for mental health. Depression can often disrupt sleep patterns, leading to insomnia or excessive sleeping. Establishing a regular sleep schedule, creating a comfortable sleep environment, and avoiding screens before bedtime can help improve sleep quality.

Social support plays a critical role in coping with depression. Maintaining relationships with friends and family, participating in social activities, or joining support groups can provide emotional support and reduce feelings of isolation often associated with depression.

Practices such as meditation, yoga, and deep breathing exercises can help individuals become more aware of their mood and thought patterns, which is a crucial step in managing depression. Yoga combines physical postures, breathing exercises, and meditation, which can be particularly beneficial in alleviating symptoms of depression. It helps in reducing stress, improving physical health, and promoting a sense of well-being.

Deep breathing exercises are a simple yet effective mindfulness technique that can be used to reduce anxiety and stress, common symptoms of depression. They can be practiced anywhere and anytime, providing immediate relief in stressful situations.

Self-care involves taking time to do activities that nurture and rejuvenate oneself. It's an essential component in managing depression. This might include activities like reading, listening to music, gardening, or any other hobbies that bring joy and relaxation.

Journaling is a powerful self-care tool for managing depression. It provides an outlet for expressing thoughts and feelings and can help in identifying patterns in mood and behaviour.

Setting realistic goals and priorities can help in managing the feelings of overwhelm that often accompany depression. Breaking tasks into smaller, manageable steps and celebrating small achievements can boost self-esteem and a sense of accomplishment.

Relaxation techniques such as progressive muscle relaxation or guided imagery can help in reducing tension and stress, which are often heightened in individuals with depression.

These strategies empower individuals to take an active role in their recovery and improve their overall quality of life. It's important to remember that while these coping strategies can be highly effective, they are most beneficial when used in conjunction with professional treatment for depression.

Assessing and Addressing SI/HI in Depression

One of the most critical aspects of managing Major Depressive Disorder (MDD) is the assessment and addressing of suicide ideation (SI) and homicidal ideation (HI). Depression significantly increases the risk of self-harm and suicidal thoughts or behaviours, making it essential for healthcare providers to regularly evaluate these risks in their patients/clients.

Assessing Risk for SI/HI

1. **Routine Evaluation**: Regular assessment for SI/HI should be an integral part of managing individuals with depression. This involves asking direct questions about thoughts, plans, or actions related to self-harm or suicide.

2. **Identifying Risk Factors**: Key risk factors for SI/HI include a history of self-harm, substance abuse, a history of trauma or abuse, significant life stresses, and previous suicide attempts. It's crucial to evaluate these factors during each assessment.

3. **Monitoring Changes**: Changes in mood, behaviour, or circumstances, such as increased withdrawal, hopelessness, or a recent loss, can elevate the risk for SI/HI. Continuous monitoring is vital for early intervention.

4. **Using Assessment Tools**: Several standardized tools and scales can help in evaluating the risk of self-harm or suicide. These tools can provide a structured approach to assessing the severity and immediacy of the risk.

Protocols and Interventions for SI/HI

1. **Safety Planning**: A safety plan involves creating a written, step-by-step plan that the individual can follow during a crisis. It includes recognizing warning signs, employing coping strategies, and identifying supportive contacts.

2. **Crisis Intervention**: In cases where there is an immediate risk of self-harm or suicide, crisis intervention is required. This may involve hospitalization or close monitoring in a safe environment.

3. **Family and Community Support**: Involving family members and close friends in the care plan can provide additional support and monitoring. Community resources, such as support groups and helplines, can also be valuable.

4. **Continuity of Care**: Ensuring continuity of care is essential, especially after a crisis or hospitalization. Follow-up appointments, regular check-ins, and a clear plan for emergency situations are crucial components.

5. **Education and Awareness**: Educating patients/clients and their families about the signs of worsening depression and the risks of SI/HI is vital. Awareness can lead to earlier intervention and better outcomes.

6. **Collaboration with Other Professionals**: For individuals at high risk of SI/HI, collaboration between mental health professionals, primary care providers, and sometimes emergency care providers is important to ensure comprehensive care.

Assessing and addressing the risk of suicide and homicidal ideation in individuals with depression is a critical component of care. It requires a multifaceted approach that includes regular assessment, crisis intervention, targeted psychotherapy, medication management, and strong support networks. By implementing these protocols and interventions, healthcare providers can significantly reduce the risk of self-harm and suicide in individuals with depression, contributing to better overall outcomes in their treatment and recovery.

Professional Knowledge and MDD

Healthcare professionals must recognize that Major Depressive Disorder (MDD) is a complex condition with diverse manifestations. It's essential to understand the various symptoms, their severity, and how they impact different aspects of a patient's/client's life. This comprehensive understanding is crucial for effective diagnosis and treatment.

The field of mental health, particularly regarding MDD, is continuously evolving. Professionals should stay informed about the latest research, including new treatment methods and understandings of the disorder's etiology. This ongoing education ensures that patients/clients receive the most current and effective care.

Accurate diagnosis is the cornerstone of effective treatment for MDD. Professionals must be adept at using diagnostic tools, such as the DSM-5, and be skilled in distinguishing MDD from other mental health disorders and physical conditions that may present similar symptoms.

Each individual's experience with MDD is unique. Healthcare providers should be skilled in creating and adjusting treatment plans that cater to the specific needs, preferences, and circumstances of each patient/client. This personalization is key to successful treatment outcomes.

Empathy is a critical skill in treating patients/clients with MDD. Understanding and empathizing with patients'/clients' experiences can help build trust and encourage patients/clients to engage fully in their treatment plans. Empathy also aids in better understanding patients'/clients' challenges and needs.

Effective communication is vital in managing MDD. Professionals should be able to convey information clearly and compassionately and be skilled listeners. Good communication helps in building a therapeutic alliance and ensuring patients/clients feel heard and understood.

MDD often requires a collaborative approach involving psychiatrists, psychologists, general practitioners, and other healthcare providers. Professionals should be adept at working within interdisciplinary teams to provide comprehensive care to patients/clients.

Healthcare providers should be advocates for their patients/clients, ensuring they have access to the necessary resources and support. This includes helping patients/clients navigate healthcare systems and advocating for their needs within these systems.

Professionals must be prepared to manage crises, such as suicidal ideation or severe depressive episodes. This involves having protocols in place and being able to make quick, informed decisions to ensure patient/client safety.

An understanding of the pharmacological treatments available for MDD, including how to choose the right medication and manage dosages and side effects, is essential. This knowledge enables professionals to effectively manage the biological aspects of the disorder.

Being skilled in various psychotherapeutic techniques are often central to treating MDD and require specific skills and training to be delivered effectively.

Patients/Clients with MDD often have comorbid conditions, such as anxiety disorders or substance abuse. Professionals need to recognize and address these co-occurring conditions as part of a comprehensive treatment plan.

With advancements in technology, including virtual therapy and digital health tools, professionals should be adept at incorporating these resources into treatment plans, enhancing accessibility and monitoring of patients/clients.

Professionals should educate patients/clients about the role of lifestyle factors in managing MDD. This includes advising on diet, exercise, sleep hygiene, and stress management techniques, which are all integral to the overall treatment plan.

Apart from managing symptoms, healthcare providers should focus on fostering resilience and personal growth in patients/clients. This approach helps patients/clients develop coping skills and confidence, contributing to long-term recovery and well-being.

Maintaining a high standard of ethics is paramount in treating MDD. This includes respecting patient/client confidentiality, obtaining informed consent for treatments, and always acting in the best interests of the patient/client.

Recognizing the role of caregivers and providing them with support and resources is an important aspect of managing MDD. Caregivers often play a crucial role in the patient's/client's support system and may need guidance and assistance.

Healthcare professionals should regularly engage in self-reflection and seek feedback to improve their practice. This ongoing self-improvement ensures that they continue to provide the highest standard of care to their patients/clients with MDD.

Professionals should be culturally competent, understanding and respecting the diverse backgrounds and experiences of their patients/clients. This awareness is crucial for providing sensitive and appropriate care. In all aspects of treatment, the focus should be on patient/client-centered care. This involves considering the patient's/client's preferences, values, and needs in all decision-making processes and ensuring that they are active participants in their own care.

Conclusion

The journey of understanding and managing Major Depressive Disorder (MDD) encompasses a comprehensive blend of knowledge from various fields. This includes understanding the multifaceted nature of MDD, recognizing its symptoms, and appreciating the complexities involved in its diagnosis and treatment. Healthcare professionals must integrate this knowledge to effectively address the needs of those with MDD.

It is essential to acknowledge that MDD is a complex disorder influenced by a myriad of factors including genetic, biological, environmental, and psychological elements. The interplay of these factors contributes to the unique manifestation of MDD in each individual, thereby necessitating a personalized approach to treatment.

Accurate diagnosis is crucial in the management of MDD. This involves not only identifying the presence of the disorder but also understanding its severity, impact on the individual's life, and any co-occurring conditions. Treatment should be tailored to the individual, combining various modalities such as medication, psychotherapy, and lifestyle interventions.

Empathy and support are indispensable in treating MDD. A compassionate approach that acknowledges the patient's/client's struggles and offers understanding can significantly enhance the therapeutic relationship and treatment outcomes. Family, friends, and caregivers also play a critical role in providing support and should be involved in the treatment process when appropriate.

Self-care and resilience-building are crucial for individuals with MDD. Encouraging patients/clients to engage in activities that promote physical and emotional well-being, such as exercise, healthy eating, and stress reduction techniques, is key to managing symptoms and improving quality of life.

For healthcare professionals, continuous education and skill development are vital in staying abreast of the latest research and treatment approaches. This ongoing learning ensures that patients/clients receive the most effective and up-to-date care.

Managing MDD often requires a collaborative approach, involving a team of healthcare providers from different specialties. This collaboration ensures a comprehensive treatment plan that addresses all aspects of the patient's/client's health.

Raising awareness about MDD and advocating for those affected is essential in breaking down stigma and barriers to treatment. Education and advocacy efforts can lead to greater understanding and support for individuals with MDD in the community.

Ultimately, the focus should always be on patient/client-centered care. This involves listening to the patient/client, respecting their experiences and preferences, and involving them in all aspects of their treatment planning and decision-making.

Recovery from MDD is often a journey, not a destination. It requires patience, persistence, and a willingness to adapt treatment strategies as needed. Celebrating small victories and acknowledging progress, no matter how incremental, is important in maintaining hope and motivation.

It's crucial to foster a sense of hope and optimism in individuals with MDD. While depression can be a challenging and sometimes long-term condition, with the right treatment and support, many individuals can manage their symptoms and lead fulfilling lives.

Understanding and managing MDD requires a multifaceted and empathetic approach that recognizes the individuality of each person's experience with the disorder. By combining professional knowledge with compassionate care, ongoing education, and a commitment to patient/client-centered treatment, healthcare providers can make a significant difference in the lives of those struggling with MDD. It is through these informed and compassionate responses that we can hope to improve outcomes and enhance the quality of life for individuals living with depression.

Week 3

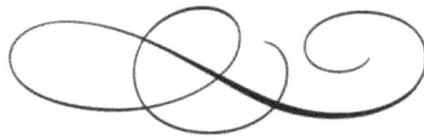

The Workbook

Week Three

MOOD DISORDER

In the previous week, we explored the multifaceted nature of Anxiety, delving into its definition, diagnostic criteria, and management strategies. We examined various aspects including Mixed Anxiety-Depressive Disorder (MAD), the complexities of diagnosis according to DSM-V, and effective treatment modalities. Through reflective exercises and guided activities, we gained a deeper understanding of the nuances in distinguishing between behaviours symptomatic of an anxiety disorder and those stemming from other causes. This exploration not only enhanced our clinical acumen but also our ability to apply evidence-based therapies and coping strategies in practice.

This week, our focus shifted to Major Depressive Disorder (MDD), a prevalent and impactful mood disorder. We have explored what MDD is and how it differentiates from general depression. Our journey included examining the DSM-V criteria for MDD, identifying common signs and symptoms, and understanding the intricate balance between behaviour and illness in the context of depression. A critical part of our exploration has been analyzing the causes of MDD, including the role of chemical imbalances, and discussing evidence-based therapies and coping strategies. The importance of ruling out suicidal and homicidal ideations (SI/HI) in depression cases has also been a key area of focus.

As professionals, it's imperative to deepen our knowledge about MDD, not just for accurate diagnosis and effective treatment, but also for better patient/client education and management. This week's learning has equipped us with the necessary tools to enhance our practice and contribute to better mental health outcomes.

Day 1: What is MDD (Major Depressive Disorder) and Depression?

1. **Reflective Exercise 1**: Describe your current understanding of MDD and how it differs from general sadness or grief.

_____

_____

_____

_____

_____

2. **Reflective Exercise 2**: Reflect on a case where MDD was initially overlooked or misdiagnosed. What were the implications?

_____

_____

_____

_____

_____

3. Reflective Exercise 2: Consider the societal misconceptions about depression and their impact on diagnosis and treatment.

_____

_____

_____

_____

_____

_____

4. Guided Activity: Develop a list of myths versus facts about depression for patient/client education.

_____

_____

_____

_____

_____

_____

Day 2: DSM-V Criteria for MDD

1. **Reflective Exercise 1**: Compare the DSM-V criteria for MDD with a real case you have encountered.

_____

_____

_____

_____

_____

_____

2. **Reflective Exercise 2**: Discuss the challenges in applying DSM-V criteria in diverse cultural and social contexts.

_____

_____

_____

_____

_____

_____

3. **Guided Activity**: Create a diagnostic checklist based on DSM-V criteria for MDD for clinical use.

_____

_____

_____

_____

_____

_____

Day 3: Common Signs and Symptoms of Depression

1. **Reflective Exercise 1**: Recall a patient/client showing classic signs of depression. How did these symptoms manifest?

_____

_____

_____

_____

_____

_____

2. **Reflective Exercise 2**: Think about a case where depression symptoms were atypical or unusual.

_____

_____

_____

_____

_____

3. **Guided Activity**: Design an infographic or chart illustrating the common signs and symptoms of depression.

_____

_____

_____

_____

_____

_____

Day 4: Distinguishing Between Behaviour and Illness in Depression

1. **Reflective Exercise 1**: Reflect on a situation where distinguishing between normal sadness and clinical depression was challenging.

_____

_____

_____

_____

_____

2. **Reflective Exercise 2**: Discuss the importance of understanding the patient's/client's overall context when diagnosing depression.

_____

_____

_____

_____

_____

_____

3. **Guided Activity**: Analyze a hypothetical case to determine if the behaviours are symptomatic of depression or a response to life events.

_____

_____

_____

_____

_____

_____

Day 5: Causes and Chemical Aspects of MDD

1. **Reflective Exercise 1**: Reflect on the various causes of MDD you have encountered in your practice.

_____

_____

_____

_____

_____

_____

2. **Reflective Exercise 2**: Discuss the role of chemicals, such as neurotransmitters, in the development of MDD.

_____

_____

_____

_____

_____

_____

3. **Guided Activity**: Research and summarize the biological, psychological, and environmental factors contributing to MDD.

_____

_____

_____

_____

_____

_____

Day 6: Therapies and Coping Strategies for Depression

1. **Reflective Exercise 1**: Discuss your experiences with different therapies for depression.

_____

_____

_____

_____

_____

2. **Reflective Exercise 2**: Reflect on coping strategies for depression that you have found effective in your practice.

_____

_____

_____

_____

_____

_____

3. **Guided Activity**: Develop a resource guide of evidence-based therapies and coping strategies for depression.

_____

_____

_____

_____

_____

Day 7: Importance of Ruling Out SI/HI in Depression Cases

1. **Reflective Exercise 1**: Reflect on the importance of assessing for suicidal ideation/homicidal ideation (SI/HI) in patients/clients with depression.

_____

_____

_____

_____

_____

2. **Reflective Exercise 2**: Recall a case where ruling out SI/HI was a critical part of managing a patient/client with depression.

_____

_____

_____

_____

_____

_____

3. **Reflective Exercise 3**: Reflect on areas of MDD management that you feel need more emphasis in professional education.

_____

_____

_____

_____

_____

_____

4. **Guided Activity 1**: Prepare a brief presentation or educational material for colleagues highlighting essential aspects of understanding and treating MDD.

_____

_____

_____

_____

_____

_____

5. **Guided Activity 2**: Create a protocol or checklist for assessing SI/HI in patients/clients presenting with depression.

_____

_____

_____

_____

_____

_____

_____

Week 4

PSYCHOSIS

Psychosis is a complex mental health condition characterized by an impaired relationship with reality. It can manifest through various symptoms, including hallucinations, delusions, disordered thinking, and disrupted behaviours. These symptoms often lead to significant distress and impairment in social, occupational, or other important areas of functioning (American Psychiatric Association, 2013).

The term 'psychosis' is broad and encompasses a variety of mental health disorders. Primary psychotic disorders include schizophrenia, schizoaffective disorder, and delusional disorder. However, psychotic symptoms can also occur in mood disorders, such as bipolar disorder, during manic or depressive episodes (Correll et al., 2016).

Hallucinations, one of the key symptoms of psychosis, involve sensing things that are not present in the environment. These can be auditory, like hearing voices, or visual, such as seeing images that others do not see. Delusions, another hallmark of psychosis, are false beliefs that are firmly held despite clear contradictory evidence. These beliefs are often paranoid, grandiose, or bizarre in nature.

Disordered thinking, also observed in psychosis, can manifest as disjointed or incoherent speech. This symptom makes it difficult for the person to organize thoughts coherently. As a result, individuals with psychosis might have trouble communicating effectively or engaging in logical discussions.

Behavioural changes in psychosis are varied and can range from agitation and restlessness to a complete lack of drive or motivation. These changes can significantly impact an individual's ability to function in daily life, affecting work, relationships, and self-care activities.

The onset of psychotic symptoms can occur at any age, but most commonly, they appear in late adolescence or early adulthood. Early intervention and treatment are crucial as they can significantly affect the course and prognosis of the condition (Correll et al., 2016).

The exact cause of psychosis is not fully understood, but it is believed to be a result of a complex interplay between genetic, biological, and environmental factors. Genetics play a significant role; individuals with a family history of psychotic disorders are at a higher risk of developing similar conditions. Brain chemistry, particularly involving neurotransmitters like dopamine and glutamate, is also implicated in the development of psychosis.

Environmental factors, including stressful life events, trauma, or drug use, can trigger the onset of psychotic symptoms in susceptible individuals. Substance use, particularly of drugs like cannabis, LSD, or amphetamines, is known to induce psychosis in some individuals. This type of psychosis is often termed drug-induced or substance-induced psychosis.

In drug-induced psychosis, the symptoms are directly related to the substance abuse and typically resolve once the substance is cleared from the body. However, in some cases, substance use can trigger a more persistent psychotic disorder, especially in those with an underlying vulnerability.

Distinguishing primary psychosis from drug-induced psychosis is crucial for appropriate treatment. While the symptoms may appear similar, the management strategies and long-term outlook can differ significantly. In cases of drug-induced psychosis, addressing the substance abuse is a primary focus, along with the management of psychotic symptoms.

The treatment for psychosis typically involves a combination of medication, psychotherapy, and social support. Antipsychotic medications are the cornerstone of treatment and are effective in reducing or eliminating symptoms like hallucinations and delusions. These medications work by affecting neurotransmitters in the brain, thereby helping to stabilize mood and improve thought processes.

Psychotherapy is also beneficial in managing psychosis. It helps individuals to identify and change problematic thought patterns and behaviours. Psychoeducation, which involves teaching individuals and their families about the condition, is also an integral part of treatment.

Support from family and friends, along with community resources, plays a crucial role in the recovery process. Social support can help reduce isolation, improve functioning, and assist with integration back into the community.

Early intervention is key in the treatment of psychosis. Studies have shown that prompt treatment can improve outcomes, reduce the severity of symptoms, and help in the recovery process (Correll et al., 2016). Therefore, recognizing the signs of psychosis and seeking professional help as soon as they are noticed is of utmost importance.

Professionals dealing with psychosis need to have a comprehensive understanding of the condition. This includes knowledge of its symptoms, causes, treatment options, and the ability to distinguish between primary and substance-induced psychosis. They should also be aware of the importance of early intervention and the role of family and community support in the treatment process.

Psychosis is a serious mental health condition that requires prompt and effective treatment. Understanding its symptoms, causes, and treatment options is essential for healthcare professionals. With appropriate care and support, individuals with psychosis can lead fulfilling lives.

Psychosis vs. Drug-Induced Psychosis

Differentiating between primary psychosis and drug-induced psychosis is essential in clinical practice, as the distinction has significant implications for treatment and prognosis. Primary psychosis, such as schizophrenia or schizoaffective disorder, arises independently of substance use and has its roots in genetic, biological, and environmental factors. In contrast, drug-induced psychosis is directly attributed to the effects of substances, including illicit drugs, prescription medications, or even alcohol (Addington *et al.*, 2007).

Substance use can both mimic and exacerbate psychotic symptoms. For instance, drugs like cannabis, hallucinogens, and amphetamines can induce hallucinations and delusions reminiscent of primary psychotic disorders. These symptoms, while chemically induced, can be indistinguishable from those of primary psychosis in terms of their presentation. This resemblance can make diagnosis challenging, particularly in individuals with a pre-existing risk or history of mental illness (Linszen, Dingemans, & Lenoir, 1994).

In some cases, substance use does not just mimic psychosis but can also worsen existing psychotic symptoms. For individuals with a predisposition to psychotic disorders, substance use can be a triggering factor, leading to an earlier onset of symptoms or exacerbating the severity of an ongoing psychotic episode. This interaction highlights the importance of substance use history in the assessment and treatment of psychosis.

The symptoms of drug-induced psychosis typically include hallucinations, delusions, disorganized thinking, and unusual behaviours, similar to primary psychosis. However, these symptoms are often more closely tied to the timing of substance use. They usually develop during or shortly after use and tend to resolve as the effects of the substance wear off. In contrast, the symptoms of primary psychosis are not tied to substance use and are generally more persistent.

Another critical aspect of differentiating the two forms of psychosis involves understanding the substance itself. Certain substances are more likely to induce psychotic symptoms. For instance, stimulants like methamphetamine and cocaine can induce a hyper-alert state that can lead to paranoia and hallucinations. Hallucinogens, such as LSD, directly alter sensory perceptions, leading to visual or auditory hallucinations.

The duration and severity of drug-induced psychosis can vary based on the type of substance used, the amount consumed, and the individual's susceptibility. In some individuals, especially those with an underlying vulnerability, drug-induced psychosis can evolve into a more chronic psychotic disorder, blurring the lines between drug-induced and primary psychosis.

Treatment approaches for drug-induced psychosis primarily involve the cessation of substance use and managing the acute psychotic symptoms. In many cases, hospitalization may be required to ensure the safety of the patient/client and to provide a controlled environment for detoxification and symptom management. Antipsychotic medications may be used to control severe symptoms, while supportive care and monitoring are also critical.

For primary psychosis, treatment is more long-term and involves a combination of antipsychotic medication, psychotherapy, and ongoing support. The focus is on managing symptoms, preventing relapse, and improving functional outcomes. Psychoeducation and family therapy can also play a significant role in treatment.

Understanding the distinction between primary psychosis and drug-induced psychosis is crucial for effective diagnosis and treatment. Substance use history, the timing of symptom onset, and the correlation between substance use and psychotic symptoms are key factors in making this differentiation. Appropriate treatment and support are essential for recovery in both forms of psychosis.

DSM-V Criteria for Psychosis

The Diagnostic and Statistical Manual of Mental Disorders, Fifth Edition (DSM-V), provides a standardized framework for diagnosing psychosis, which is pivotal for effective treatment planning. Accurate diagnosis ensures that patients/clients receive appropriate and targeted interventions, which is essential for improving outcomes and quality of life.

According to the DSM-V, the core feature of psychosis is the presence of one or more of the following symptoms: hallucinations, delusions, disorganized thinking (speech), grossly disorganized or abnormal motor behaviour (including catatonia), and negative symptoms (American Psychiatric Association, 2013). Each of these symptoms contributes to the comprehensive assessment and diagnosis of psychotic disorders.

Hallucinations are defined as perception-like experiences that occur without an external stimulus. They are vivid and clear, with the full force and impact of normal perceptions, and not under voluntary control. They can occur in any sensory modality, but auditory hallucinations, particularly hearing voices, are the most common in psychosis.

Hallucinations are one of the most identifiable symptoms of psychosis. These are sensory experiences that appear real but are created by the mind. They can affect any of the senses – auditory hallucinations (hearing voices or sounds that aren't there) being the most common in psychotic disorders. Visual hallucinations (seeing things that aren't present) are also frequent. These hallucinations are often distressing and can lead to confusion and fear in the affected individual.

Delusions are firmly held erroneous beliefs that usually involve a misinterpretation of perceptions or experiences. Their content may include a variety of themes, such as persecutory, referential, somatic, religious, or grandiose. The key to identifying delusions is the degree of conviction with which they are held, despite their implausibility and the lack of supporting evidence.

Delusions are another cardinal feature of psychosis. These are false beliefs that are strongly held despite clear evidence to the contrary. Delusions in psychosis can be varied, including persecutory delusions (belief that one is being harmed or harassed), grandiose delusions (belief in possessing extraordinary power, talent, or importance), and referential delusions (belief that certain gestures or comments are directed at oneself). Delusions can lead to significant impairments in social and occupational functioning as they can provoke behaviours that are based on these false beliefs.

Disorganized Thinking is typically inferred from the individual's speech. Effective communication can be impaired, and answers to questions may be partially or completely unrelated. Severely disorganized or incoherent speech is a hallmark of this symptom and is often observed in more severe psychotic episodes.

Disorganized Thinking is often inferred from disorganized speech. Individuals with psychosis may have trouble organizing their thoughts and may speak in a way that is hard to follow, with tangential or irrelevant responses to questions. In severe cases, speech may be so disorganized that it becomes incoherent, known as "word salad." This symptom can make it challenging for individuals to engage in meaningful communication, impacting their social interactions and daily activities.

Grossly Disorganized or Abnormal Motor Behaviour may manifest in a variety of ways, ranging from childlike silliness to unpredictable agitation. Problems may be noted in any form of goal-directed behaviour, leading to difficulties in performing activities of daily living. Catatonic behaviour, a marked decrease in reactivity to the environment, is a specific type of abnormal motor behaviour associated with psychosis.

Abnormal Motor Behaviour, including catatonia, can also be a symptom of psychosis. This may range from excessive and pointless motor activity to complete lack of verbal and motor responses. Catatonic behaviour can be particularly distressing for both the individual and their caregivers, as it can significantly interfere with daily functioning.

Negative Symptoms account for a significant portion of the morbidity associated with schizophrenia, but they are also seen in other types of psychosis. These symptoms include diminished emotional expression, avolition (decrease in motivated self-initiated purposeful activities), alogia (diminished speech output), anhedonia (decreased ability to experience pleasure), and asociality (lack of interest in social interactions).

Negative Symptoms such as reduced emotional expression, lack of motivation, withdrawal from social situations, reduced speech, and an inability to experience pleasure, are also common in psychosis. These symptoms can be particularly debilitating as they impact the individual's ability to initiate and maintain activities and relationships. Negative symptoms often contribute to the difficulty in maintaining employment and social relationships.

For a diagnosis of a psychotic disorder, these symptoms must cause significant social or occupational dysfunction. Duration criteria also vary based on the specific psychotic disorder. For instance, schizophrenia requires a significant portion of the symptoms to be present for a minimum of six months, while brief psychotic disorder is characterized by symptoms that last more than a day but less than a month.

The DSM-V also emphasizes the need to rule out substance-induced psychosis and psychotic disorders due to another medical condition. This involves a thorough evaluation of the individual's history, physical examination, and often, laboratory testing.

The importance of an accurate diagnosis cannot be overstated. It guides the entire treatment process, including the choice of medication, psychotherapy, and support services. Misdiagnosis can lead to inappropriate treatment, which can exacerbate symptoms or lead to unnecessary side effects. Thus, the DSM-V criteria serve as an essential tool in the identification and management of psychosis.

Signs and Symptoms of Psychosis

Understanding the signs and symptoms of psychosis is critical in recognizing and managing this complex mental health condition. Psychosis significantly impacts an individual's perception, beliefs, and behaviours, leading to considerable distress and dysfunction.

The impact of these symptoms on behaviour and cognition can be profound. Hallucinations and delusions can lead to erratic or unpredictable behaviour, often based on the content of the hallucination or delusion. Disorganized thinking can result in difficulty in performing tasks that require sequential steps or logical planning. Negative symptoms can result in a withdrawal from personal and professional responsibilities.

Understanding and recognizing these symptoms are crucial steps in the diagnosis and treatment of psychosis. They not only help in identifying the need for professional intervention but also guide the choice of treatment modalities. Early identification and intervention can significantly improve outcomes for individuals with psychosis, helping them to manage their symptoms more effectively and maintain a higher quality of life.

Recognizing Drug-Induced Psychosis

Drug-induced psychosis, a form of psychosis precipitated by the use of substances, has distinct characteristics that differentiate it from primary psychotic disorders. Recognizing these specific signs and symptoms, as well as understanding the role of intoxication and withdrawal, is crucial for accurate diagnosis and appropriate treatment.

Characteristic Symptoms of Drug-Induced Psychosis: The symptoms of drug-induced psychosis often mirror those of primary psychosis, including hallucinations, delusions, and disorganized thinking. However, there are certain nuances. For instance, the content of hallucinations and delusions in drug-induced psychosis often relates to the specific substance used. Hallucinogens like LSD and psilocybin can cause vivid, complex visual hallucinations, while stimulants like methamphetamine may lead to intense paranoia or persecutory delusions.

Another distinctive feature of drug-induced psychosis is the rapid onset of symptoms following substance use. Unlike primary psychotic disorders, which develop gradually over time, drug-induced psychosis typically manifests shortly after drug use begins or is intensified. The severity of symptoms can also fluctuate based on the level of drug use.

The Role of Intoxication: During intoxication, especially with substances such as stimulants or hallucinogens, individuals may experience acute psychotic symptoms. These symptoms can include severe paranoia, hallucinations, and a loss of touch with reality. The intensity of these symptoms often correlates with the amount of the substance used and its pharmacological properties.

The Role of Withdrawal: Withdrawal from substances, particularly those that are addictive, can also trigger psychotic symptoms. For instance, withdrawal from alcohol or sedatives can lead to symptoms like hallucinations, agitation, and confusion. These symptoms are part of a broader withdrawal syndrome and typically resolve as the substance is metabolized and cleared from the body.

Fluctuating Symptoms: The symptoms of drug-induced psychosis are closely tied to the substance use pattern. They tend to escalate with increased use or higher doses of the substance and diminish as the effects of the substance wear off. This fluctuation is a key indicator that psychosis might be substance-induced rather than primary.

Risk of Persistent Psychosis: In some individuals, particularly those with a predisposition to mental illness, prolonged or heavy substance use can lead to a more persistent psychotic state. This situation complicates the diagnosis, as it can be challenging to determine whether the psychosis is solely drug-induced or indicative of an underlying primary psychotic disorder.

Treatment Implications: The treatment for drug-induced psychosis primarily involves cessation of the substance causing the symptoms. This might require detoxification in a controlled environment, especially for substances with a high risk of dangerous withdrawal symptoms. In many cases, antipsychotic medications are used to manage acute symptoms, alongside supportive care and monitoring.

Recognizing drug-induced psychosis and differentiating it from primary psychosis is vital due to the different treatment approaches required for each. Understanding the specific signs and symptoms, and the role of intoxication and withdrawal, is key to this process. Accurate diagnosis ensures that individuals receive the most appropriate care, which can significantly improve their prognosis and overall well-being.

Substances and Illicit Drugs Leading to Psychosis

Various substances and illicit drugs are known to induce psychotic episodes, with some having a higher propensity than others to cause such symptoms. Understanding which substances are commonly associated with psychosis, as well as their prevalence and associated risks, is crucial in both clinical settings and public health perspectives.

Amphetamines: This category of stimulants, including methamphetamine, is well-known for its potential to induce psychosis. Amphetamine-induced psychosis can manifest with symptoms such as paranoia, hallucinations, and disorganized thinking, often resembling acute schizophrenia. The risk of psychosis increases with higher doses and chronic use of these substances. Amphetamines can alter brain chemistry, particularly affecting dopamine pathways, which play a significant role in the development of psychotic symptoms.

Cocaine: Cocaine, another powerful stimulant, can also lead to psychosis. Cocaine-induced psychosis is characterized by paranoid delusions and auditory hallucinations. Similar to amphetamines, the risk of experiencing psychotic symptoms increases with the amount and frequency of cocaine use. The psychosis induced by cocaine is primarily attributed to its effects on the brain's dopaminergic systems.

Hallucinogens: Substances such as LSD (lysergic acid diethylamide), psilocybin (found in magic mushrooms), and PCP (phencyclidine) are known for their strong hallucinogenic properties. These drugs can cause profound alterations in perceptions, leading to visual and auditory hallucinations, a distorted sense of time, and disconnection from reality. While the psychosis-like experiences induced by hallucinogens are often temporary and coincide with the duration of the drug's effects, they can be profoundly disorienting and distressing.

Cannabis: Though traditionally considered less harmful, cannabis is increasingly recognized for its potential to induce psychotic symptoms, especially in high-potency forms and among vulnerable individuals. The relationship between cannabis use and psychosis is complex, with evidence suggesting that early and heavy use can increase the risk of developing chronic psychotic disorders like schizophrenia, particularly in genetically predisposed individuals.

Prevalence and Risks: The prevalence of substance-induced psychosis is closely linked to the patterns of illicit drug use in the population. The widespread availability and use of substances like amphetamines, cocaine, and cannabis contribute to the occurrence of drug-induced psychosis. Urban areas with higher rates of drug trafficking and use often report more cases of substance-induced psychotic disorders.

The risks associated with these substances are multifaceted. Acute risks include the immediate onset of severe psychotic symptoms, which can lead to dangerous behaviours and require emergency medical attention. Chronic risks involve the potential for long-term psychiatric disorders, cognitive impairment, and the development of a substance use disorder.

Substances including amphetamines, cocaine, hallucinogens, and cannabis are among the most common culprits in substance-induced psychosis. The prevalence of psychosis associated with these drugs highlights the need for public health strategies to address substance misuse and for healthcare providers to be vigilant in recognizing and treating drug-induced psychotic episodes. Recognizing the link between substance use and psychosis is essential for effective prevention, early intervention, and treatment strategies.

Impact of Drugs on the Brain

The impact of drugs on the brain, particularly in relation to the induction of psychotic symptoms, is a critical area of study in both psychiatry and neurology. Various substances alter brain chemistry in ways that can lead to the development of psychotic symptoms, and prolonged use can have lasting effects on mental health.

Altering Brain Chemistry: Many drugs associated with psychosis exert their effects by altering neurotransmitter systems in the brain. For example:

- **Stimulants**, such as amphetamines and cocaine, increase the levels of dopamine, a neurotransmitter associated with pleasure, motivation, and reward. Excess dopamine, especially in certain brain regions like the mesolimbic pathway, is linked to the development of psychotic symptoms, including hallucinations and delusions.

- **Hallucinogens** primarily affect serotonin, another key neurotransmitter that influences mood, perception, and cognition. By stimulating serotonin receptors, these drugs can cause altered sensory experiences and perceptions that may mimic psychotic episodes.

- **Cannabis** affects the endocannabinoid system, which plays a role in various brain functions, including mood regulation and perception. THC, the psychoactive component in cannabis, can disrupt normal neurotransmitter function, leading to altered thought processes and perceptions.

Long-Term Effects: The long-term impact of drug use on mental health can be profound. Chronic use of substances that induce psychosis can lead to persistent changes in brain chemistry and structure. These changes can manifest as:

- **Cognitive Impairment**: Prolonged drug use can lead to difficulties with memory, attention, and decision-making. These cognitive deficits can persist even after drug use has ceased, affecting an individual's ability to function in daily life.

- **Increased Risk of Chronic Psychotic Disorders**: There is evidence to suggest that continuous use of drugs like cannabis, especially at a young age, can increase the risk of developing chronic psychotic disorders like schizophrenia, particularly in genetically predisposed individuals.

- **Mood Disorders**: The use of psychoactive substances can also lead to the development of mood disorders like depression and anxiety. The altered brain chemistry can disrupt emotional regulation, leading to heightened vulnerability to mood disturbances.

- **Dependence and Addiction**: Repeated drug use can lead to dependence and addiction, conditions that themselves are associated with a range of mental health issues, including increased risk of suicide, mood disorders, and cognitive impairments.

- **Brain Structure Changes**: Imaging studies have shown that chronic drug use can lead to changes in brain structure, particularly in areas involved in decision-making, judgment, learning, memory, and behaviour control. These structural changes can further exacerbate mental health issues and hinder recovery.

Understanding the impact of drugs on brain chemistry and the potential for long-term mental health effects is essential for both prevention and treatment. It underscores the importance of early intervention in cases of substance abuse and the need for comprehensive treatment approaches that address both the substance use and its psychiatric consequences. Educating individuals, especially youths, about the risks associated with drug use is a critical component of public health strategies aimed at reducing the incidence of drug-induced psychosis and its long-term effects on mental health.

Differentiating Behaviour from Illness

Differentiating between behaviours indicative of a psychotic disorder and those related to substance use or other conditions is a critical aspect of psychiatric assessment. This distinction is essential for accurate diagnosis and effective treatment planning. The process involves a combination of clinical techniques and a comprehensive evaluation of the individual's history, symptoms, and overall functioning.

Clinical Techniques for Differentiation: To distinguish between psychotic disorders and behaviours related to substance use or other conditions, clinicians use several techniques:

- **Detailed Medical and Psychiatric History**: A thorough exploration of the individual's medical, psychiatric, and substance use history is crucial. This includes understanding the timeline of symptom development in relation to substance use, previous psychiatric symptoms, and family history of mental health disorders.

- **Assessment of Symptom Onset and Course**: Clinicians pay close attention to when symptoms appeared and how they have progressed over time. Symptoms that coincide closely with substance use or withdrawal might suggest a substance-induced psychosis, whereas symptoms that persist regardless of substance use are more indicative of a primary psychotic disorder.

- **Physical and Neurological Examination**: A comprehensive physical and neurological examination can help identify any medical or neurological conditions that may present with psychotic-like symptoms. This may include conditions such as brain injuries, tumors, or infections.

- **Laboratory Testing and Imaging**: Drug screening and other laboratory tests can detect the presence of substances that might induce psychotic symptoms. Brain imaging techniques, like MRI or CT scans, can be used to rule out neurological disorders.

- **Evaluation of Symptom Context**: Understanding the context in which symptoms occur is important. For instance, hallucinations experienced only in the context of substance use or withdrawal are more suggestive of drug-induced psychosis.

- **Psychological Evaluation**: This involves assessing the individual's mental status, looking for signs of disordered thinking, delusions, hallucinations, and assessing their insight and judgment.

Importance of Comprehensive Assessment:

- **Accurate Diagnosis**: A comprehensive assessment ensures that the diagnosis is accurate, which is crucial for determining the appropriate treatment. Misdiagnosis can lead to ineffective treatment and potentially worsen the individual's condition.

- **Treatment Planning**: Understanding the underlying cause of the symptoms guides the treatment plan. For example, treatment for drug-induced psychosis primarily focuses on substance abuse treatment, whereas primary psychotic disorders require a different therapeutic approach.

- **Risk Assessment**: A thorough assessment helps in identifying any risks associated with the psychotic symptoms, such as the potential for self-harm or harm to others, which is crucial for ensuring the safety of the individual and others.

- **Baseline for Monitoring Progress**: Establishing a comprehensive baseline is important for monitoring the individual's progress over time. This includes tracking the response to treatment and making necessary adjustments.

Differentiating between behaviours that are symptomatic of a psychotic disorder and those related to substance use or other conditions requires a meticulous and comprehensive approach.

This process is vital for ensuring that individuals receive appropriate and effective care tailored to their specific needs and circumstances.

Causes of Psychosis

Psychosis is a complex mental health condition with multifaceted causes. Understanding these causes involves exploring genetic, neurological, and environmental factors, each contributing in varying degrees to the development of the disorder. The interplay of these elements adds to the complexity in understanding and treating psychosis.

Genetic Factors: Genetics play a significant role in the susceptibility to psychotic disorders. Studies have shown that individuals with a family history of psychotic disorders such as schizophrenia are at a higher risk of developing similar conditions. Genetic predisposition does not guarantee the development of psychosis but increases the likelihood, especially when combined with environmental triggers.

- Research has identified several genes associated with an increased risk of psychosis, although no single gene is considered responsible. These genetic factors likely interact with each other and with non-genetic factors to influence the risk of developing psychotic disorders.

Neurological Factors: The brain's structure and function are critical in understanding the development of psychosis. Abnormalities in certain brain areas, neurotransmitter systems, and neural pathways are linked to psychotic symptoms.

Environmental Factors: Environmental factors play a crucial role in the development and triggering of psychosis, especially in individuals with a genetic predisposition.

- **Stressful Life Events**: Traumatic experiences, chronic stress, and significant life changes can trigger the onset of psychotic symptoms or exacerbate existing symptoms in vulnerable individuals.

- **Substance Use**: As previously discussed, certain substances, including cannabis, hallucinogens, and amphetamines, can induce psychosis, particularly in susceptible individuals.

- **Socioeconomic Factors**: Factors such as socioeconomic status, urbanicity, migration, and social isolation have been linked to an increased risk of developing psychotic disorders. These factors may interact with biological vulnerabilities to trigger the onset of psychosis.

- **Perinatal Factors**: Complications during pregnancy and birth, such as prenatal exposure to infections, malnutrition, or hypoxia, have been associated with a higher risk of psychotic disorders later in life.

Understanding the Complexity:

- The causes of psychosis are not isolated; they interact with each other in complex ways. For example, a person with a genetic predisposition may not develop psychosis unless triggered by environmental factors like drug use or significant stress.

- The relative contribution of each factor can vary greatly among individuals. While one person may develop psychosis primarily due to genetic reasons, another might do so due to a combination of environmental stresses and subtle genetic factors.

- This complexity makes predicting who will develop psychosis challenging and underscores the need for a personalized approach in both prevention and treatment.

Understanding these elements is crucial for developing effective prevention strategies, identifying individuals at risk, and providing tailored treatments. This multifaceted causality also highlights the importance of a holistic approach in managing psychotic disorders, one that considers the entire spectrum of an individual's life and experiences.

Neurochemical Aspects of Psychosis

The neurochemical aspects of psychosis provide significant insight into the understanding and treatment of this complex mental health condition. Central to this discussion is the role of brain chemicals, particularly neurotransmitters like dopamine, and how their imbalances contribute to the development and manifestation of psychotic symptoms.

Dopamine and Psychosis: Dopamine, a key neurotransmitter in the brain, plays a crucial role in the neurochemical pathology of psychosis. The dopamine hypothesis of schizophrenia and other psychotic disorders suggests that an overactivity of dopamine transmission in certain brain pathways is associated with psychotic symptoms.

- **Dopamine Pathways**: The brain has several dopamine pathways, and their dysregulation can lead to different symptoms of psychosis. For instance, excessive dopaminergic activity in the mesolimbic pathway is thought to contribute to positive symptoms of psychosis, such as hallucinations and delusions.

- **Antipsychotic Medications**: Most antipsychotic drugs work by blocking dopamine receptors, particularly the D2 receptors, which helps in reducing psychotic symptoms. This mechanism of action supports the theory that dopamine plays a central role in psychosis.

Other Neurotransmitters: While dopamine is a key player, other neurotransmitters are also involved in psychosis.

- **Glutamate**: This neurotransmitter is important for learning and memory. The glutamate hypothesis of schizophrenia suggests that a dysfunction in glutamatergic transmission, particularly involving NMDA (N-methyl-D-aspartate) receptors, may contribute to psychosis.

- **Serotonin**: Some newer antipsychotic drugs target serotonin receptors as well as dopamine receptors. The role of serotonin in psychosis is less clear than dopamine, but it is believed to modulate various brain functions, including mood, perception, and cognition, which are altered in psychosis.

Neurochemical Imbalances:

- **Positive Symptoms**: The positive symptoms of psychosis, such as hallucinations and delusions, are thought to be related to an overactivity of dopamine and possibly other neurotransmitters in certain brain regions.

- **Negative and Cognitive Symptoms**: The negative symptoms (like emotional flatness and social withdrawal) and cognitive symptoms (such as impaired memory and attention) may be related to reduced dopamine activity in other brain pathways, such as the mesocortical pathway.

- **Complex Interactions**: The interaction between different neurotransmitter systems adds complexity to the neurochemical understanding of psychosis. For example, glutamate and dopamine interact in ways that may affect the symptoms and course of psychotic disorders.

The neurochemical aspects of psychosis involve a complex interplay of neurotransmitters, with dopamine playing a central role. This understanding has been pivotal in developing pharmacological treatments for psychosis. However, the full picture of neurochemical involvement in psychosis is intricate, with ongoing research continuing to uncover new insights. The complexity of these neurochemical interactions underlines the challenges in developing effective treatments for all aspects of psychotic disorders and highlights the need for ongoing research in this field.

Evidence-Based Therapies for Psychosis

The treatment of psychosis involves a multi-faceted approach, incorporating evidence-based therapies such as antipsychotic medications, psychotherapy, and integrated care models. Personalized treatment plans, tailored to meet the specific needs of each individual, are crucial for effective management of this complex condition.

Antipsychotic Medications: Antipsychotic drugs form the cornerstone of pharmacological treatment for psychosis, particularly for managing acute psychotic episodes and preventing relapses.

- **First-Generation Antipsychotics**: These older medications, such as haloperidol and chlorpromazine, primarily target dopamine receptors to reduce psychotic symptoms. However, they are often associated with significant side effects, including movement disorders (Tandon, Nasrallah, & Keshavan, 2008).

- **Second-Generation Antipsychotics**: Newer antipsychotics, like risperidone, olanzapine, and quetiapine, have a broader spectrum of action, affecting both dopamine and serotonin receptors. They are generally preferred due to a lower risk of movement disorders, though they can have other side effects such as weight gain and metabolic syndrome (Leucht, Cipriani, Spineli, Mavridis, Orey, Richter, ... & Davis, 2013).

Psychotherapy: Various forms of psychotherapy are used in conjunction with medication to treat psychosis.

- **Cognitive-Behavioural Therapy (CBT)**: CBT for psychosis is tailored to help individuals recognize and alter distorted thinking and perceptions. It can be particularly effective in addressing delusions and hallucinations (Wykes, Steel, Everitt, & Tarrier, 2008).

- **Family Therapy**: Involving family members in therapy can be beneficial, providing education about psychosis, improving family communication, and reducing relapse rates (Pharoah, Mari, Rathbone, & Wong, 2010).

- **Other Therapeutic Approaches**: Techniques such as supportive psychotherapy, psychosocial interventions, and social skills training are also valuable, particularly for addressing negative symptoms and improving social functioning.

Integrated Care Models: Integrated care models that combine pharmacological treatment, psychotherapy, and support services are considered best practice in treating psychosis.

- **Assertive Community Treatment (ACT)**: ACT teams provide comprehensive, community-based psychiatric treatment, rehabilitation, and support to individuals with severe mental illness (Burns et al., 2007).

- **Early Intervention Services**: These services, targeting individuals in the early stages of psychotic disorders, are shown to improve outcomes, reduce hospitalization, and support recovery (Bertolote & McGorry, 2005).

  Personalized Treatment Plans: Personalizing treatment involves considering the individual's specific symptoms, preferences, medical history, and life circumstances.

- **Pharmacogenomics**: This emerging field studies how genetic makeup affects an individual's response to drugs, holding potential for more personalized medication choices in the treatment of psychosis.

- **Holistic Approach**: A holistic approach, addressing physical health, mental health, social needs, and lifestyle, is critical for the overall well-being of individuals with psychosis.

The treatment of psychosis requires a comprehensive and personalized approach, combining evidence-based pharmacological and psychotherapeutic interventions. Ongoing research continues to refine these approaches, with an increasing emphasis on early intervention and individualized care to improve outcomes for individuals with psychotic disorders.

Coping Strategies for Psychosis

Managing the symptoms of psychosis requires a combination of clinical treatment and practical coping strategies. These strategies are crucial for individuals to maintain their daily functioning and quality of life. Emphasizing the importance of support networks, self-care, and routine is fundamental in the management of psychosis.

Building a Strong Support Network: A strong support network is invaluable for individuals with psychosis. This network can include family members, friends, mental health professionals, and peer support groups.

- **Family and Friends**: Educating family and friends about psychosis can help them understand the condition, provide appropriate support, and recognize early warning signs of relapse.

- **Professional Support**: Regular contact with mental health professionals ensures ongoing monitoring and management of symptoms. Mental health teams can also provide guidance and support in crisis situations.

- **Peer Support**: Connecting with others who have experienced similar challenges can provide a sense of community and understanding. Peer support groups offer a platform for sharing coping strategies and encouragement.

Developing Self-Care Practices: Self-care practices are essential for managing stress and promoting overall well-being.

- **Healthy Lifestyle Choices**: Regular physical activity, a balanced diet, and adequate sleep can positively impact mental health. Avoiding alcohol and drugs is particularly important, as they can exacerbate symptoms.

- **Mindfulness and Relaxation Techniques**: Practices such as mindfulness, meditation, and deep breathing exercises can help reduce stress and improve focus and mental clarity.

- **Creative Outlets**: Engaging in creative activities like art, music, or writing can be therapeutic and provide a means of expression and distraction from distressing symptoms.

Establishing a Routine: A regular routine provides structure and predictability, which can be reassuring for individuals with psychosis.

- **Daily Schedules**: Having a set schedule for daily activities, including meals, medication, work or study, exercise, and leisure time, can help maintain stability and balance.

- **Goal Setting**: Setting small, achievable goals can provide a sense of purpose and accomplishment. Breaking larger tasks into smaller steps can make them more manageable.

Managing Symptoms: Practical strategies for dealing with symptoms like hallucinations and delusions are also important.

- **Reality Testing**: Individuals can be encouraged to check their perceptions with others, which can help distinguish between what is real and what is a symptom of psychosis.

- **Coping with Hallucinations**: Techniques such as listening to music, engaging in conversation, or focusing on physical sensations can help divert attention from auditory hallucinations.

- **Addressing Delusions**: While challenging delusions directly can be counterproductive, encouraging engagement in activities that distract from delusional thinking can be helpful.

Emphasizing the Role of Education: Educating oneself about psychosis can empower individuals to understand their condition better, recognize symptoms, and take an active role in their treatment plan.

Coping with psychosis involves a comprehensive approach that includes building a strong support network, practicing self-care, establishing a routine, and employing practical strategies to manage symptoms. These coping strategies, combined with professional treatment, can significantly improve the ability of individuals with psychosis to manage their condition and lead fulfilling lives.

Addressing SI/HI in Psychosis

Managing and addressing the risks of self-harm (SI) and suicidal ideation (HI) in individuals with psychosis is a critical aspect of care. The prevalence of these risks in psychosis necessitates a vigilant and proactive approach to ensure the safety and well-being of affected individuals.

Importance of Assessing Risks for SI/HI:

- **High Risk in Psychosis**: Individuals with psychosis are at a significantly higher risk for self-harm and suicidal ideation compared to the general population. This risk is compounded by factors such as the severity of symptoms, comorbid mental health conditions, and substance abuse.

- **Early Identification**: Early and accurate identification of SI/HI is vital. This involves regular and thorough assessments, not only of suicidal thoughts but also of plans, means, and intentions.

- **Impact of Symptoms**: Certain symptoms of psychosis, such as command hallucinations, severe depression, or overwhelming delusions, can increase the risk of SI/HI. Understanding the impact of these symptoms is essential in risk assessment.

Protocols for Managing SI/HI:

- **Safety Planning**: Developing a safety plan with the individual and their support network is crucial. This plan should include identifying warning signs, coping strategies, and emergency contact information.

- **Crisis Intervention**: In cases where there is an immediate risk of self-harm or suicide, crisis intervention protocols must be in place. This may involve hospitalization, increased monitoring, and adjustments in medication.

- **Collaborative Approach**: Working collaboratively with the individual, their family, and other healthcare providers is essential in managing SI/HI. This approach ensures that all parties are informed and involved in the care plan.

Support Systems for Crisis Situations:

- **Emergency Services**: Access to emergency services, such as crisis hotlines or emergency rooms, should be readily available. Individuals and their families should be aware of how and when to seek these services.

- **Mental Health Teams**: Community mental health teams can provide ongoing support and monitoring, especially for individuals identified as high risk for SI/HI. These teams often include psychiatrists, nurses, and social workers.

- **Support Groups and Therapy**: Support groups and therapy, particularly those focusing on coping skills and resilience, can be beneficial. These resources provide a space for individuals to share their experiences and learn from others.

Ongoing Monitoring and Review:

- **Regular Assessment**: Regularly assessing the risk of SI/HI is crucial, as the risk can change over time based on various factors like medication changes, life stressors, or symptom fluctuations.

- **Medication Management**: Certain antipsychotic medications can affect mood and cognition, which in turn can impact SI/HI risk. Continuous monitoring and adjustment of medication are necessary.

- **Psychoeducation**: Educating the individual and their support network about the signs of increasing SI/HI risk and strategies to manage them is an integral part of ongoing care.

Addressing SI/HI in psychosis requires a multi-faceted and proactive approach that involves regular risk assessment, safety planning, and access to crisis intervention services. Collaboration among healthcare providers, patients/clients, and their support networks is key to effectively managing these risks. Continuous monitoring and adaptation of the care plan are essential to ensure the safety and well-being of individuals with psychosis.

Professional Knowledge on Psychosis

For healthcare providers, possessing comprehensive knowledge about psychosis and adhering to best practices in care, communication, and management is crucial for effectively treating and supporting individuals with this complex condition.

Essential Information for Healthcare Providers:

- **Understanding of Psychosis**: A thorough understanding of the signs, symptoms, and underlying mechanisms of psychosis is fundamental. This includes knowledge of various psychotic disorders, their presentations, and differentiating them from other mental health conditions.

- **Pharmacological Treatments**: Familiarity with antipsychotic medications, their side effects, and the principles of pharmacotherapy in psychosis is essential. Providers should stay updated on the latest pharmacological advancements and guidelines.

- **Psychotherapeutic Interventions**: Knowledge of evidence-based psychotherapeutic interventions, for psychosis, family therapy, and psychosocial interventions, is important for holistic treatment.

- **Risk Assessment and Management**: Understanding how to assess and manage risks associated with psychosis, particularly the risks of self-harm and suicidal ideation, is critical for ensuring patient/client safety.

Best Practices in Care:

- **Person-Centered Approach**: Adopting a person-centered approach that respects the individual's preferences, needs, and values is essential. This approach fosters a therapeutic alliance and enhances treatment adherence and effectiveness.

- **Early Intervention**: Recognizing the importance of early intervention in psychosis and implementing strategies for early detection and treatment can significantly improve outcomes.

- **Integrated Care**: Coordinating care among psychiatrists, psychologists, primary care physicians, social workers, and other healthcare professionals ensures comprehensive treatment. This integrated approach addresses not only the psychological aspects but also the social and physical health needs of the individual.

Best Practices in Communication:

- **Empathy and Active Listening**: Communicating with empathy and active listening is vital in building trust and understanding with individuals experiencing psychosis. This approach facilitates a more accurate assessment and encourages patient/client engagement in treatment.

- **Clear and Concise Information**: Providing clear, concise, and jargon-free information about the condition, treatment options, and prognosis helps patients/clients and their families make informed decisions about their care.

- **Psychoeducation**: Offering psychoeducation to patients/clients and their families about psychosis enhances understanding, reduces stigma, and supports coping and management strategies.

Management of Psychotic Disorders:

- **Monitoring and Follow-Up**: Regular monitoring of symptoms, medication effects, and overall functioning is crucial for timely adjustments in treatment plans.

- **Crisis Management**: Being prepared for and skilled in managing crises, including acute psychotic episodes and situations involving SI/HI, is crucial for healthcare providers.

- **Continuity of Care**: Ensuring continuity of care, especially during transitions between care settings (e.g., hospital to community), is important for maintaining treatment gains and preventing relapse.

Conclusion

Professional knowledge and best practices in the care, communication, and management of psychosis are integral to providing effective and compassionate care to individuals with psychotic disorders. Healthcare providers must continually update their knowledge and skills, consider the holistic needs of their patients/clients, and collaborate with a team of professionals to deliver optimal care. This comprehensive approach is key to supporting the recovery and well-being of individuals with psychosis.

Week 4

The Workbook

Week Four

PSYCHOSIS

In the previous week, we deepened our understanding of Major Depressive Disorder (MDD), exploring its diagnostic criteria, manifestations, and treatment modalities. Our exploration highlighted the complexities inherent in differentiating MDD from normal mood fluctuations, the role of various biochemical factors, and the efficacy of evidence-based therapeutic interventions. We also emphasized the importance of professional competence in identifying and managing suicidal or homicidal ideations (SI/HI) in the context of MDD.

This week, we shift our focus to Psychosis, a mental health condition characterized by an impaired relationship with reality. Our aim has been to dissect the multifaceted nature of psychosis, understanding its clinical presentation, causative factors, and the critical distinction between primary psychosis and drug-induced psychosis. We have examined the DSM-V criteria for psychosis, delving into the common signs and symptoms, and exploring how substances and illicit drugs can precipitate psychotic episodes. Our exploration extended to the neurological underpinnings of psychosis, scrutinizing the role of specific chemicals and neurotransmitters in its pathogenesis. Emphasizing the necessity of distinguishing between behavioural anomalies and clinical illness, we reviewed evidence-based therapies and coping strategies for managing psychosis. The week we concluded with an emphasis on the professional's role in ruling out SI/HI and broadening their knowledge base to effectively address the challenges posed by psychosis in clinical practice. This endeavour aimed not only to enhance our clinical acumen but also to refine our approach to patient/client care in the realm of mental health.

Day 1: What is Psychosis?

1. **Reflective Exercise 1**: Describe your understanding of psychosis and its impact on patients/clients.

   _____

   _____

   _____

   _____

   _____

2. **Reflective Exercise 2**: Reflect on a case involving psychosis. What were the key challenges and learnings?

   _____

   _____

   _____

   _____

   _____

3. **Guided Activity**: Research and summarize the historical perspective on psychosis and its evolution in psychiatric understanding.

   _____

   _____

   _____

   _____

   _____

Day 2: Psychosis vs Drug-Induced Psychosis

1. **Reflective Exercise 1**: Consider the differences between primary psychosis and drug-induced psychosis based on your experiences.

_____

_____

_____

_____

_____

_____

2. **Reflective Exercise 2**: Reflect on a case of drug-induced psychosis and its management.

_____

_____

_____

_____

_____

_____

3. **Guided Activity**: Develop a comparison chart outlining the key differences between psychosis and drug-induced psychosis.

_____

_____

_____

_____

_____

Day 3: DSM-V Criteria for Psychosis

1. **Reflective Exercise 1**: Compare the DSM-V criteria for psychosis with a real case you have encountered.

_____

_____

_____

_____

_____

_____

2. **Reflective Exercise 2**: Discuss the challenges of applying the DSM-V criteria for psychosis in different patient/client populations.

_____

_____

_____

_____

_____

_____

3. **Guided Activity**: Create a diagnostic checklist based on DSM-V criteria for psychosis.

_____

_____

_____

_____

_____

Day 4: Signs and Symptoms of Psychosis

1. **Reflective Exercise 1**: Recall a patient/client showing classic signs of psychosis. How did these symptoms manifest?

_____

_____

_____

_____

_____

_____

2. **Reflective Exercise 2**: Reflect on a case where psychosis symptoms were atypical or unusual.

_____

_____

_____

_____

_____

_____

3. **Guided Activity**: Design an educational tool, like an infographic, illustrating the common signs and symptoms of psychosis.

_____

_____

_____

_____

_____

Day 5: Signs and Symptoms of Drug-Induced Psychosis

1. **Reflective Exercise 1**: Reflect on the typical signs and symptoms of drug-induced psychosis you have observed.

    _____

    _____

    _____

    _____

    _____

2. **Reflective Exercise 2**: Consider a case of drug-induced psychosis. How was it diagnosed and managed?

    _____

    _____

    _____

    _____

    _____

3. **Guided Activity**: Create a table outlining the common signs and symptoms of drug-induced psychosis and their distinguishing features.

    _____

    _____

    _____

    _____

Day 6: Substances and Illicit Drugs Causing Psychosis

1. **Reflective Exercise 1**: Discuss your experiences with patients/clients who developed psychosis as a result of substance or drug use.

_____

_____

_____

_____

_____

2. **Reflective Exercise 2**: Reflect on the types of substances commonly linked to psychosis in your practice.

_____

_____

_____

_____

3. **Guided Activity**: Research and create a summary of how various substances and illicit drugs can induce psychosis.

_____

_____

_____

_____

_____

Day 7: Therapies and Coping Strategies for Psychosis

1. **Reflective Exercise 1**: Share your experience with evidence-based therapies for psychosis.

_____

_____

_____

_____

_____

2. **Reflective Exercise 2**: Reflect on coping strategies for psychosis that you have found effective.

_____

_____

_____

_____

3. **Guided Activity**: Compile a resource list or guide of effective therapies and coping strategies for psychosis.

_____

_____

_____

_____

_____

_____

Week 5

PERSONALITY **DISORDERS**

Personality disorders (PD) represent a significant and complex area of mental health, characterized by deeply ingrained and enduring behaviour patterns that deviate markedly from the expectations of the individual's culture. These patterns typically manifest in two or more of the following areas: cognition, affectivity, interpersonal functioning, and impulse control. Notably, personality disorders are often misunderstood and can be challenging to diagnose and treat due to their pervasive nature and the variability in how symptoms present in individuals.

The understanding of personality disorders is crucial as they have a profound impact on an individual's life, influencing their thinking, feeling, and behaviour. These disorders often lead to significant impairments in personal, social, and occupational functioning. Moreover, they are associated with high rates of comorbidity with other mental health disorders, including anxiety, depression, and substance abuse disorders.

The prevalence of personality disorders in the general population is a subject of ongoing research, with estimates varying due to differences in diagnostic criteria and assessment methods. According to the Diagnostic and Statistical Manual of Mental Disorders, Fifth Edition (DSM-5), personality disorders are categorized into three clusters based on descriptive similarities. Cluster A includes paranoid, schizoid, and schizotypal personality disorders; Cluster B encompasses antisocial, borderline, histrionic, and narcissistic personality disorders; and Cluster C consists of avoidant, dependent, and obsessive-compulsive personality disorders.

Personality disorders are thought to result from a complex interplay of genetic, environmental, and psychological factors. Studies suggest that genetic predispositions play a significant role in the development of these disorders, particularly in the context of environmental stressors. For example, research has shown a significant genetic contribution to antisocial and borderline personality disorders (Torgersen et al., 2000). Furthermore, adverse childhood experiences, such as trauma or neglect, are strongly associated with the development of personality disorders in adulthood.

The treatment of personality disorders often involves a multifaceted approach, combining psychotherapy, pharmacotherapy, and social support interventions. Psychotherapy remains the cornerstone of treatment, with modalities such as Dialectical Behaviour Therapy (DBT) and Cognitive Behavioural Therapy (CBT) being particularly effective. Pharmacotherapy can be used to manage specific symptoms or comorbid conditions, although no medications are specifically approved for the treatment of personality disorders.

Despite the challenges associated with personality disorders, recent advancements in understanding and treating these conditions offer hope. Increasing awareness and education about personality disorders can lead to earlier diagnosis and intervention, potentially improving outcomes for those affected.

It is important for mental health professionals to have a thorough understanding of personality disorders, given their complexity and the impact they have on individuals and society. This understanding includes not only knowledge of diagnostic criteria and treatment options but also an awareness of the stigma and challenges faced by those living with these disorders.

Personality disorders represent a significant area of mental health, characterized by complex and enduring patterns of behaviour, thought, and emotion. Understanding these disorders is crucial for effective diagnosis and treatment, and ongoing research continues to shed light on their etiology and management.

Understanding BPD and Narcissism

Borderline Personality Disorder (BPD) and Narcissistic Personality Disorder (NPD) are two distinct types of personality disorders that often present with significant challenges both to the individuals affected and those around them. Understanding these disorders requires an appreciation of their unique characteristics, as well as common misconceptions that surround them.

Borderline Personality Disorder (BPD): BPD is characterized by a pervasive pattern of instability in interpersonal relationships, self-image, and emotions, as well as marked impulsivity. Individuals with BPD often experience intense episodes of anger, depression, and anxiety that may last only a few hours or, at most, a few days. These emotional swings are typically accompanied by a chronic fear of abandonment and may lead to efforts to avoid real or imagined separation or rejection. Self-harming behaviour, suicidal threats, and actions are not uncommon in individuals with BPD. Additionally, individuals with BPD often have an unclear or shifting self-image, which can affect their goals, values, opinions, and relationships.

Narcissistic Personality Disorder (NPD): NPD is characterized by a long-standing pattern of grandiosity (in fantasy or behaviour), a constant need for admiration, and a lack of empathy for others. People with this disorder often believe they are of primary importance in everybody's life or to anyone they meet. While they may project substantial self-confidence, this facade often masks a fragile self-esteem that is vulnerable to the slightest criticism. NPD may cause significant impairments in interpersonal functioning, as individuals with this disorder often exploit relationships and lack empathy, making it difficult for them to recognize the needs and feelings of others.

BPD Characteristics

Borderline Personality Disorder (BPD) is a complex mental health condition characterized by a range of distinctive features that significantly impact an individual's life. One of the most prominent characteristics of BPD is emotional instability. Individuals with BPD experience intense emotional episodes that may include severe bouts of anger, anxiety, and depression. These emotional swings are often rapid and unpredictable, making it challenging for them to maintain stable relationships and emotional equilibrium.

Impulsive behaviours are another hallmark of BPD. Individuals with this disorder might engage in risky and potentially self-damaging activities. These can range from substance abuse and reckless driving to binge eating and other forms of self-harm. Such behaviours often serve as a coping mechanism for dealing with overwhelming emotions or a sense of emptiness.

A deep-seated fear of abandonment is also central to BPD. This fear can stem from early life experiences and can lead to intense and frantic efforts to avoid real or imagined separation from loved ones. This fear significantly influences their relationships and can result in behaviours that appear clingy or overly dependent.

Relationships for those with BPD are often intense but unstable. They may idealize someone one moment and then suddenly believe the person does not care enough or is cruel. This pattern of idealization and devaluation, known as splitting, can lead to tumultuous and stormy relationships with family, friends, and romantic partners.

Additionally, individuals with BPD often struggle with identity issues. They may have a shifting sense of self, frequently changing their views, interests, values, or plans for the future. This instability can further complicate their interpersonal relationships and lead to feelings of emptiness and uncertainty about their role in the world.

Understanding these characteristics of BPD is crucial for effective treatment and support. It allows mental health professionals to tailor their therapeutic approach to the specific needs of individuals with BPD, helping them develop healthier coping mechanisms and build more stable and fulfilling relationships. It also fosters a deeper empathy and awareness, which is essential for reducing the stigma and misunderstanding often associated with this disorder.

NPD Characteristics

Narcissistic Personality Disorder (NPD) presents with distinct characteristics that significantly affect an individual's interpersonal relationships and self-perception. At the core of NPD is an exaggerated sense of self-importance and superiority. Individuals with this disorder often have an inflated view of their abilities and accomplishments and believe they are unique or special. This grandiosity is not just a matter of feeling confident; it's an unrealistic sense of superiority over others.

A defining feature of NPD is a preoccupation with fantasies of unlimited success, power, brilliance, beauty, or ideal love. These fantasies serve as a critical component of their self-esteem regulation and are often far removed from reality. They help the individual maintain their perception of being exceptional or superior.

Another significant characteristic of NPD is the constant need for excessive admiration and validation. Individuals with NPD often seek out attention and praise from others to support their grandiose self-image. This need for admiration is so fundamental that they may become distressed or agitated when they do not receive the desired level of recognition.

Perhaps the most challenging aspect of NPD in interpersonal contexts is the lack of empathy. People with this disorder often struggle to recognize or empathize with the feelings and needs of others. This lack of empathy is not necessarily intentional but rather a result of their own self-absorption and focus on their own needs and desires. It can lead to difficulties in forming and maintaining close, genuine relationships, as they may not fully understand or respond to the emotional needs of others.

Additionally, relationships for individuals with NPD are often superficial and are primarily used to enhance their own self-esteem or achieve personal goals. They may exploit or take advantage of others to get what they want, showing little regard for the feelings or interests of those around them.

Understanding the characteristics of NPD is essential in recognizing and addressing this personality disorder. It enables mental health professionals to devise appropriate treatment strategies that address the core issues of grandiosity, need for admiration, and lack of empathy. Moreover, a clear understanding of NPD helps in managing the interpersonal difficulties these individuals face and in reducing the stigma associated with the disorder. Empathy and informed care are critical in supporting individuals with NPD, helping them develop healthier ways of relating to themselves and others.

Common Misconceptions about BPD and NPD

Common misconceptions surrounding personality disorders, particularly Borderline Personality Disorder (BPD) and Narcissistic Personality Disorder (NPD), often lead to stigma and misunderstandings, impacting how individuals with these conditions are perceived and treated.

Addressing these misconceptions is vital for fostering a more informed and empathetic approach to mental health care.

Misconceptions about Borderline Personality Disorder (BPD)

1. **Intentional Manipulation:** A prevalent misconception about BPD is that individuals with this disorder are manipulative and deliberately troublesome. In reality, their behaviours, such as intense emotional reactions or fear of abandonment, are often involuntary responses to deep-seated pain, fear, or insecurity. These actions are more about managing overwhelming emotions than consciously manipulating others.

2. **Violent or Dangerous Tendencies:** There's a misconception that people with BPD are inherently violent or dangerous. While impulsive behaviour is a symptom, it does not inherently lead to violence. Understanding the context of their actions is essential. These behaviours often stem from an inability to regulate emotions rather than a tendency toward violence.

3. **Incurability:** Another common myth is that BPD is untreatable. However, with appropriate therapy and support, many individuals with BPD can lead fulfilling lives. Therapies like Dialectical Behaviour Therapy (DBT) have been particularly effective in managing BPD symptoms.

Misconceptions about Narcissistic Personality Disorder (NPD):

1. **Pure Selfishness and Confidence:** NPD is often mistaken for merely being overly confident or selfish. However, the disorder is more complex and rooted in deep-seated feelings of inadequacy and low self-esteem. The apparent confidence and self-centeredness are often defenses against profound internal vulnerability.

2. **Lack of Emotion:** There's a belief that individuals with NPD are incapable of feeling emotions, particularly love or empathy. While they may struggle with empathy and emotional expression, it does not mean they are devoid of feelings. Their emotional expressions might be distorted by their narcissistic traits.

3. **Chosen Behaviour:** The behaviours associated with NPD are often viewed as deliberate choices. However, these behaviours are manifestations of a mental health disorder, influenced by various underlying psychological factors. It's important to recognize that NPD behaviours, like those in other mental health conditions, are part of a disorder, not a simple choice.

4. **Inability to Benefit from Therapy:** Another misconception is that people with NPD cannot benefit from therapy or change their behaviours. While treatment can be challenging due to the nature of the disorder, psychotherapy, particularly those focusing on understanding underlying issues and building empathy, can be beneficial.

Understanding and dispelling these misconceptions is crucial for the effective treatment and support of individuals with BPD and NPD. Awareness and education can lead to more compassionate care and reduce the stigma and isolation often experienced by those with these disorders. This understanding also aids in the development of more effective and tailored treatment approaches, improving outcomes for individuals with personality disorders.

Borderline vs. Narcissistic Behaviours

Distinguishing between Borderline Personality Disorder (BPD) and Narcissistic Personality Disorder (NPD) can be challenging, as both disorders exhibit certain overlapping symptoms, yet they also possess distinct characteristics that set them apart. Understanding these nuances is crucial for accurate diagnosis and effective treatment.

1. **Emotional Regulation:** Individuals with BPD often experience intense emotional fluctuations and may struggle with feelings of emptiness or fear of abandonment. In contrast, those with NPD typically display a more stable yet inflated sense of self-importance and exhibit less emotional variability.

2. **Interpersonal Relationships:** BPD is frequently associated with unstable and intense interpersonal relationships, where individuals might rapidly oscillate between idealization and devaluation of others. On the other hand, individuals with NPD tend to have relationships characterized by a lack of empathy and an exploitative approach, often viewing relationships as a means to elevate their status or self-esteem.

3. **Self-Image:** People with BPD often have a distorted and unstable self-image, which can fluctuate depending on their current relationships and circumstances. Conversely, those with NPD usually maintain a grandiose sense of self and an over-inflated ego, despite underlying insecurities.

4. **Reaction to Criticism:** Individuals with BPD may react to criticism with intense fear, sadness, or anger due to their fragile self-image. In contrast, people with NPD often react with rage or disdain, typically perceiving criticism as a threat to their perceived superiority.

While BPD and NPD are distinct disorders, they share certain features, such as a tendency for impulsive behaviours and difficulty with maintaining stable relationships. Both disorders can also co-occur, complicating the clinical picture. Understanding these nuances is critical in distinguishing between the two, which is essential for tailoring treatment approaches.

Studies indicate that both disorders might have common developmental trajectories, such as childhood trauma or neglect. However, the response to these early life experiences often diverges, leading to the distinct symptomatology observed in BPD and NPD (Levy, 2005).

The treatment approach for each disorder varies. For instance, Dialectical Behaviour Therapy (DBT) is particularly effective for BPD, focusing on improving emotional regulation and interpersonal effectiveness. In contrast, treatment for NPD often involves helping individuals develop greater empathy and understanding the root causes of their grandiosity and need for admiration (Ronningstam, 2005).

DSM-V Criteria for Personality Disorders

The Diagnostic and Statistical Manual of Mental Disorders, Fifth Edition (DSM-5), provides specific criteria for diagnosing personality disorders (PDs), including Borderline Personality Disorder (BPD) and Narcissistic Personality Disorder (NPD). Understanding these criteria is crucial for clinicians to make accurate diagnoses and develop effective treatment plans.

General Criteria for Personality Disorders: The DSM-5 outlines general criteria for diagnosing PDs, which are applicable to all specific types. These include:

1. **Enduring Patterns:** An enduring pattern of inner experience and behaviour that deviates markedly from the expectations of the individual's culture.

2. **Pervasiveness and Inflexibility:** This pattern is pervasive and inflexible, consistent across a broad range of personal and social situations.

3. **Significant Distress or Impairment:** It leads to clinically significant distress or impairment in social, occupational, or other important areas of functioning.

4. **Stability and Long Duration:** The pattern is stable and of long duration, with its onset traceable back to at least adolescence or early adulthood.

5. **Not Better Explained:** The pattern is not better explained as a manifestation or consequence of another mental disorder.

6. **Not Attributable to Substance Use or Medical Condition:** The pattern is not attributable to the physiological effects of a substance or another medical condition.

Diagnostic Criteria for BPD in DSM-5

The Diagnostic and Statistical Manual of Mental Disorders, Fifth Edition (DSM-5), outlines specific criteria for the diagnosis of BPD. These criteria include a pervasive pattern of instability in interpersonal relationships, self-image, and affect, as well as marked impulsivity, beginning by early adulthood and present in a variety of contexts.

1. **Frantic Efforts to Avoid Real or Imagined Abandonment**: Individuals with BPD often exhibit intense fears of abandonment, which can lead to desperate behaviours to avoid being alone or left out. These fears are typically not grounded in reality and can arise even in stable relationships. This criterion reflects the hypersensitivity to abandonment, often stemming from early life experiences.

2. **A Pattern of Unstable and Intense Interpersonal Relationships**: Relationships of those with BPD are often characterized by a pattern of instability and intensity. They may quickly shift from idealizing someone to devaluing them, a phenomenon known as "splitting." This

instability often stems from an effort to cope with fears of abandonment and a need for closeness and validation.

3. **Identity Disturbance: Markedly and Persistently Unstable Self-Image or Sense of Self**: Individuals with BPD may experience significant uncertainty about their identity, self-image, values, and aspirations. Their opinions of themselves can change rapidly and may be influenced by their current relationships and circumstances. This lack of a stable sense of self may lead to frequent changes in jobs, friends, lovers, religion, values, goals, or even sexual identity.

4. **Impulsivity in at Least Two Areas that are Potentially Self-Damaging**: Impulsivity in behaviours that are potentially harmful is common in BPD. This can include substance abuse, binge eating, reckless driving, and risky sexual behaviour. Such behaviours are often ways of coping with emotional pain or feelings of emptiness but lead to further instability and distress.

5. **Recurrent Suicidal Behaviour, Gestures, Threats, or Self-Mutilating Behaviour**: BPD is often associated with suicidal behaviour and self-harm. This may include suicide attempts, threats, or self-injury (like cutting). These behaviours are usually in response to feelings of rejection, criticism, or abandonment.

6. **Affective Instability Due to a Marked Reactivity of Mood**: Individuals with BPD experience intense emotional swings that can change rapidly. This emotional instability can include intense episodic dysphoria, irritability, or anxiety usually lasting a few hours and only rarely more than a few days. These mood swings are often reactive to interpersonal stresses.

7. **Chronic Feelings of Emptiness**: Many with BPD describe a chronic feeling of emptiness or boredom. This feeling is different from sadness or loneliness, as it is a pervasive sense of emptiness or lack of fulfillment. This emptiness may result from the lack of a stable self and frequent changes in goals, values, and aspirations.

8. **Inappropriate, Intense Anger or Difficulty Controlling Anger**: People with BPD may display intense and inappropriate anger or have trouble controlling their anger. This might manifest as frequent temper outbursts, constant anger, or physical fights. The anger is often triggered by perceived slights or abandonment and may be disproportionate to the situation.

9. **Transient, Stress-Related Paranoid Ideation or Severe Dissociative Symptoms**: Under stress, individuals with BPD may experience paranoid ideation or dissociative symptoms. These may include feeling disconnected from reality or oneself, experiencing distortions in perception, or having brief paranoid thoughts. These symptoms are transient and often related to stressful situations.

The diagnostic criteria for BPD in the DSM-5 emphasize the pattern of instability in interpersonal relationships, self-image, and affect, along with marked impulsivity. These criteria must be met consistently over time and not just be a response to a particular situation or in a specific state of mind. The diagnosis of BPD, like all mental health diagnoses, requires a comprehensive assessment by a qualified mental health professional, taking into account the individual's life history, symptoms, and behaviour patterns.

Borderline Personality Disorder is a complex mental health disorder that requires a nuanced understanding and a compassionate approach. Accurate diagnosis, comprehensive treatment planning, and ongoing support are crucial for individuals with BPD to navigate the challenges of the disorder and lead fulfilling lives. By raising awareness and understanding of BPD, we can foster a more empathetic and effective approach to managing this condition.

Diagnostic Criteria for NPD in DSM-5

The diagnostic criteria for NPD in the DSM-5 underscore the pervasive patterns of grandiosity, need for admiration, and a lack of empathy. These symptoms must be consistent across various contexts and not exclusively during periods of illness or distress. Diagnosing NPD, like all personality disorders, requires a comprehensive clinical evaluation, considering an individual's long-term patterns of behaviour and the impact on their functioning in various life areas. It's important to note that these criteria are meant for use by trained clinicians and should be considered within the broader context of the individual's personal and psychological history.

1. **Grandiose Sense of Self-importance**: Individuals with NPD often have an inflated sense of self-importance. They may exaggerate achievements and talents, expecting to be recognized as superior without commensurate achievements. This grandiosity is often the most noticeable feature and can manifest in both overt and covert forms.

2. **Preoccupied with Fantasies of Unlimited Success, Power, Brilliance, Beauty, or Ideal Love**: People with NPD frequently indulge in daydreams about achieving power, success, brilliance, beauty, or ideal love. These fantasies are out of proportion to the reality of the individual's life and may serve as a coping mechanism for feelings of inadequacy. These fantasies can significantly impact their decision-making and relationships.

3. **Believes That They Are "Special" and Unique**: Individuals with NPD often believe that they are unique or "special" and can only be understood by or should associate with other special or high-status people (or institutions). They may display snobbish or patronizing attitudes.

4. **Requires Excessive Admiration**: A constant need for attention, affirmation, and admiration characterizes NPD. This requirement is not just a desire but seen as an entitlement. This need for admiration is linked to their fragile self-esteem.

5. **Has a Sense of Entitlement**: Individuals with NPD typically exhibit unreasonable expectations of especially favourable treatment or automatic compliance with their expectations. They often expect others to cater to their needs without reciprocation.

6. **Interpersonally Exploitative:** People with NPD often take advantage of others to achieve their own ends. They may use others without consideration for their feelings or interests. This exploitation is often a central aspect of their interpersonal relationships.

7. **Lacks Empathy: Unwilling to Recognize or Identify with the Feelings and Needs of Others:** A key feature of NPD is a lack of empathy. Individuals with NPD have difficulty recognizing or identifying with the feelings and needs of others. They may be dismissive or oblivious to the hurt their behaviour can cause.

8. **Often Envious of Others or Believes That Others Are Envious of Them:** Envy is common in NPD, both feeling envious of others and believing that others are envious of them. This stems from their need to be superior in all aspects. They may be resentful of others' success or happiness.

9. **Arrogant and Haughty Behaviours or Attitudes:** Individuals with NPD often exhibit arrogance and haughty behaviours or attitudes. They may be contemptuous, patronizing, or disdainful towards others, particularly those they perceive as inferior. This arrogance often serves as a facade to mask their deep-seated insecurity.

Importance of a Comprehensive Diagnostic Process

The importance of a comprehensive diagnostic process cannot be overstated. Accurate diagnosis requires a thorough understanding of the individual's history, symptoms, and how their behaviour deviates from cultural norms. Clinicians must consider the complexity of personality disorders, which often co-occur with other mental health disorders, complicating the diagnostic process. Additionally, understanding the individual's personal and cultural background is crucial, as this can influence the expression of personality traits and disorder manifestations.

A comprehensive diagnostic assessment typically involves a combination of clinical interviews, self-report questionnaires, and, in some cases, reports from family members or close associates. The clinician must also differentiate between personality disorders and other mental health conditions, as well as assess for the presence of co-occurring disorders. This careful and thorough approach ensures that the diagnosis is accurate, which is crucial for developing an effective treatment plan.

Proper diagnosis of personality disorders is challenging yet vital. It not only guides treatment but also helps in understanding the individual's world view, coping mechanisms, and interpersonal dynamics. Clinicians must be sensitive to the complexities involved and the potential impact of these disorders on the individual's life and relationships.

Signs and Symptoms of Borderline Personality Disorder

Understanding the signs and symptoms of Borderline Personality Disorder (BPD) is crucial for recognizing and managing this complex mental health condition. BPD is characterized by intense emotional experiences, unstable relationships, and a chronic fear of abandonment. These symptoms can significantly affect an individual's daily life and functioning.

Emotional Instability: One of the most prominent features of BPD is emotional instability or affective dysregulation. Individuals with BPD experience intense emotions that can fluctuate rapidly. They might feel ecstatic one moment and deeply distressed the next, often without a clear trigger. This emotional turbulence can lead to significant distress and impairs their ability to maintain a stable sense of well-being.

Fear of Abandonment: People with BPD often struggle with an intense fear of abandonment or rejection. This fear can stem from early life experiences and can lead to desperate efforts to avoid real or imagined abandonment. It manifests in various ways, such as clinging to relationships, rapid involvement in intimate relationships, or conversely, distancing oneself to pre-empt perceived rejection.

Intense and Unstable Relationships: Relationships of individuals with BPD are typically marked by intensity and instability. They may idealize someone at the beginning of a relationship but suddenly shift to devaluing them at the first sign of disappointment or conflict. This pattern, often referred to as 'splitting,' results from their struggles to integrate both positive and negative aspects of others and themselves.

Impulsive Behaviours: Impulsivity is another key symptom of BPD. It might manifest in risky behaviours such as reckless driving, substance abuse, binge eating, or engaging in unsafe sex. These behaviours are often attempts to manage or escape from overwhelming emotions but can lead to further problems and regrets.

Chronic Feelings of Emptiness: Many individuals with BPD describe feeling empty or bored. This chronic emptiness is more than just occasional feelings of loneliness or sadness; it's a persistent sense of dissatisfaction with life and oneself. It can lead to a lack of motivation, feeling disconnected from others, and difficulty finding meaning or pleasure in activities.

Intense Anger and Problems with Anger Management: Individuals with BPD may experience intense and inappropriate anger. They may have a hard time controlling their anger, leading to outbursts, ongoing feelings of irritability, or even physical confrontations. This anger often arises from perceived mistreatment or injustice and can significantly strain interpersonal relationships.

Self-Harming Behaviours and Suicidal Ideation: Self-harm and suicidal thoughts are unfortunately common in individuals with BPD. These actions might be used as a way to cope with overwhelming emotional pain or as expressions of deep despair. It's crucial to approach these behaviours with understanding and to seek professional help.

Transient Stress-Related Paranoia or Dissociative Symptoms: Under stress, people with BPD may experience paranoid ideation or dissociative symptoms. They might feel detached from reality, have out-of-body experiences, or experience brief episodes of paranoid thinking. These symptoms usually occur in response to stress and typically resolve as the stress diminishes.

The manifestation of these symptoms can significantly disrupt daily life, affecting work, education, and relationships. It's not uncommon for individuals with BPD to have turbulent work histories, interrupted education, and tumultuous relationships. Moreover, the emotional turmoil can make it challenging to maintain a consistent life structure, impacting everything from self-care to long-term planning.

Recognizing these symptoms is the first step toward managing BPD. Understanding the impact of these symptoms on daily life is essential for both individuals with BPD and those around them. It paves the way for empathy, effective communication, and the development of appropriate coping strategies and treatment plans.

Recognizing Narcissistic Behaviours

Recognizing the signs of Narcissistic Personality Disorder (NPD) is essential for understanding and managing this condition, which is often characterized by grandiosity, a lack of empathy, and a significant need for admiration. These behaviours not only affect the individual with the disorder but also significantly impact their relationships and interactions with others.

Grandiosity: A hallmark of narcissistic behaviour is grandiosity, which manifests as an exaggerated sense of self-importance. Individuals with NPD often believe they are superior to others and may exaggerate their achievements and talents. This grandiosity isn't just a case of high self-esteem; it's an unrealistic view of oneself that is often out of touch with reality. They may expect special treatment and believe that normal rules or standards don't apply to them.

Lack of Empathy: A critical aspect of NPD is a marked lack of empathy. Individuals with this disorder often have difficulty recognizing or understanding the feelings and needs of others. They may be indifferent to the emotional distress of others or unable to acknowledge it. This lack of empathy can lead to relationships that are superficial or exploitative, as the individual with NPD primarily focuses on their own needs and disregards those of others.

Need for Admiration: People with NPD have a significant need for admiration and validation from others. This need is so strong that it can drive many of their actions and interactions. They may constantly seek compliments and positive reinforcement, and they may react negatively to criticism or feedback that isn't overwhelmingly positive. Their self-esteem is often dependent on how others view them, leading to behaviours aimed at drawing attention and affirmation.

Sense of Entitlement: A sense of entitlement is common in those with NPD. They may expect special treatment from others and believe that they deserve to have their needs met without regard for the needs of others. This entitlement can manifest in various ways, from expecting others to comply with their demands to believing they should receive favourable treatment in social or professional settings.

Exploitative Relationships: Due to their lack of empathy and sense of entitlement, individuals with NPD often engage in exploitative relationships. They may use others for their own gain without consideration for the impact of their actions. This exploitation can be emotional, financial, or professional and often leads to strained or broken relationships.

Envy and Belief of Others' Envy: Envy is a common emotion for those with NPD. They may be envious of others' successes, relationships, or possessions. Conversely, they might believe that others are envious of them, regardless of whether there is any basis for this belief. This perception of envy can affect how they interact with others and how they perceive their social and professional environments.

Arrogance and Haughty Behaviours: Arrogance is frequently observed in individuals with NPD. They may come across as snobbish, disdainful, or patronizing. This arrogance is a defense mechanism masking their vulnerabilities and is often used to maintain their sense of superiority over others.

The Impact of Narcissistic Behaviours on Self and Relationships

The behaviours associated with NPD can significantly impact the individual's life and relationships. Their need for admiration and lack of empathy can make it challenging to form and maintain close, genuine relationships. In personal relationships, they may struggle to connect deeply with others, leading to a sense of loneliness or dissatisfaction. Professionally, their sense of entitlement and exploitation of others can lead to conflicts and strained working relationships.

The grandiosity and constant need for admiration can also lead to internal challenges. Individuals with NPD may struggle with underlying feelings of emptiness or dissatisfaction, particularly when they don't receive the external validation they seek. Their self-esteem is often fragile and dependent on external factors, leading to a constant pursuit of affirmation.

Understanding these narcissistic behaviours and their impact is crucial for both individuals with NPD and those interacting with them. It helps in developing strategies to manage these behaviours and in creating more stable and fulfilling relationships. For the individual with NPD, recognizing these traits can be the first step toward seeking help and learning healthier ways to relate to themselves and others.

Impact of BPD and Narcissistic Behaviours

The impacts of Borderline Personality Disorder (BPD) and Narcissistic Personality Disorder (NPD) extend far beyond the individuals diagnosed with these conditions. Both disorders significantly affect personal, social, and professional interactions and present unique challenges in various life settings.

Personal Relationships: Individuals with BPD often experience intense and unstable personal relationships. Their fear of abandonment, coupled with a tendency to idealize or devalue others, can lead to a series of tumultuous and often short-lived relationships. They may quickly form intense attachments, but these can just as rapidly deteriorate into conflicts and breakups.

Emotional Turmoil: The emotional instability characteristic of BPD means that individuals often experience intense mood swings and emotional episodes. This can result in unpredictable behaviour and reactions, making it difficult for them to maintain steady, long-term relationships and friendships.

Professional Challenges: In the workplace, the impulsivity and emotional intensity associated with BPD can lead to difficulties in maintaining consistent performance and relationships with colleagues and superiors. The stress of the work environment can exacerbate symptoms, leading to conflicts and potential job losses.

Self-Image and Identity Issues: The fluctuating self-image and sense of identity can create a persistent sense of uncertainty and dissatisfaction. Individuals with BPD may struggle to understand who they are, which can impact their life choices, relationships, and overall stability.

Interpersonal Relationships: People with NPD often have difficulty forming and maintaining healthy relationships. Due to their lack of empathy and exploitative tendencies, their relationships can be superficial and primarily serve their needs for admiration and validation. This can lead to a lack of genuine, deep connections with others.

Professional Environment: In the workplace, individuals with NPD may seek positions of power and may be driven to achieve, but their sense of entitlement and lack of consideration for others can create conflicts. They may be seen as arrogant or difficult to work with, which can hamper teamwork and collaboration.

Long-term Relationship Challenges: In long-term relationships, whether romantic, familial, or platonic, the narcissistic individual's need for admiration and tendency to devalue others when they do not meet their expectations can lead to significant strain. Relationships may be marked by a lack of mutual support and understanding, often leading to their breakdown.

Self-Esteem and Vulnerability: Despite their outward appearance of confidence and superiority, individuals with NPD often have fragile self-esteem. Their self-worth is heavily dependent on external validation, and they can be very sensitive to criticism or perceived slights. This can lead to internal distress and challenges in maintaining a stable sense of self-worth.

Both BPD and NPD significantly impact individuals' lives and their ability to form and maintain healthy and stable relationships. In personal settings, these disorders can lead to strained and tumultuous relationships, while in professional environments, they can create challenges in teamwork and performance. Understanding these impacts is crucial for individuals with these disorders, their loved ones, and professionals working with them. This understanding can guide the development of more effective communication strategies, relationship management techniques, and therapeutic approaches to improve overall functioning and quality of life for those affected by BPD and NPD.

Differentiating Traits or Behaviours

Distinguishing between personality traits or behaviours and personality disorders like BPD and NPD is a critical aspect of diagnosis and understanding these complex conditions. This differentiation is not always straightforward, as certain characteristics of personality disorders can be observed in various degrees in the general population. However, certain techniques and criteria, particularly focusing on patterns, intensity, and functional impairment, help in making this distinction. Here are some techniques to Distinguish Personality Traits or Behaviours from Personality Disorders

1. **Consistency Across Time and Situations:** One of the primary indicators of a personality disorder, as opposed to a personality trait, is the consistency of behaviours and patterns across various situations and over time. While many individuals may exhibit traits like impulsivity or sensitivity to criticism at points in their life, those with personality disorders will show these traits consistently and persistently.

2. **Intensity and Extremity of Behaviours:** The intensity and extremity of behaviours and emotional responses are also key in differentiating personality disorders from traits. In personality disorders, behaviours and emotional reactions are often more extreme and intense compared to the general population. For example, while many may experience moments of self-doubt, individuals with BPD may experience profound identity disturbances.

3. **Impact on Functioning:** Another important aspect to consider is the impact of these behaviours on an individual's functioning. Personality disorders are associated with significant impairments in personal, social, and occupational functioning. For instance, whereas occasional arrogance or self-centeredness can be a personality trait, in NPD, this behaviour is pervasive and significantly impairs interpersonal relationships and functioning.

4. **Response to Stress and Conflict:** Observing how an individual responds to stress and conflict can also aid in differentiating between personality traits and disorders. Those with personality disorders often exhibit exacerbated patterns of behaviour under stress, which are disproportionate to the situation and can lead to dysfunctional coping mechanisms.

5. **Self-Perception and Insight:** People with personality disorders often have limited insight into their behaviour and how it affects others. They may not recognize that their behaviour is problematic or differs from societal norms. This lack of self-awareness is less common in individuals with personality traits.

The diagnosis of personality disorders requires a careful consideration of the pattern, intensity, and impairment caused by the individual's behaviours and traits. It's not just the presence of certain characteristics but how they are woven into the fabric of the person's life that matters.

- **Pattern:** A persistent and enduring pattern of behaviour that deviates from cultural expectations.

- **Intensity:** The severity with which these behavioural patterns manifest, often leading to extreme reactions and interactions.

- **Impairment:** The key factor that distinguishes disorders from traits is the level of impairment in daily functioning, including work, relationships, and self-care.

Differentiating personality traits or behaviours from personality disorders is crucial in providing appropriate care and support. It helps in understanding the severity of the condition and tailoring treatment approaches that address not just the symptoms but the underlying patterns and impacts on the individual's life. This differentiation also aids in reducing the stigma associated with personality disorders by highlighting the distinction between occasional personality traits and more severe, enduring patterns indicative of a disorder.

Causes of Personality Disorders

Understanding the causes of personality disorders like BPD and NPD involves exploring a complex interplay of genetic, environmental, and psychological factors. These disorders are not the result of a single cause but rather emerge from a combination of various influences that interact in unique ways for each individual.

Genetic Factors

1. **Heritability:** Research indicates a significant genetic component in the development of personality disorders. Studies involving twins and families suggest that genetic factors can predispose individuals to these conditions. For example, there's evidence suggesting a higher prevalence of BPD and NPD among first-degree relatives of those with these disorders.

2. **Genetic Vulnerability:** Certain genes have been associated with traits and behaviours central to personality disorders. For instance, genes affecting the regulation of neurotransmitters like serotonin and dopamine may play a role in emotional regulation and impulsive behaviours seen in BPD.

Environmental Factors

1. **Childhood Trauma and Abuse:** A strong environmental factor in the development of personality disorders is the experience of trauma, particularly during childhood. Physical, emotional, and sexual abuse, as well as neglect, have been significantly associated with the development of conditions like BPD.

2. **Invalidating or Dysfunctional Family Environments:** Growing up in an environment where emotions are ignored, trivialized, or punished can contribute to the development of personality disorders. An invalidating environment can exacerbate the difficulty in managing emotions and forming a stable self-identity, particularly in BPD.

3. **Cultural and Social Influences:** Societal norms and cultural expectations can also influence the development and expression of personality disorders. Cultural factors may shape the way symptoms are expressed and can also impact the perception and stigma around mental health disorders.

Psychological Factors

1. **Coping and Defense Mechanisms:** Individuals with personality disorders often develop maladaptive coping mechanisms in response to stress or trauma. For example, individuals with NPD may develop grandiosity and a lack of empathy as a defense against deep-seated feelings of inadequacy.

2. **Attachment and Relationships:** Early attachment experiences and relationship patterns can significantly influence the development of personality disorders. Disruptions in early attachment, such as inconsistent caregiving or abandonment, can lead to difficulties in forming stable relationships later in life.

The Complexity of Influencing Factors

The etiology of personality disorders is multifaceted and complex. It's rarely possible to pinpoint a single cause; rather, it's the interaction of genetic predispositions, environmental experiences, and individual psychological processes that culminate in the development of these disorders. This complexity can make understanding and treating personality disorders challenging, as each individual's unique combination of influences shapes their experience of the disorder.

Moreover, the interplay between these factors can vary greatly from one person to another, even among those with the same diagnosis. For example, while one individual with BPD may have a history of childhood trauma, another might not, suggesting different pathways to the development of similar symptomatology.

Understanding the causes of personality disorders is crucial for developing effective treatment approaches. It allows for a more personalized understanding of each individual's condition, paving the way for tailored interventions that address not only the symptoms but also the underlying causes. This holistic approach is essential for providing comprehensive care and support to individuals with personality disorders, helping them navigate the challenges posed by their condition.

Evidence-Based Therapies for Personality Disorders

Effective treatment of personality disorders requires a nuanced approach that includes evidence-based therapies. The key to successful treatment lies in tailoring these approaches to meet the individual needs and specific characteristics of the disorder.

Dialectical Behaviour Therapy (DBT)

1. **DBT for BPD:** Dialectical Behaviour Therapy (DBT) is one of the most well-researched and effective treatments for BPD. Developed by Dr. Marsha Linehan, DBT combines cognitive-behavioural techniques with mindfulness practices. It focuses on teaching skills in four key areas: mindfulness, distress tolerance, emotion regulation, and interpersonal effectiveness.

2. **Application:** DBT is particularly effective in reducing self-harming behaviours, a common symptom in BPD, and in improving emotional regulation. The therapy involves both individual counselling and group skills training, providing a comprehensive approach to managing BPD symptoms.

3. **Adaptability:** While DBT was originally developed for BPD, its principles and techniques can also be adapted to treat other personality disorders, especially where emotion dysregulation and impulsive behaviours are present.

Cognitive Behavioural Therapy (CBT)

1. **CBT Principles:** Cognitive Behavioural Therapy (CBT) is another cornerstone in the treatment of personality disorders. CBT focuses on identifying and changing negative and distorted thinking patterns, beliefs, and behaviours.

2. **Effectiveness in Personality Disorders:** In the context of personality disorders, CBT helps patients/clients challenge their long-standing patterns of thinking and behaviour. For NPD, CBT can be tailored to address issues like grandiosity, entitlement, and sensitivity to criticism, by working on developing empathy and realistic self-assessment.

3. **Integrating CBT:** CBT can be integrated with other therapeutic modalities and can be effective in both individual and group settings. Its structured approach can be particularly beneficial in providing clarity and direction in therapy for individuals with personality disorders.

Psychotherapy

1. **Long-term Psychotherapy:** For many individuals with personality disorders, long-term psychotherapy can be beneficial. This approach allows for a deeper exploration of the underlying causes of the disorder, such as childhood trauma, family dynamics, and attachment issues.

2. **Psychodynamic Psychotherapy:** This form of therapy delves into understanding the unconscious processes and past experiences that influence current behaviour. For personality disorders, it can be particularly useful in exploring the development of the disorder over time and in various contexts.

3. **Schema Therapy:** Schema Therapy, which integrates elements of CBT, psychodynamic, and attachment theories, is another effective approach for treating personality disorders. It focuses on identifying and changing deep-seated patterns or schemas that underlie the individual's maladaptive behaviours and thoughts.

Tailoring Treatments to Individual Needs and Disorder Specifics

1. **Personalized Approach:** No single therapy is universally effective for all individuals with a personality disorder. A personalized approach, often involving a combination of different therapeutic modalities, is essential.

2. **Comorbid Conditions:** Many individuals with personality disorders also have comorbid conditions like depression, anxiety, or substance abuse. Treatment plans need to address these co-occurring disorders for effective overall management.

3. **Therapist-Patient/Client Relationship:** The relationship between the therapist and patient/client is a critical component of successful treatment. Building trust, understanding, and a strong therapeutic alliance is key, especially given the complex and sensitive nature of personality disorders.

4. **Continuity and Follow-up:** Consistency and long-term follow-up are crucial in treating personality disorders. These conditions are deeply ingrained and require ongoing effort to manage. Continuity of care ensures that progress is maintained and adjustments are made as needed.

The treatment of personality disorders is a multifaceted and ongoing process. Effective management requires a combination of evidence-based therapies tailored to individual needs, along with a strong therapeutic alliance and a commitment to long-term treatment. This approach not only addresses the symptoms but also works towards a deeper understanding and lasting change in the patterns of thought and behaviour characteristic of personality disorders.

Addressing SI/HI in Personality Disorders

The assessment and management of self-harm (SI) and homicidal ideation (HI) are critical components of treating personality disorders, particularly Borderline Personality Disorder (BPD) and Narcissistic Personality Disorder (NPD). These disorders can be associated with a higher risk of self-harm and suicidal thoughts, making it essential for clinicians to be vigilant in identifying and addressing these risks.

Importance of Assessing Risks for Self-Harm and Suicidal Ideation

Individuals with personality disorders, especially BPD, may exhibit behaviours like self-harm or express suicidal thoughts as a response to emotional pain, stress, or feelings of emptiness and abandonment. In NPD, suicidal ideation can occur in response to perceived failures, rejections, or criticism, often linked to fragile self-esteem. Assessing the risk of SI/HI is vital as it can:

1. **Prevent Potential Harm:** Early identification and intervention can prevent self-harm or suicide attempts.

2. **Understand Underlying Issues:** Assessing these risks can provide insights into the severity of the disorder and the underlying emotional distress.

3. **Guide Treatment Planning:** Recognizing the presence of SI/HI helps in tailoring treatment plans to ensure they address these critical aspects.

Strategies and Interventions for Managing These Risks

1. **Regular Monitoring and Assessment:** Continuous assessment of SI/HI risk is crucial in the treatment of personality disorders. This involves not just evaluating the presence of such thoughts but also understanding their frequency, intensity, and triggers.

2. **Crisis Intervention Plans:** Developing individualized crisis intervention plans is an effective strategy. These plans include steps that individuals can take when experiencing intense urges or thoughts related to self-harm or suicide, such as contacting a therapist or using coping strategies.

3. **Therapeutic Relationship:** A strong therapeutic relationship is key in managing SI/HI risks. Patients/Clients should feel safe and supported in discussing their thoughts and feelings with their therapist, which requires building trust and understanding over time.

4. **Safety Planning:** Safety planning is a practical tool in managing SI/HI. It involves identifying warning signs, developing coping strategies, and creating a support system that the patient/client can turn to during crises.

5. **Skill Building in Therapy:** Therapies like DBT, which emphasize skills in emotional regulation, distress tolerance, and interpersonal effectiveness, are particularly beneficial. These skills help patients/clients manage their emotions and reduce the likelihood of resorting to self-harm or suicidal behaviours.

6. **Family and Support System Involvement:** Involving family members or close friends in the treatment process, where appropriate, can provide additional support. Educating them about the nature of the disorder and how to respond to crises can be invaluable.

7. **Addressing Co-occurring Disorders:** Many individuals with personality disorders may have co-occurring mental health issues like depression or substance abuse. Addressing these in conjunction with the personality disorder is crucial as they can significantly increase the risk of SI/HI.

8. **Medication Management:** While no medications are specifically approved for personality disorders, certain medications can help manage co-occurring disorders or symptoms like mood swings, anxiety, or depression, which in turn may reduce SI/HI risks.

In managing personality disorders, the assessment and management of risks for self-harm and suicidal ideation are of paramount importance. This requires a multifaceted approach that includes regular assessment, crisis intervention, skill-building, and the involvement of the patient's/client's support system. By addressing these risks directly and comprehensively, clinicians can significantly improve patient/client safety and treatment outcomes.

Professional Insights on Personality Disorders

Treating personality disorders like BPD and NPD requires specific knowledge and skills from healthcare professionals. These disorders are complex and multifaceted, and successful treatment hinges on a deep understanding of their nature as well as a compassionate approach to care.

1. **Comprehensive Understanding of the Disorders:** A thorough grasp of the characteristics, diagnostic criteria, and typical course of personality disorders is essential. Professionals should be familiar with the nuances of each disorder to provide accurate diagnoses and effective treatment plans.

2. **Empathy and Compassion:** Given the often challenging nature of these disorders, empathy and compassion are crucial. Patients/Clients with personality disorders may have histories of trauma, and their behaviours, though sometimes difficult, are coping mechanisms. Understanding and empathy can foster a therapeutic alliance and encourage patient/client engagement.

3. **Communication Skills:** Effective communication is key, particularly in managing the intense emotions and potential conflicts that can arise in treatment. This includes active listening, clear and respectful expression, and the ability to set and maintain appropriate boundaries.

4. **Flexibility and Patience:** Treatment of personality disorders often requires a long-term commitment. Professionals should be prepared for a potentially slow process with ups and downs. Flexibility in approach and patience with progress are important.

5. **Skills in Specific Therapies:** Proficiency in therapies proven effective for personality disorders is crucial. Continuing education in these areas ensures that clinicians stay updated with the latest treatment modalities and research.

6. **Crisis Management:** Professionals should be adept at handling crises, particularly regarding risks of self-harm or suicidal ideation. This includes risk assessment, crisis intervention strategies, and the ability to develop and implement safety plans.

7. **Collaborative Approach:** A collaborative approach involving psychiatrists, psychologists, social workers, and other healthcare providers can be beneficial. Collaboration ensures comprehensive care and support for the patient/client.

Understanding the complexities involved in personality disorders is critical. These disorders often arise from deep-seated issues and can significantly impact a person's life. A compassionate approach, which acknowledges the patient's/client's struggles and strengths, is essential. This involves seeing beyond the symptoms to the person beneath, understanding their experiences, and providing support that fosters growth and healing.

Conclusion

Understanding and managing personality disorders like BPD and NPD is a challenging yet vital aspect of mental health care. These conditions, characterized by complex patterns of thinking, feeling, and behaving, require a nuanced and empathetic approach.

1. **Comprehensive Care:** Effective treatment combines a deep understanding of the disorders with evidence-based therapies tailored to individual needs. This includes recognizing and managing the risks associated with these disorders, such as self-harm and suicidal ideation.

2. **Empathy and Patience:** A compassionate approach, marked by empathy and patience, is crucial. Understanding the individual's experiences and struggles, and providing support that respects their dignity and promotes healing, is key to successful treatment.

3. **Collaboration and Continuing Education:** Collaboration among healthcare professionals and ongoing education in the latest treatment modalities are essential for providing the best possible care.

4. **Long-Term Commitment:** Managing personality disorders is often a long-term process. It requires dedication from both healthcare professionals and patients/clients, with an understanding that progress may be gradual.

5. **Holistic Approach:** Addressing not just the symptoms but the underlying causes of personality disorders is important. This holistic approach ensures that treatment is comprehensive and more likely to be effective.

Treating personality disorders requires a blend of specialized knowledge, therapeutic skills, and a compassionate approach. By understanding the complexities of these disorders and employing empathetic and informed strategies, healthcare professionals can significantly improve the quality of life for individuals with personality disorders and facilitate their journey towards healing and self-discovery.

Week 5

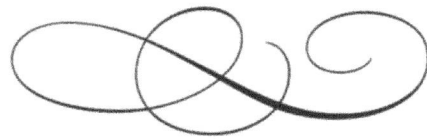

The Workbook

Week Five

PERSONALITY **DISORDERS**

In the previous week, we delved deeply into the realm of Psychosis, exploring its multifaceted nature, including its symptoms, causes, and the profound impact it has on individuals and their surroundings. We examined both the intrinsic complexities of psychosis and its drug-induced variants, gaining insights into the diagnostic challenges and the importance of distinguishing between various presentations. This exploration not only enhanced our understanding of Psychosis but also underscored the critical role of evidence-based therapies and the necessity of ruling out suicidal/homicidal ideation (SI/HI) in such cases.

This week, we turned our focus to Personality Disorders, a topic that demands our attention due to its intricate and often misunderstood nature. Personality Disorders, including Borderline Personality Disorder (BPD) and Narcissism, present unique challenges in both diagnosis and management. As we navigated through this week, we dissected the subtle yet distinct differences between these disorders, scrutinize the DSM-V criteria, and delve into the signs and symptoms that characterize them. We have aimed to unravel the complexities surrounding the effects of these disorders on individuals and their interpersonal relationships, differentiating between behaviours symptomatic of a disorder and those stemming from other causes.

Our journey have encompassed the various factors responsible for Personality Disorders, the efficacy of different therapeutic interventions, and the essential coping strategies beneficial for managing these conditions. As with previous topics, the critical importance of assessing for SI/HI in the context of Personality Disorders has been a focal point, enhancing our professional acumen in handling these challenging yet fascinating facets of mental health.

Day 1: What is PD?

1. **Reflective Exercise 1**: Describe your current understanding of personality disorders and how they differ from other mental health disorders.

_____

_____

_____

_____

_____

2. **Reflective Exercise 2**: Reflect on a case where a personality disorder was initially overlooked. What were the implications?

_____

_____

_____

_____

_____

3. **Guided Activity**: Research and summarize the evolution of the concept of personality disorders in psychiatric literature.

_____

_____

_____

_____

_____

Day 2: What is PBD, Narcissism?

1. **Reflective Exercise 1**: Reflect on your understanding of Borderline Personality Disorder and Narcissism and their impact on individuals.

_____

_____

_____

_____

_____

_____

2. **Reflective Exercise 2**: Consider a patient/client you've encountered with either BPD or Narcissism. What were the key challenges?

_____

_____

_____

_____

_____

_____

3. **Guided Activity**: Develop a brief overview of BPD and Narcissism, highlighting their key characteristics for educational purposes.

_____

_____

_____

_____

_____

_____

Day 3: Difference Between BPD and Narcissistic Behaviours

1. **Reflective Exercise 1**: Discuss the differences between BPD and Narcissistic behaviours based on your clinical experiences.

_____

_____

_____

_____

_____

2. **Reflective Exercise 2**: Reflect on a case where distinguishing between BPD and Narcissistic behaviours was challenging.

_____

_____

_____

_____

_____

3. **Guided Activity**: Create a comparison chart outlining the key differences between BPD and Narcissistic behaviours.

_____

_____

_____

_____

_____

Day 4: DSM-V Criteria for Personality Disorders

1. **Reflective Exercise 1**: Compare the DSM-V criteria for personality disorders with a case you have encountered.

_____

_____

_____

_____

_____

_____

2. **Reflective Exercise 2**: Discuss the challenges of applying DSM-V criteria for personality disorders in diverse populations.

_____

_____

_____

_____

_____

_____

3. **Guided Activity**: Develop a checklist or guide based on DSM-V criteria for diagnosing personality disorders.

_____

_____

_____

_____

_____

_____

Day 5: Signs and Symptoms of BPD and Narcissism

1. **Reflective Exercise 1**: Reflect on the common signs and symptoms of BPD you've observed in your practice.

_____

_____

_____

_____

_____

_____

2. **Reflective Exercise 2**: Consider the common signs and symptoms of Narcissistic behaviours and their impact.

_____

_____

_____

_____

_____

_____

3. **Guided Activity**: Design a tool like an infographic to illustrate the signs and symptoms of BPD and Narcissism.

_____

_____

_____

_____

_____

_____

Day 6: Effects of BPD and Narcissistic Behaviours

1. **Reflective Exercise 1**: Discuss how BPD affects individuals and their relationships based on your experience.

_____

_____

_____

_____

_____

_____

2. **Reflective Exercise 2**: Reflect on how Narcissistic behaviours affect the individual and others around them.

_____

_____

_____

_____

_____

_____

3. **Guided Activity**: Create a case study that illustrates the effects of BPD or Narcissism on individual and interpersonal dynamics.

_____

_____

_____

_____

_____

Day 7: Distinguishing Behaviour from Illness in Personality Disorders

1. **Reflective Exercise 1**: Reflect on a situation where distinguishing between problematic behaviour and a personality disorder was challenging.

_____

_____

_____

_____

_____

_____

2. **Reflective Exercise 2**: Discuss the importance of understanding the broader context when diagnosing personality disorders.

_____

_____

_____

_____

_____

_____

3. **Guided Activity**: Analyze a hypothetical case to determine if the behaviours are symptomatic of a personality disorder or a reaction to life events.

_____

_____

_____

_____

_____

_____

Week 6

ADDICTIONS

Substance abuse and addiction are complex issues that significantly impact individuals, families, and communities. Substance abuse refers to the harmful or hazardous use of psychoactive substances, including alcohol, cannabis and illicit drugs. Addiction, or substance use disorder, is a more severe condition characterized by an intense focus on using a certain substance(s) to the point where it takes over the individual's life.

To understand these concepts fully, it's crucial to recognize that substance abuse and addiction are not simply a matter of choice or moral failing. They are recognized as chronic diseases that affect the brain and behaviour (American Psychiatric Association, 2013). The development of addiction is a gradual process, often beginning with experimental or social use and evolving into more frequent and intense usage.

One of the key features of addiction is the development of tolerance, where increased amounts of the substance are needed to achieve the same effect. This escalation often leads to physical dependence, wherein the body adapts to the presence of the drug, and withdrawal symptoms occur if the use is reduced or stopped (Volkow, Koob, & McLellan, 2016).

It's also important to differentiate between physical dependence and addiction. Physical dependence can occur with the regular use of many drugs, including prescription medication, and may not necessarily be harmful. Addiction is marked by compulsive drug seeking and use, despite harmful consequences, and changes in the brain, which can be long-lasting. These changes in the brain can lead to harmful behaviours seen in people who abuse substances.

Addiction is a multifaceted problem, influenced by a variety of factors. Genetics play a significant role, with some individuals being more predisposed to addiction than others. Additionally, environmental factors such as exposure to drugs at a young age, peer pressure, stress, and trauma can significantly impact the development of substance abuse and addiction (Volkow et al., 2016)

The DSM-V (Diagnostic and Statistical Manual of Mental Disorders, Fifth Edition) provides specific criteria for the diagnosis of substance use disorders. It focuses on a pattern of use that leads to significant impairment or distress. This includes issues like using more of a substance than intended, unsuccessful efforts to cut down, craving, and failure to fulfill major role obligations at work, school, or home due to substance use.

Common signs and symptoms of addiction can vary depending on the substance used but generally include behavioural changes such as increased secrecy, changes in social circles, risky behaviours, and neglect of responsibilities. Physical signs might include changes in appetite, sleep patterns, and physical appearance. Psychological symptoms can encompass mood swings, irritability, and decreased motivation.

Understanding the signs of addiction is crucial for early intervention and treatment. Early recognition of these symptoms can lead to more effective treatment outcomes. Treatment for addiction is multifaceted and typically includes a combination of medication, counselling, and support groups. The goal is to help the individual stop using the substance, maintain a drug-free lifestyle, and achieve productive functioning in the family, at work, and in society.

Evidence-based therapies for addiction include pharmacotherapy, where medications are used to manage withdrawal symptoms and prevent relapse. Behavioural therapies help patients/clients engage in the treatment process, modify their attitudes and behaviours related to drug abuse, and increase healthy life skills. These therapies can also enhance the effectiveness of medications and help people remain in treatment longer.

One of the key aspects of treating addiction is understanding that it is a chronic illness, much like diabetes or hypertension. This means that while it can be managed effectively, a one-time treatment is often not sufficient. Ongoing care, monitoring, and adjustments to treatment are often necessary. Relapses can occur, but they are not a sign of failure; rather, they indicate that the treatment needs to be reinstated or adjusted.

Substance Use vs. Addiction

Understanding the distinction between substance use and addiction is essential in the field of mental health. Substance use involves the consumption of alcohol or other drugs, which might occur for a variety of reasons, such as social enjoyment, relaxation, or even for medical purposes. In contrast, addiction, also known as a substance use disorder, is a more severe form of substance involvement characterized by a problematic pattern of use leading to significant impairment or distress.

Casual or Controlled Substance Use

- Casual or controlled use refers to the consumption of substances in a way that does not disrupt one's daily life, responsibilities, and relationships.

- It is characterized by the user's ability to limit the amount and frequency of consumption. For example, having a glass of wine with dinner or using a prescribed medication as directed falls under controlled use.

- This form of use does not typically lead to physical dependence or addiction, and it is often socially acceptable within certain boundaries.

Transitioning from Use to Addiction

1. **Increased Tolerance**: Over time, individuals may develop a tolerance to the substance, meaning they require more of it to achieve the same effects. This increased tolerance can be one of the first steps towards addiction.

2. **Physical Dependence**: With continued use, some individuals develop physical dependence, where their body comes to rely on the substance to function normally. Dependence is often a precursor to addiction but is not equivalent to addiction.

3. **Loss of Control**: A key factor in the transition to addiction is the loss of control over substance use. This might manifest as using more of the substance than intended or being unable to cut down despite wanting to.

4. **Continued Use Despite Negative Consequences**: As use becomes more compulsive, individuals may continue using the substance despite experiencing significant negative consequences, such as health problems, strained relationships, or legal issues.

5. **Preoccupation with the Substance**: Addiction often involves a significant amount of time spent obtaining, using, and recovering from the effects of the substance. The substance becomes a central part of the individual's life.

6. **Psychological Dependence**: In addition to physical dependence, psychological dependence plays a major role in addiction. This dependence is characterized by cravings for the substance and using it to cope with stress, emotions, or other psychological issues.

7. **Neglect of Other Activities**: Individuals may begin to neglect hobbies, responsibilities, and social activities they once enjoyed in favour of substance use.

8. **Risk-Taking Behaviours**: Increased risk-taking, particularly when it comes to obtaining and using the substance, is common. This might include driving under the influence or using illegal means to acquire the substance.

Understanding the difference between substance use and addiction is critical for early intervention. Recognizing when controlled or casual use is transitioning into problematic use can help prevent the development of a full-blown addiction. This knowledge is essential for health professionals patients/clients, and their families in addressing substance use issues effectively and compassionately.

Review of DSM-V Criteria for Addictions

The Diagnostic and Statistical Manual of Mental Disorders, Fifth Edition (DSM-V), provides a standardized framework for diagnosing addictions, known clinically as Substance Use Disorders (SUDs). This framework is critical for clinicians in making accurate diagnoses, which is a crucial step in planning effective treatment strategies.

The DSM-V outlines specific criteria for diagnosing Substance Use Disorders (SUDs), which is a vital tool for clinicians. These criteria encompass a range of behavioural, psychological, and physical symptoms that signify problematic substance use. Here's a detailed exploration of each criterion:

1. **Substance Taken in Larger Amounts or Over a Longer Period Than Intended**: This criterion is met when an individual consistently consumes more of a substance than they initially intended or uses it for a longer duration than planned. It indicates a loss of control over substance use.

2. **Persistent Desire or Unsuccessful Efforts to Cut Down or Control Substance Use**: This involves repeated unsuccessful attempts to reduce or control substance use, reflecting the compulsive nature of addiction. It shows the individual's recognition of the problem but an inability to change behaviour.

3. **Significant Time Spent in Activities Necessary to Obtain, Use, or Recover from Substance**: A large portion of the individual's time is dedicated to obtaining the substance, using it, and recovering from its effects. This often leads to neglect of other important activities and responsibilities.

4. **Craving, or a Strong Desire or Urge to Use the Substance**: Cravings are intense desires or urges for the substance that can dominate an individual's thoughts. Cravings are often triggered by environmental cues and internal emotional states.

5. **Recurrent Substance Use Resulting in a Failure to Fulfill Major Role Obligations at Work, School, or Home**: The individual fails to meet major responsibilities at work, school, or home due to substance use. This includes poor performance, absenteeism, neglecting household tasks, or failure to care for children.

6. **Continued Substance Use Despite Having Persistent or Recurrent Social or Interpersonal Problems Caused or Exacerbated by the Effects of the Substance**: This criterion is met when substance use leads to or worsens social and interpersonal problems, yet the individual continues to use. It can include arguments with family members, loss of friendships, or social isolation.

7. **Important Social, Occupational, or Recreational Activities Given Up or Reduced Because of Substance Use**: The individual abandons or reduces involvement in important social, occupational, or recreational activities. They might stop participating in hobbies, social events, or career opportunities because of their substance use.

8. **Recurrent Substance Use in Situations in Which It Is Physically Hazardous**: The individual continues to use the substance in situations where it poses a danger to themselves or others, such as driving while intoxicated or operating machinery under the influence.

9. **Substance Use is Continued Despite Knowledge of Having a Persistent or Recurrent Physical or Psychological Problem That is Likely to Have Been Caused or Exacerbated by the Substance**: The individual is aware that their physical or psychological health issues are likely linked to their substance use, yet they continue to use. This could include liver damage from excessive alcohol use or depressive symptoms from drug use.

10. **Tolerance, as Defined by Either of the Following**: Tolerance involves needing to consume more of the substance to achieve the desired effect or noticing a markedly reduced effect when using the same amount. This physiological change is a hallmark of many substance use disorders.

11. **Withdrawal, as Manifested by Either of the Following**: Withdrawal symptoms occur when the substance use is reduced or stopped. Symptoms vary based on the substance but can include physical sickness, mood changes, and other disturbances. In some cases, the substance is taken to relieve or avoid withdrawal symptoms.

These criteria capture the multifaceted nature of substance use disorders. They provide a comprehensive framework for clinicians to assess the severity and impact of substance use, which is crucial for diagnosing and developing an effective treatment plan. The DSM-V emphasizes the behavioural patterns associated with addiction, moving beyond physical dependence to include the broader psychological and social impacts of substance use. This approach helps in recognizing addiction as a complex and chronic disease, requiring a holistic treatment strategy.

Importance of DSM-V Criteria in Identifying and Treating Addiction

The DSM-V criteria for diagnosing Substance Use Disorders (SUDs) play a pivotal role in the fields of mental health and addiction treatment. These criteria are not just tools for diagnosis; they significantly influence the entire process of identifying, understanding, and treating addiction.

Ensuring Accurate Diagnosis

- **Uniformity in Diagnosis**: The DSM-V provides a universally accepted standard for diagnosing addiction, which is crucial for uniformity across different healthcare settings. This standardization ensures that patients/clients receive a consistent diagnosis regardless of where they seek treatment.

- **Comprehensive Evaluation**: The criteria cover a broad spectrum of symptoms and behaviours associated with substance use, from physical dependence to impact on daily functioning. This comprehensive approach ensures that all aspects of the disorder are considered.

Guiding Effective Treatment

- **Tailoring Treatment Plans**: A diagnosis based on DSM-V criteria helps clinicians in creating personalized treatment plans. It allows healthcare providers to evaluate the severity and specific characteristics of the addiction, guiding them in selecting appropriate therapeutic interventions.

- **Monitoring Progress**: The criteria can be used to monitor the patient's/client's progress over time. Changes in the severity of symptoms as outlined in the DSM-V can indicate the effectiveness of treatment and guide adjustments in the therapeutic approach.

Facilitating Communication Among Professionals

- **Common Language**: The DSM-V criteria provide a common language for healthcare professionals. This shared terminology is crucial for effective communication among different professionals involved in a patient's/client's care, including psychiatrists, psychologists, primary care physicians, and substance abuse counsellors.

- **Interdisciplinary Collaboration**: The clear diagnostic criteria facilitate better collaboration among the interdisciplinary team involved in addiction treatment. Understanding the specifics of a patient's/client's diagnosis helps in coordinating care and ensuring that all aspects of the disorder are addressed.

Enhancing Research and Understanding

- **Research and Studies**: The criteria enable researchers to define their study populations more precisely. This clarity is essential for conducting epidemiological studies and clinical trials, leading to a better understanding of addiction and the development of more effective treatments.

- **Policy and Advocacy**: Accurate and standardized diagnosis plays a crucial role in shaping public policy and advocacy efforts related to addiction. It informs policymakers about the prevalence and severity of addiction, influencing the allocation of resources for treatment and prevention.

Impacting Insurance and Access to Care

- **Insurance Coverage**: For many patients/clients, access to treatment is contingent upon a formal diagnosis as defined by the DSM-V. Insurance companies often require a DSM-V-based diagnosis to approve coverage for treatment services.

- **Access to Treatment Programs**: Many treatment programs use the DSM-V criteria as a guideline for admission. An accurate diagnosis ensures that individuals receive the appropriate level of care, whether it be inpatient, outpatient, or a specialized program.

Addressing Stigma and Misunderstanding

- **Reducing Stigma**: By framing addiction as a medical disorder with clearly defined criteria, the DSM-V helps in reducing the stigma associated with substance abuse. It emphasizes that addiction is a health issue rather than a moral failing or a matter of willpower.

- **Educating Patients/Clients and Families**: The criteria can be used as an educational tool to help patients/clients and their families understand addiction as a medical condition. This understanding is crucial for fostering a supportive environment that is conducive to recovery.

The DSM-V criteria for addiction are more than just diagnostic tools; they are integral to the entire process of addressing substance use disorders. They ensure accurate and consistent diagnosis, guide effective treatment, enhance communication among professionals, support research, influence policy, and play a role in reducing stigma. Understanding and applying these criteria is essential for any healthcare professional involved in the treatment of addiction.

Signs and Symptoms of Addictions

Recognizing the signs and symptoms of addiction is crucial in the early detection and treatment of Substance Use Disorders (SUDs). Addiction manifests through a variety of physical, behavioural, and psychological symptoms that can significantly impact an individual's daily life.

Physical Symptoms

- **Changes in Appetite and Weight**: Fluctuations in weight and eating habits are common, with some substances causing increased appetite and others leading to weight loss due to decreased appetite (National Institute on Drug Abuse [NIDA], 2020).

- **Sleep Disturbances**: Insomnia or oversleeping can occur, depending on the substance used.

- **Withdrawal Symptoms**: These may include sweating, shaking, nausea, and headaches when the substance is not used.

- **Tolerance**: Needing more of the substance to achieve the same effect is a clear sign of physical dependency (Volkow, Koob, & McLellan, 2016).

Behavioural Symptoms

- **Compulsive Use**: The individual may take the substance in larger amounts or over a longer period than intended.

164 | P a g e

- **Loss of Control**: Persistent desire or unsuccessful attempts to cut down or control substance use.

- **Time Spent**: Significant time is spent obtaining, using, or recovering from the effects of the substance.

- **Neglect of Responsibilities**: Failing to fulfill obligations at work, school, or home due to substance use (American Psychiatric Association, 2013).

Psychological Symptoms

- **Craving**: A strong desire or urge to use the substance.

- **Mood Swings**: Emotional instability, including irritability, anxiety, or depression, can be signs of addiction.

- **Decreased Interest**: Loss of interest in activities that were once enjoyed.

- **Denial**: The individual may fail to acknowledge the extent of their substance use or its impact on their life.

Impact on Daily Life

- **Interpersonal Relationships**: Addiction can strain relationships with family, friends, and colleagues. It often leads to social isolation or conflicts with loved ones.

- **Occupational and Academic Impairment**: Substance use can impair cognitive and physical abilities, leading to decreased performance at work or school.

- **Financial Problems**: The cost of obtaining substances, along with reduced work productivity, can lead to financial strain.

- **Legal Issues**: Engaging in illegal activities to obtain substances or legal problems due to substance-induced behaviours is common.

Understanding the signs and symptoms of addiction is vital for early intervention. Addiction affects every aspect of an individual's life, from physical health to personal relationships and societal functioning. Recognizing these symptoms as early as possible can lead to timely and effective treatment, greatly improving the chances of recovery and reducing the long-term impacts of addiction.

Common Types of Addictions

Addiction is a complex condition that can manifest in various forms, encompassing both substance-related and behavioural addictions. Each type of addiction has its unique characteristics and challenges, yet they all share the underlying feature of compulsive engagement despite adverse consequences.

Substance-related addictions are perhaps the most recognized forms of addiction. Alcohol addiction, for instance, is widespread and can lead to severe physical and psychological health issues. The abuse of drugs, whether they are legal prescription medications or illicit drugs like heroin or cocaine, also falls into this category. These substances alter brain chemistry and can quickly lead to physical dependence and addiction. Prescription drug abuse, particularly of opioids, sedatives, and stimulants, has become a significant public health concern due to the risk of overdose and addiction.

In addition to substance-related addictions, behavioural addictions are increasingly being recognized. These involve compulsive behaviours that provide a reward or 'high' that can become addictive. Gambling addiction is a prime example, characterized by the uncontrollable urge to continue gambling despite the toll it takes on one's life. This addiction can lead to financial ruin, strained relationships, and mental health issues like depression and anxiety.

The rise of technology has seen the emergence of internet addiction, which can encompass various behaviours such as compulsive use of social media, online gaming, or obsessive internet browsing. While these activities are a normal part of life for many, for some individuals, they can become addictive, leading to social isolation, neglect of responsibilities, and other detrimental effects.

The spectrum of addictive behaviours and substances is broad, and understanding this diversity is crucial in recognizing and treating addiction. Each type of addiction carries its own set of challenges and impacts on individuals' lives in different ways. However, the common thread across all addictions is the persistent and compulsive nature of the behaviour, which continues despite negative consequences.

In addressing addiction, it's important to consider the specific type of addiction and tailor treatment accordingly. While there are commonalities in the approach to treating different types of addiction, each requires a nuanced understanding of its particular challenges and triggers. By recognizing the diverse nature of addictions, healthcare providers can offer more effective and targeted interventions, helping individuals overcome their addictive behaviours and lead healthier, more fulfilling lives.

Addictions and the Brain

The impact of addictions on the brain is profound and multifaceted, affecting both its structure and function. Understanding how addictions alter the brain's neurobiology is crucial for comprehending the tenacity of these disorders and for developing effective treatment strategies.

Addiction significantly alters the brain's reward system. Initially, substance use or addictive behaviours activate this system, which is designed to reinforce behaviours essential for survival, such as eating and social interaction. However, addictive substances or behaviours hijack this system, leading to the overstimulation of the reward circuit and the release of excessive amounts of neurotransmitters like dopamine (Volkow, Koob, & McLellan, 2016).

This overstimulation creates a euphoric high or a sense of intense pleasure, which strongly reinforces the behaviour, encouraging repeated engagement despite potential risks. Over time, this leads to changes in other brain circuits involved in stress, self-control, and decision-making. These changes can decrease an addicted individual's ability to resist the substance or behaviour, despite being aware of its negative consequences.

Chronic addiction can also lead to structural changes in the brain. For instance, neuroimaging studies have shown alterations in areas of the brain involved in decision making, judgment, learning, memory, and behaviour control. These changes can persist long after the individual stops using the substance, contributing to the risk of relapse (Volkow, Koob, & McLellan, 2016).

Dopamine plays a central role in the development of addiction. It is released in large amounts by substances and addictive behaviours, creating a strong association between the behaviour and pleasure. This dopamine release reinforces the behaviour, making the individual more likely to repeat it.

However, with continued substance use or engagement in addictive behaviours, the brain starts to produce less dopamine or reduces the number of dopamine receptors in the reward circuit. This reduction diminishes the user's ability to enjoy the substance and other activities they once found pleasurable, leading to increased substance use or engagement in the behaviour in an attempt to achieve the same dopamine high. This cycle is a key factor in the transition from voluntary use to compulsive use, characteristic of addiction.

Glutamate, another neurotransmitter, is also involved in addiction. Changes in glutamate levels affect the reward circuit and the brain's ability to learn and adapt. This can impact the brain's ability to form memories associated with substance use or certain behaviours, further reinforcing addiction (Kalivas & Volkow, 2005).

Addiction's impact on the brain is extensive, affecting both its structure and functioning. The alterations in neurotransmitters and neural pathways contribute to the compulsive nature of addiction and the difficulty in overcoming it. Understanding these changes is essential for developing effective treatments and helping individuals recover from addiction.

Causes of Addictions

Addiction is a complex disorder influenced by an interplay of various factors. It is not the result of a single cause but rather a combination of genetic, environmental, and psychological factors. Understanding this complexity is crucial in addressing addiction effectively.

Genetic Factors

Research indicates that genetics plays a significant role in the likelihood of developing an addiction. Studies of familial patterns and twins have shown that individuals are more likely to develop addiction if they have a family member, especially a first-degree relative, with a history of substance use disorders (SUDs). Estimates suggest that genetics account for about 40% to 60% of the vulnerability to addiction (Goldman, Oroszi, & Ducci, 2005). Specific genes may affect how an individual metabolizes substances or how their brain's reward system responds to substances, influencing their risk of addiction.

Environmental Factors

Environmental influences are also critical in the development of addiction. These include factors such as family life, social networks, socio-economic status, and exposure to drugs or addictive behaviours. Early exposure to substance use, childhood trauma, peer pressure, and social environments that normalize substance use can significantly increase the risk of developing an addiction. Moreover, chronic stress or living in an environment with easy access to substances can contribute to the initiation and continuation of substance use.

Psychological Factors

Psychological factors are integral in the development of addiction. Mental health disorders such as depression, anxiety, and post-traumatic stress disorder (PTSD) are often found in individuals with addiction. The concept of "self-medication," where individuals use substances to cope with mental health issues, is common. This can create a vicious cycle where substance use exacerbates mental health problems, which in turn leads to increased substance use. Additionally, personality traits such as impulsivity, sensation-seeking, and a high need for approval can predispose individuals to addiction.

The Bio-Psycho-Social Model of Addiction

Addiction is best understood through a bio-psycho-social model, which acknowledges that biological, psychological, and social factors all play a role in its development. This model suggests that the interplay of these factors creates a unique risk profile for each individual. For example, a person with a genetic predisposition to addiction may never develop a disorder unless they are exposed to certain environmental or psychological stressors. Conversely, someone with no family history of addiction may develop an SUD due to significant environmental pressures or psychological issues.

The complexity of addiction as a bio-psycho-social disorder requires a holistic approach to treatment and prevention. It underscores the importance of addressing not just the physical aspects of addiction but also the psychological and social factors. Tailoring interventions to the individual's specific circumstances and needs is crucial for effective treatment and sustained recovery.

Understanding the multifaceted nature of addiction is vital for both prevention and treatment. Recognizing the various factors that contribute to the development of addiction helps in creating comprehensive treatment plans that address all aspects of the disorder, offering a better chance for successful recovery and long-term management.

Neurochemical Aspects of Addictions

The development and perpetuation of addiction are deeply rooted in the neurochemical changes in the brain. Central to understanding these changes is the role of neurotransmitters, particularly dopamine, and the concept of reward and reinforcement in addiction.

Dopamine is a key neurotransmitter involved in the brain's reward system. It plays a significant role in regulating feelings of pleasure and reinforcement, which are crucial in motivating behaviour. In the context of addiction, dopamine creates a powerful reward loop. When an individual engages in substance use or addictive behaviours, dopamine levels in the brain's reward circuits spike, resulting in feelings of euphoria or a 'high.' This surge in dopamine reinforces the behaviour, making the individual more likely to repeat it to experience those feelings again.

Substances like opioids, nicotine, and alcohol, as well as behaviours like gambling, can all trigger this dopamine release. Over time, the brain's reward system adapts to the excess dopamine. This adaptation can lead to a diminished response to the substance or behaviour and a decreased ability to feel pleasure from other activities, a phenomenon known as tolerance. As tolerance builds, individuals often increase their substance use or engagement in the behaviour to achieve the same level of dopamine release and pleasure, further driving the cycle of addiction.

The concept of reward and reinforcement is central to understanding addiction. The brain's reward system evolved to reinforce behaviours that are essential for survival, such as eating and procreating. However, addictive substances and behaviours hijack this natural reward system, providing an immediate and intense reward. This reward exceeds what is experienced from natural rewards, leading to the prioritization of the substance or addictive behaviour over other healthy activities.

The reinforcement experienced during substance use or addictive behaviours strengthens neural pathways in the brain, making the desire for the substance or behaviour more powerful. This reinforcement can create a compulsion to seek out the substance or behaviour despite knowing the negative consequences. Additionally, environmental cues and stressors can trigger cravings, due to the strong association built in the brain between these cues and the substance or behaviour, further perpetuating the cycle of addiction.

Over time, this cycle of reward and reinforcement can lead to significant changes in the brain's structure and function, particularly in areas involved in decision making, impulse control, and judgment. These changes can make overcoming addiction challenging, as they affect an individual's ability to control or resist the impulse to engage in addictive behaviours.

Understanding the neurochemical aspects of addiction, especially the role of dopamine and the process of reward and reinforcement, is essential in developing effective treatment strategies. This knowledge helps in designing therapies that aim to normalize the brain's chemistry and retrain the brain's response to rewards and stressors. Medications that target neurotransmitter systems and behavioural therapies that focus on managing cravings and triggers can be particularly effective in treating addiction.

The neurochemical aspects of addiction highlight the complex interaction between brain chemistry and behaviour. They underscore the fact that addiction is not just a matter of willpower or choice, but a chronic brain disorder influenced by a variety of biological and environmental factors. Understanding these aspects is crucial for both the prevention and treatment of addiction.

Evidence-Based Therapies for Addictions

Effective treatment of addiction requires a comprehensive approach that often includes medication-assisted treatment (MAT), cognitive-behavioural therapy (CBT), support groups, and personalized treatment plans. These evidence-based therapies are designed to address the multifaceted nature of addiction, ensuring a more holistic and long-term recovery strategy.

Medication-Assisted Treatment (MAT)

Medication-Assisted Treatment (MAT) is a comprehensive approach to the treatment of substance use disorders, particularly those involving opioids and alcohol. It combines the use of medications with counselling and behavioural therapies, offering a "whole- patient/client" approach to treatment. The efficacy of MAT in improving patient/client outcomes and its critical role in a holistic treatment strategy is well-documented in various studies. Key Aspects of MAT include:

1. **Medications Used in MAT**: MAT for opioid addiction often involves medications like methadone, buprenorphine, and naltrexone. Methadone and buprenorphine help reduce withdrawal symptoms and cravings by acting on the same opioid receptors as the addictive drug but without causing the same high. Naltrexone, another medication used in both opioid and alcohol addiction treatment, works by blocking the euphoric and sedative effects of opioids and the pleasurable effects of alcohol.

2. **Effectiveness of MAT**: MAT has been proven to be clinically effective and to significantly reduce the need for inpatient detoxification services for these individuals. MAT provides a more comprehensive, individually tailored program of medication and behavioural therapy that addresses the needs of most patients/clients (Substance Abuse and Mental Health Services Administration [SAMHSA], 2020).

3. **Goals of MAT**: The primary goal of MAT is full recovery, including the ability to live a self-directed life. This approach helps to improve patient/client survival, increase retention in treatment, reduce illicit opiate use and other criminal activity among people with substance use disorders, and improve patients'/clients' ability to gain and maintain employment.

4. **Safety and Regulations of MAT**: Medications used in MAT are approved by the Food and Drug Administration (FDA) and are administered under the supervision of a physician.

The prescribed medication operates to normalize brain chemistry, block the euphoric effects of alcohol and opioids, relieve physiological cravings, and normalize body functions without the negative effects of the abused drug.

5. **Integration with Counselling and Behavioural Therapies**: While medications can effectively manage withdrawal symptoms and cravings, counselling and behavioural therapies in MAT help patients/clients engage in the treatment process and modify their attitudes and behaviours related to drug use. These therapies also increase healthy life skills and improve patients'/clients' relationships and social functioning.

6. **Stigma and Challenges of MAT**: Despite its proven efficacy, MAT is sometimes stigmatized, both within and outside of the recovery community. This stigma often stems from misconceptions about substituting one drug for another. Education and advocacy are essential to change these perceptions and highlight MAT as a legitimate and effective treatment for substance use disorders.

7. **Long-term Perspective in MAT**: Treatment duration in MAT varies depending on the individual's needs. For some, MAT is a long-term treatment approach, while others might use it as a step toward other forms of treatment. Long-term maintenance treatment has been shown to be more effective than short-term detoxification programs in preventing relapse.

MAT is a critical component of the treatment spectrum for substance use disorders. Its efficacy in reducing the negative consequences of addiction, such as criminal activity, disease transmission, and overdose deaths, is well-supported by research. As part of a comprehensive treatment plan, MAT can offer a path to long-term recovery, especially when combined with counselling and behavioural therapies.

MAT's role in treating addiction underscores the importance of a multifaceted approach, acknowledging the biological aspects of addiction and addressing them alongside psychological and social factors. This integrated treatment model aligns with the current understanding of addiction as a complex disorder requiring comprehensive and sustained intervention strategies.

Cognitive Behavioural Therapy (CBT) and Thought Developmental Practice (TDP)

Cognitive Behavioural Therapy (CBT) Thought Developmental Practice (TDP) are widely recognized and effective treatment modality for addiction. It is a structured, time-limited, and goal-oriented psychotherapeutic approach that focuses on identifying, understanding, and changing thinking and behaviour patterns. CBT and TDP are grounded in the principle that thoughts, feelings, and behaviours are interconnected, and that altering one can lead to changes in the others. The Core Concepts of CBT and TDP in Addiction are:

*   **Identification of Negative Thought Patterns**: CBT and TDP helps individuals recognize and challenge distorted or irrational thoughts that contribute to substance use. It also helps to divert the cravings that comes with the thought pattern. For example, a person might

believe that they need a substance to cope with stress, which CBT would help to reframe those thoughts, and TDP helps to rewire the cravings with several diversion methods.

- **Behavioural Change**: It encourages patients/clients to engage in positive behavioural changes by choosing several options to distract the mind when the craving occurs. This might involve learning new coping skills, avoiding triggers that lead to substance use, or practicing healthier lifestyle choices.

- **Skill Development**: CBT and TDP equips individuals with skills to manage cravings and avoid relapse. This includes strategies for dealing with stress, regulating emotions, and improving communication skills. TDP helps to recondition the mind with healthy coping strategies which can become a lifestyle.

- **Problem-Solving**: CBT and TDP enhances problem-solving skills, helping individuals to address challenges and setbacks in a more constructive way, reducing the likelihood of turning to substances as a solution.

CBT and TDP have been extensively studied and proven effective in treating various substance use disorders. CBT is particularly effective in addressing co-occurring conditions such as anxiety and depression, which are common among individuals with addiction (McHugh, Hearon, & Otto, 2010). The skills learned through CBT and TDP remain with the individual long after the completion of treatment, contributing to long-term recovery.

Integration of TDP with Other Treatments

Thought Developmental Practice (TDP) for addiction is often most effective when integrated with other treatment modalities. This integrative approach acknowledges the complexity of addiction as a disorder that affects individuals on multiple levels – biological, psychological, and social.

A key aspect of this integration is the combination of TDP with medication-assisted treatment (MAT). MAT involves the use of medications to manage withdrawal symptoms and reduce cravings, particularly in addictions with a strong physiological component like opioid or alcohol dependence. When MAT is used in conjunction with TDP, the medication helps stabilize the patient's/client's physical symptoms. This allows them to engage more effectively in the exercises to recondition their minds and restructure their thinking with diversion methods. This combination addresses both the neurobiological underpinnings of addiction and the learned behaviours and thought patterns that contribute to the cycle of substance abuse.

Support groups, such as Alcoholics Anonymous (AA) or Narcotics Anonymous (NA), provide another layer of support that complements TDP. These groups offer a community of individuals who share similar experiences and challenges with addiction. The sense of belonging and peer support found in these groups can reinforce the skills and strategies learned in TDP, providing a social context for recovery and an additional layer of accountability.

The integration of TDP with other treatments also extends to addressing co-occurring mental health disorders, such as anxiety or depression. Often, individuals with addiction are also struggling with other psychological issues, which may have contributed to the development of their substance use disorder. Combining TDP with therapies targeted at these co-occurring disorders can provide a more comprehensive treatment approach, addressing all facets of the individual's health.

Personalized treatment plans are essential in this integrative approach. Each person's experience with addiction is unique, and so are their treatment needs. Personalization might involve adjusting the focus and techniques used in TDP, selecting appropriate medications in MAT, and recommending specific types of support groups or additional therapies. This tailored approach ensures that treatment addresses the individual's specific circumstances, challenges, and strengths, increasing the likelihood of successful recovery.

Integrating TDP with other treatments in addiction therapy recognizes the multifaceted nature of addiction and the need for a comprehensive treatment approach. By addressing the biological, psychological, and social aspects of addiction, this integrative approach offers a more holistic path to recovery, tailored to the individual needs of each patient/client.

TDP and Personalization in Treatment

Thought Developmental Practice (TDP) is highly adaptable, making it an ideal choice for a personalized approach in addiction treatment. The personalization of TDP begins with an understanding that each individual's journey into addiction is unique, influenced by a complex interplay of psychological, environmental, and biological factors. This individualized approach is particularly beneficial because it allows therapists to tailor the therapy to address the specific challenges, needs, and circumstances of each patient/client.

One of the key strengths of TDP in personalization is its flexibility to choose a module or several modules that a patient/client may feel comfortable with. The workbook at hand is meticulously constructed around modules devised to assist individuals dealing with substance abuse, addictions, and pertinent mental disorders. These modules are organized into twelve distinct sections, each replete with practical and stimulating activities.

Contained within TDP are activities expressly selected for their ability to stimulate the brain. The essence lies in the employment of straightforward activities, principles, and concepts systematically arranged to cultivate the mind and reshape thought patterns. It serves as a guide for patients/clients to access and understand their "memory cards," which are often the root causes of anxiety, mood disorders, and addiction issues. It is a tool to bring insight and clarity, enabling individuals to grasp their internal dynamics and interpersonal relationships. The process assists in closing chapters on issues stemming from unresolved past situations and crafting new positive memory cards to replace the old, negative ones.

The ambition of TDP is not to obliterate emotions or the individual's thought process but to enrich coping strategies with practical, uplifting ideas. It seeks to guide individuals in harnessing existing knowledge and behaviours to aid themselves and others. The thrust of TDP is to enable people to unearth the underlying sources of their unhappiness by excavating detrimental habits, thoughts, and ideas and supplanting them with value-driven concepts that instill a sense of self-worth. Exploring causes, effects, and solutions is embarked upon, striving to identify and overcome the emotional and cognitive obstacles impeding progress. For instance, if a patient/client turns to substances as a way of coping with stress, TDP can be directed towards developing healthier stress management techniques. Similarly, for someone whose substance use is linked to social anxiety, the therapy can focus on skills for managing anxiety in social situations.

Moreover, TDP can be adjusted to accommodate the severity of the addiction. For someone in the early stages of addiction, the focus might be on preventing the development of more severe problems. In contrast, for someone with a long history of substance use, TDP might concentrate more on managing cravings and avoiding relapse.

Incorporating personal experiences and preferences is another aspect of personalization in TDP. The therapy sessions can be structured around an individual's life experiences, cultural background, and personal values, ensuring that the therapy resonates more deeply with them. This aspect of personalization is not just about making the patient/client comfortable; it's about enhancing the relevance and effectiveness of the therapy.

TDP's adaptability also extends to its integration with other treatments. For example, in cases where medication is part of the treatment plan, TDP can support medication adherence and address any psychological side effects or misconceptions about medication use. When combined with support groups, TDP's focus on skill development can complement the peer support and shared experiences found in group settings.

Another important aspect of personalization in TDP is the duration and intensity of therapy, which can be adjusted according to the individual's progress and needs. Some may benefit from short-term, intensive TDP, while others may need longer-term therapy to address more deep-rooted issues.

However, TDP is not without challenges too. Challenges and considerations in implementing TDP for addiction are multifaceted, reflecting the complexity of both the treatment modality and the nature of addiction itself. One of the primary challenges in TDP is patient/client engagement and motivation. The effectiveness of TDP heavily relies on the individual's active participation in therapy sessions and their commitment to applying learned strategies outside of these sessions. This can be particularly challenging for individuals struggling with substance use disorders, as factors such as ambivalence about change, fluctuating motivation levels, and the presence of withdrawal symptoms or cravings can impact their ability to fully engage in the therapeutic process.

Another significant consideration is the skill and experience of the therapist. The success of TDP is not solely dependent on the method itself but also on how it is administered. Therapists need to be skilled in establishing a trusting therapeutic relationship, tailoring interventions to meet the unique needs of each patient/client, and adapting the therapy to suit the individual's stage of readiness for change. This requires a deep understanding of the principles of TDP, as well as the ability to be flexible and responsive to the patient's/client's evolving needs.

Moreover, TDP for addiction needs to be sensitive to the complex and often intertwined psychological and emotional issues that accompany substance use disorders. Many individuals with addiction also struggle with co-occurring mental health disorders such as depression, anxiety, or trauma-related disorders. Therefore, TDP must be integrated with treatments addressing these concurrent issues, which adds an additional layer of complexity to therapy.

The therapeutic approach must also consider cultural and socio-economic factors that can influence the patient's/client's experience with addiction and recovery. Cultural sensitivity in TDP involves recognizing and respecting the individual's cultural background and its impact on their perceptions of addiction and treatment. Socio-economic factors like access to resources, social support, and environmental stressors also play a crucial role in both the development of addiction and the recovery process.

Lastly, a critical consideration in TDP for addiction is the maintenance of gains post-treatment. The risk of relapse is a persistent challenge in the treatment of substance use disorders. Ensuring that patients/clients have the necessary support and skills to maintain their recovery after the completion of therapy is essential. This might involve ongoing support groups, booster sessions, or continued engagement in other forms of therapy or self-help programs.

While TDP is a highly effective treatment for addiction, its successful implementation requires careful consideration of patient/client engagement and motivation, therapist expertise, the presence of co-occurring disorders, cultural and socio-economic factors, and strategies for maintaining long-term recovery. Addressing these challenges and considerations is essential for maximizing the effectiveness of TDP in the context of addiction treatment.

Support Groups

Support groups, such as Alcoholics Anonymous (AA) and Narcotics Anonymous (NA), provide a community-based, peer-led environment where individuals can share experiences and support each other in recovery. These groups often use a step-based approach that emphasizes spiritual and personal growth. Participation in support groups can be an effective complement to other treatments and has been associated with longer-lasting recovery (Kelly, Magill, & Stout, 2009).

Personalized Treatment Plans

Personalized treatment plans are central to the effective management of addictions. Each individual's journey with addiction is unique, influenced by a myriad of factors including genetic predisposition, environmental influences, psychological conditions, and the specific substances or behaviours involved. Consequently, a one-size-fits-all approach to treatment is insufficient. Personalized plans take into account the multifaceted nature of addiction, tailoring interventions to meet the specific needs of the individual for a more effective and sustainable recovery process.

The development of a personalized treatment plan begins with a comprehensive assessment that includes medical history, patterns of substance use, co-occurring mental health disorders, family dynamics, and social circumstances. This assessment helps healthcare providers understand the breadth and depth of the individual's addiction and the various factors contributing to it. Based on this assessment, a treatment plan is developed that addresses the unique combination of these factors.

A key aspect of personalized treatment plans is their adaptability. As individuals progress through treatment, their needs may change. Regular assessments allow for adjustments to the treatment plan to ensure it remains aligned with the individual's evolving needs. This ongoing assessment and adaptation are essential for long-term recovery, as the journey to recovery is rarely linear.

Personalized treatment plans are not just about the interventions and therapies used; they also involve empowering the individual in their recovery journey. This includes setting achievable goals, developing coping strategies, and building a supportive network. Empowering individuals in their treatment increases their engagement and commitment to the recovery process.

Long-Term Recovery Strategies

Long-term recovery from addiction involves ongoing support and maintenance. This may include continued participation in support groups, ongoing counselling or therapy, lifestyle changes, and, in some cases, continued medication. Recovery is a lifelong process, and long-term strategies focus on maintaining sobriety and preventing relapse.

Evidence-based therapies for addiction combined with personalized treatment plans and long-term recovery strategies, provide a comprehensive approach to treating addiction. This multifaceted approach is essential for addressing the complex nature of addiction and ensuring sustained recovery.

The integration of these therapies provides a well-rounded approach to addiction treatment, recognizing it as a chronic condition that requires ongoing management and support. This approach aligns with the current understanding of addiction as a complex bio-psycho-social disorder, necessitating diverse and sustained interventions.

Coping Strategies for Addictions

Developing effective coping strategies is crucial for individuals recovering from addictions. These strategies are essential for managing cravings, avoiding triggers, building resilience, and maintaining sobriety. They empower individuals to deal with the challenges of addiction recovery and reduce the risk of relapse.

Managing Cravings

- **Mindfulness and Awareness**: Practicing mindfulness, TDP, grounding techniques can help individuals recognize and accept their cravings without acting on them. It involves being aware of the present moment and understanding that cravings are temporary and will pass.

- **Distraction Techniques**: Engaging in activities that distract from cravings, such as exercise, hobbies, or socializing, can be effective. These activities provide a positive outlet and reduce the focus on cravings.

- **Delaying Tactics**: Postponing the decision to use a substance can help manage immediate cravings. This could involve waiting for a certain amount of time, during which the urge may subside.

Avoiding Triggers

- **Identifying Triggers**: Recognizing the specific situations, emotions, or people that trigger cravings is essential. Once identified, individuals can develop strategies to avoid or cope with these triggers.

- **Changing Routines**: Altering daily routines can help avoid situations or people associated with substance use. This might include taking different routes to avoid places where substances were used or changing social activities that involve substance use.

- **Seeking Support**: Talking to a therapist, counsellor, or support group about triggers can provide insight and strategies for coping with them.

Building Resilience

- **Developing a Support Network**: Building a strong support network of family, friends, and peers who understand and support the recovery process is crucial. Support groups can also offer a sense of community and shared experience.

- **Setting Realistic Goals**: Setting achievable goals can provide a sense of purpose and accomplishment. Goals should be specific, measurable, achievable, relevant, and time-bound (SMART).

- **Learning Stress Management Techniques**: Stress is a common trigger for substance use. Techniques such as deep breathing, meditation, and yoga can help manage stress effectively.

Maintaining Sobriety

- **Continued Therapy or Counselling**: Ongoing therapy or counselling can provide continuous support and guidance throughout the recovery process. It can also help address underlying issues that may have contributed to the addiction.

- **Healthy Lifestyle Choices**: Maintaining a healthy lifestyle, including regular exercise, a balanced diet, and adequate sleep, can improve overall well-being and support recovery.

- **Relapse Prevention Planning**: Developing a relapse prevention plan that outlines strategies to cope with high-risk situations is important. This plan should include steps to take if a relapse occurs.

Coping strategies for addiction are diverse and should be tailored to each individual's unique circumstances and needs. These strategies are not only about avoiding substance use but also about building a fulfilling and substance-free life. They play a critical role in empowering individuals in recovery, helping them manage the challenges they face, and providing the tools needed to maintain long-term sobriety.

Addressing SI/HI in Addiction

The intersection of self-harm (SI) and suicidal ideation (HI) with addiction presents a critical challenge in the treatment and management of Substance Use Disorders (SUDs). The heightened risk of SI and HI among those struggling with addiction necessitates a careful, nuanced approach to assessment, intervention, and ongoing support.

Understanding the complex relationship between addiction, SI, and HI is essential for effective intervention. Substance use often exacerbates underlying mental health issues, potentially increasing the risk of self-harm and suicidal thoughts. Additionally, substances may be used as a coping mechanism for pre-existing suicidal ideation or tendencies toward self-harm. Regular and comprehensive screening for SI and HI should be an integral part of the treatment process for addiction. This screening not only aids in early detection but also helps in understanding the severity and specific nature of the risk, which is crucial for tailoring interventions.

In situations where an immediate risk of self-harm or suicide is identified, swift and decisive action is required. This may entail hospitalization or other emergency interventions to ensure the safety of the individual. Alongside immediate measures, the development of a crisis response plan is paramount. Such a plan should detail emergency contacts, specific steps to take during a crisis, and methods for accessing emergency services. It serves as a crucial roadmap for both individuals and caregivers in times of acute crisis.

Another vital component in addressing SI/HI in the context of addiction is the development of a safety plan in collaboration with the individual. This plan should outline recognizable warning signs, list coping strategies and distractions, and identify people and resources that can provide support during a crisis. The involvement of family members and the wider community in the creation and implementation of this plan can offer additional layers of support and monitoring, thereby enhancing its effectiveness.

Therapeutic interventions are integral in managing SI/HI risks in individuals with addiction and should focus on equipping individuals with coping mechanisms, skills for emotional regulation, and strategies for managing distressing thoughts and impulses. Such therapeutic approaches not only address the immediate risks associated with SI/HI but also contribute to the long-term stability and well-being of the individual.

Continuous monitoring and follow-up are crucial, especially considering that the risks associated with SI/HI can fluctuate over time and in response to various external and internal factors. Long-term engagement with mental health services and support networks ensures that individuals at risk receive the necessary care and intervention in a timely manner.

Addressing the risks of self-harm and suicidal ideation in individuals with addictions is a complex, ongoing process that requires a multi-faceted approach. It involves regular risk assessment, immediate crisis intervention, the development of comprehensive safety and crisis response plans, therapeutic interventions, and long-term monitoring and support. Through these measures, it is possible to significantly mitigate the risks associated with SI/HI in the context of addiction, thereby safeguarding the well-being and enhancing the recovery prospects of affected individuals.

Conclusion

Understanding and managing addictions require a comprehensive and multifaceted approach. Addiction is a complex disorder that affects individuals physically, psychologically, and socially. Effective treatment involves a combination of medication-assisted treatment, cognitive-behavioural therapy, support groups, and personalized treatment plans. Coping strategies focused on managing cravings, avoiding triggers, building resilience, and maintaining sobriety are essential for long-term recovery.

Addressing co-occurring issues such as self-harm and suicidal ideation is crucial, as these can significantly impact the recovery process and overall well-being. Regular screening, crisis intervention strategies, and ongoing support are key components in managing these risks.

Addiction is a chronic condition that requires ongoing management. Recovery is a journey that involves not just the cessation of substance use but also rebuilding a fulfilling, substance-free life. A supportive and non-judgmental approach is vital in this process. Encouraging open communication, understanding, and empathy can make a significant difference in the lives of those struggling with addiction. By fostering a supportive environment and utilizing evidence-based treatment approaches, individuals with addiction can achieve sustained recovery and improve their quality of life.

Week 6

The Workbook

Week Six

ADDICTIONS

Building on our comprehensive exploration of personality disorders in the previous week, where we delved into the complexities of conditions like Borderline Personality Disorder and Narcissism, Week Six of our program shifted our focus to a pervasive and critical issue in mental health: Addictions. This week, we aimed to unpack the multifaceted nature of substance abuse and addiction, distinguishing between casual substance use and addictive behaviours.

Our journey this week encompassed a deep dive into the DSM-V criteria for addiction, examining its signs, symptoms, and the diverse types of addictions encountered in clinical practice. Understanding how addictions impacted the brain, both chemically and neurologically, has been a key aspect of our learning. Moreover, we explored the intricacies of evidence-based therapies including TDP and coping strategies, enhancing our toolkit for managing these challenging cases.

Crucially, we maintained a focus on the holistic well-being of individuals struggling with addiction, emphasizing the importance of ruling out suicidal and homicidal ideation. As we have progressed through this week, our objective remains to equip professionals with a robust understanding of addictions, fostering competence and empathy in navigating these often complex and sensitive cases.

Day 1: Understanding Substance Abuse and Addictions

1. **Reflective Exercise 1**: Describe your perception of the difference between substance abuse and addictions.

_____

_____

_____

_____

_____

_____

2. **Reflective Exercise 2**: Reflect on a case where substance abuse evolved into addiction. What were the key factors?

_____

_____

_____

_____

_____

_____

3. **Guided Activity**: Research the historical context and evolution of the understanding of substance abuse and addictions.

_____

_____

_____

_____

_____

_____

Day 2: Substance Use vs Addictions

1. **Reflective Exercise 1**: Reflect on your experiences with patients/clients who used substances but weren't addicted.

_____

_____

_____

_____

_____

_____

2. **Reflective Exercise 2**: Consider the key behavioural and psychological differences between substance use and addiction.

_____

_____

_____

_____

_____

_____

3. **Guided Activity**: Develop a checklist or guide to help distinguish between substance use and addiction.

_____

_____

_____

_____

_____

_____

Day 3: DSM-V Criteria for Addictions

1. **Reflective Exercise 1**: Compare a real case of addiction with the DSM-V criteria for addiction.

_____

_____

_____

_____

_____

_____

2. **Reflective Exercise 2**: Discuss the challenges in applying the DSM-V criteria to diverse cases of addiction.

_____

_____

_____

_____

_____

_____

3. **Guided Activity**: Create a diagnostic flowchart based on the DSM-V criteria for addiction.

_____

_____

_____

_____

_____

_____

Day 4: Signs and Symptoms of Addictions

1. **Reflective Exercise 1**: Reflect on the common signs and symptoms of addiction observed in your practice.

_____

_____

_____

_____

_____

_____

2. **Reflective Exercise 2**: Consider a case where addiction symptoms were atypical or unusual.

_____

_____

_____

_____

_____

_____

3. **Guided Activity**: Design an educational tool like an infographic highlighting the signs and symptoms of addiction.

_____

_____

_____

_____

_____

Day 5: Common Types of Addictions

1. **Reflective Exercise 1**: Discuss various types of addictions you have encountered and their unique challenges.

_____

_____

_____

_____

_____

_____

2. **Reflective Exercise 2**: Reflect on a particularly challenging type of addiction and its management.

_____

_____

_____

_____

_____

_____

3. **Guided Activity**: Research and summarize the different types of addictions and their prevalence.

_____

_____

_____

_____

_____

_____

Day 6: Addictions and the Brain

1. **Reflective Exercise 1**: Reflect on how addiction affects the brain based on your clinical experience.

_____

_____

_____

_____

_____

2. **Reflective Exercise 2**: Discuss the role of chemicals or neurotransmitters in the development of addiction.

_____

_____

_____

_____

_____

3. **Guided Activity**: Develop a simple diagram or chart explaining the brain's changes due to addiction.

_____

_____

_____

_____

_____

Day 7: Therapies, Coping Strategies, and Professional Knowledge for Addictions

1. **Reflective Exercise 1**: Share your experience with evidence-based therapies for addiction.

_____

_____

_____

_____

_____

_____

2. **Reflective Exercise 2**: Reflect on effective coping strategies for managing addiction.

_____

_____

_____

_____

_____

_____

3. **Guided Activity**: Prepare a brief presentation or educational material for colleagues highlighting the essential aspects of understanding and treating addiction.

_____

_____

_____

_____

_____

_____

Week 7

EMOTIONAL WOUNDS

Emotional wounds are psychological injuries that arise from experiences of trauma, loss, or significant stress. These wounds often linger long after the physical scars have healed, impacting mental health and well-being. Unlike physical injuries, emotional wounds are invisible and often unrecognized, yet they profoundly affect an individual's life.

Trauma, a significant contributor to emotional wounds, occurs when individuals experience events that are overwhelmingly stressful or disturbing. This could include incidents like accidents, natural disasters, or experiences of violence. Trauma can disrupt a person's sense of safety, leading to feelings of helplessness and a diminished sense of self.

Abuse, another source of emotional wounds, involves harmful treatment from another person, which could be physical, emotional, or sexual. Abuse often leaves deep psychological scars, affecting trust, self-esteem, and the ability to form healthy relationships.

Emotional wounds can manifest in various forms, including anxiety, depression, and Post-Traumatic Stress Disorder (PTSD). These psychological impacts are not just fleeting emotions but persistent states that can significantly hinder an individual's ability to function normally.

A pivotal study by Cloitre, Stolbach, Herman, van der Kolk, Pynoos, Wang, and Petkova (2009) investigated the impact of complex trauma, highlighting how repeated trauma exposure, especially during childhood, leads to a wide range of emotional and psychological difficulties. This study underscores the profound impact emotional wounds can have on mental health (Cloitre et al., 2009).

Recognition and understanding of emotional wounds are vital for healing. In contrast to physical injuries, where the healing process is often straightforward, emotional healing is complex and multifaceted. It requires time, patience, and often professional intervention.

The journey to heal emotional wounds involves acknowledging the pain, understanding its roots, and engaging in therapeutic processes. Therapy can be a transformative process that helps individuals process their experiences, develop coping strategies, and rebuild a sense of safety and trust.

Emotional wounds are serious psychological injuries that arise from traumatic experiences. They have a significant impact on an individual's mental health and require careful attention and treatment.

Trauma and Abuse: Definitions and Differences

Trauma is defined as a response to a deeply distressing or disturbing event that overwhelms an individual's ability to cope, causing feelings of helplessness and diminishing their sense of self and ability to feel a full range of emotions and experiences. Trauma can stem from a single event or a series of events and can have lasting adverse effects on an individual's functioning and mental, physical, social, emotional, or spiritual well-being.

Abuse, on the other hand, refers to the mistreatment by any person that violates another's rights or causes harm. Abuse can be physical, emotional, sexual, or psychological, and it often occurs in relationships where there is an imbalance of power. Repeated abuse often leads to trauma, but not all traumatic events are a result of abuse.

The primary difference between trauma and abuse lies in their origins. While trauma can be caused by natural disasters, accidents, or life-threatening events, abuse is always a result of actions by another person or group. Abuse is characterized by a pattern of behaviour that is intentionally harmful and controlling.

Understanding this distinction is crucial for providing appropriate support and intervention. Trauma-informed care involves recognizing the presence of trauma symptoms and acknowledging the role trauma may play in an individual's life. Similarly, addressing abuse requires understanding the dynamics of power and control that are central to abusive relationships.

A key study by Briere and Scott (2006) focuses on the principles of trauma therapy, emphasizing the importance of recognizing and addressing trauma symptoms in therapeutic settings. This research highlights the complexity of trauma and the necessity of specialized approaches in treatment (Briere & Scott, 2006).

Both trauma and abuse can lead to significant emotional and psychological distress. Symptoms may include anxiety, depression, flashbacks, nightmares, and avoidance behaviours. These symptoms can persist long after the traumatic event or abusive relationship has ended, indicating the lasting impact of these experiences.

Treatment for trauma and abuse often includes therapy, which can help individuals process their experiences, develop coping strategies, and rebuild a sense of safety and trust. Trauma-focused therapies are particularly effective.

While trauma and abuse can overlap, they are distinct experiences that require tailored approaches in treatment. Understanding the differences between these two is crucial in providing appropriate care and support for those affected.

Trauma vs. Abuse

Distinguishing between trauma and abuse is crucial in understanding their impacts and guiding effective treatment. While all abuse can cause trauma, not all trauma stems from abuse. This distinction is important because it influences the therapeutic approach and the healing process.

Trauma typically refers to the psychological and emotional response to an event or series of events that are extraordinarily stressful. These events are often life-threatening or perceived as life-threatening, such as natural disasters, accidents, or violent attacks. Trauma can disrupt a person's belief systems, making the world seem a dangerous and unpredictable place.

Abuse, in contrast, is an intentional act of harm or mistreatment by one person towards another. It can be physical, sexual, emotional, or psychological. The key element of abuse is the presence of power and control exerted by the abuser over the victim. Abuse often occurs in a relationship context, such as in families, intimate partnerships, or caretaking situations.

The impacts of trauma and abuse can be similar, including symptoms like anxiety, depression, PTSD, and relationship difficulties. However, the root causes and the context in which they occur are different, necessitating distinct approaches in therapy and support.

Treatment for trauma often focuses on helping individuals process and make sense of their traumatic experiences, develop coping strategies, and rebuild a sense of safety.

Abuse recovery, on the other hand, often involves addressing issues related to power, control, and self-esteem. Therapy may focus on rebuilding the individual's sense of autonomy, addressing the effects of prolonged exposure to an abusive environment, and developing healthy relationship skills.

The overlap between trauma and abuse is evident in many cases, especially in situations of repeated or prolonged abuse. Understanding this overlap is crucial for healthcare professionals, as it informs the choice of treatment and support strategies.

Both trauma and abuse require a compassionate, patient/client, and trauma-informed approach in therapy. Recognizing and validating the individual's experiences is the first step towards healing. Providing a safe and supportive environment is essential for individuals to explore their feelings and start the recovery process.

While trauma and abuse may present with similar symptoms, their underlying causes and dynamics are different. Distinguishing between the two is vital for effective treatment and recovery. Understanding these differences allows healthcare professionals to provide the most appropriate and effective care for those affected by trauma and abuse.

DSM-V Criteria for PTSD

Post-Traumatic Stress Disorder (PTSD) is a significant mental health condition identified in the Diagnostic and Statistical Manual of Mental Disorders, Fifth Edition (DSM-V). According to DSM-V, PTSD is characterized by exposure to actual or threatened death, serious injury, or sexual violence, either by directly experiencing it, witnessing it, learning that it happened to a close family member or friend, or experiencing repeated or extreme exposure to aversive details of traumatic events.

The DSM-V criteria for PTSD include the presence of specific symptoms from four different categories: intrusion symptoms, avoidance behaviours, negative alterations in cognitions and mood, and alterations in arousal and reactivity. These symptoms must persist for more than one month after the trauma and cause significant distress or impairment in social, occupational, or other important areas of functioning.

Intrusion symptoms refer to recurrent, involuntary, and intrusive distressing memories of the traumatic event(s), recurrent distressing dreams related to the event(s), dissociative reactions (such as flashbacks), intense or prolonged psychological distress, and marked physiological reactions to internal or external cues that symbolize or resemble an aspect of the traumatic event(s).

Avoidance behaviours include efforts to avoid distressing memories, thoughts, or feelings about or closely associated with the traumatic event(s) and efforts to avoid external reminders (people, places, conversations, activities, objects, situations) that arouse distressing memories, thoughts, or feelings about or closely associated with the traumatic event(s).

Negative alterations in cognitions and mood associated with the traumatic event(s) involve the inability to remember an important aspect of the traumatic event(s) (typically due to dissociative amnesia and not to other factors such as head injury, alcohol, or drugs), persistent and exaggerated negative beliefs or expectations about oneself, others, or the world, persistent, distorted cognitions about the cause or consequences of the traumatic event(s) that lead the individual to blame themselves or others, persistent negative emotional state (e.g., fear, horror, anger, guilt, or shame), markedly diminished interest or participation in significant activities, feelings of detachment or estrangement from others, and persistent inability to experience positive emotions.

Alterations in arousal and reactivity associated with the traumatic event(s) include irritable behaviour and angry outbursts, reckless or self-destructive behaviour, hypervigilance, exaggerated startle response, problems with concentration, and sleep disturbance.

The DSM-V also acknowledges that the duration of the disturbance (symptoms in Criteria B, C, D, and E) is more than 1 month and specifies that the disturbance causes clinically significant distress or impairment in social, occupational, or other important areas of functioning.

The DSM-V provides a comprehensive framework for diagnosing PTSD, recognizing the complexity of the disorder and the various ways it can manifest in individuals. This framework is crucial for mental health professionals in accurately diagnosing and treating PTSD.

Common Signs and Symptoms of Trauma, Including PTSD

Trauma and Post-Traumatic Stress Disorder (PTSD) can manifest through a variety of signs and symptoms, impacting individuals differently. Common signs and symptoms of trauma include intrusive thoughts, emotional numbness, hyperarousal, avoidance behaviours, nightmares, flashbacks, hypervigilance, and changes in mood and cognition.

Intrusive thoughts are recurrent, unwanted memories or images of the traumatic event. These may include distressing dreams or flashbacks, where individuals feel as though they are reliving the trauma. Flashbacks can be so vivid that individuals lose touch with reality during these episodes.

Emotional numbness refers to a detachment from emotions. Individuals may find it difficult to connect with their feelings or with others. This symptom is often a coping mechanism to avoid the pain of the trauma.

Hyperarousal is characterized by being in a constant state of alertness or heightened awareness. Individuals may experience an exaggerated startle response, feel jittery, or find it difficult to relax. This state of arousal can also lead to difficulties with sleep and concentration.

Avoidance behaviours are efforts to avoid thoughts, feelings, conversations, places, or people that remind the individual of the trauma. This avoidance can significantly impact one's daily life and relationships.

Changes in mood and cognition can include persistent negative beliefs about oneself or the world, feelings of guilt or blame, and a persistent negative emotional state, such as fear, horror, anger, guilt, or shame.

Individuals with PTSD may also experience irritability, angry outbursts, reckless or self-destructive behaviour, and a feeling of being "on edge." These symptoms can strain relationships and make it difficult to go about daily activities.

Physical symptoms of trauma and PTSD can include headaches, gastrointestinal issues, fatigue, and other stress-related physical reactions. These physical symptoms are often a response to the psychological stress of the trauma.

It is important to note that not everyone who experiences trauma will develop PTSD. The severity and duration of these symptoms can vary widely, and some individuals may experience a delayed onset of symptoms.

Recognizing Signs and Symptoms of Abuse

Abuse, whether physical, emotional, sexual, or psychological, leaves distinct signs and symptoms in its victims. Recognizing these indicators is crucial for early intervention and support.

Physical abuse often leaves visible marks, such as bruises, cuts, burns, or fractures. However, not all physical abuse is immediately apparent, as abusers may target parts of the body that are easily concealed.

Emotional abuse, though less visible, can be equally damaging. It includes verbal assaults, threats, intimidation, humiliation, and manipulation. Victims of emotional abuse may exhibit signs of anxiety, depression, low self-esteem, and withdrawal from social interactions. They might also show symptoms of post-traumatic stress, such as hypervigilance, nightmares, and flashbacks.

Sexual abuse, involving any non-consensual sexual activity, can lead to severe emotional and psychological distress. Symptoms may include feelings of shame, guilt, sexual dysfunction, and avoidance of intimacy.

Psychological abuse involves tactics to control, frighten, isolate, or belittle the victim. Victims may exhibit confusion, fearfulness, dependence on the abuser, and changes in personality or behaviour

In children, signs of abuse can include changes in behaviour or school performance, reluctance to go home, fear of certain individuals, and age-inappropriate sexual behaviours or knowledge.

Abuse impacts mental health significantly, often leading to disorders such as depression, anxiety, and PTSD. Abuse can also affect behaviour, manifesting in either increased aggression or withdrawal. Victims might engage in substance abuse or self-harm as coping mechanisms. They may also struggle with forming healthy relationships, often either becoming overly dependent or excessively distant.

Victims of abuse often suffer from a profound loss of trust, not only in others but also in themselves. This erosion of trust can lead to difficulties in decision-making and a general sense of insecurity in various aspects of life. They may constantly seek validation or, conversely, reject any form of assistance or intimacy due to fear of being hurt again.

Long-term impacts of abuse include challenges in establishing and maintaining healthy relationships, potential difficulties in occupational functioning, and ongoing struggles with self-worth and self-identity. Abuse, especially when experienced in childhood, can have lasting effects on an individual's development and personality.

The signs and symptoms of abuse are diverse and encompass physical, emotional, and behavioural aspects. The impact of abuse extends far beyond the immediate physical or emotional harm, affecting the mental health and overall well-being of the victim. Recognizing these signs is critical for providing timely and effective support to those affected by abuse.

Impact of Emotional Wounds

Emotional wounds, resulting from experiences such as trauma and abuse, have profound and far-reaching effects on individuals and their relationships. On a personal level, emotional wounds can lead to a range of psychological problems, including anxiety, depression, PTSD, and various personality disorders. These conditions often stem from the individual's attempt to process and cope with their traumatic experiences.

In relationships, emotional wounds can manifest as difficulties in trusting others, fear of intimacy, or an inability to form secure emotional attachments. Individuals with unhealed emotional wounds might either cling to relationships out of fear of abandonment or avoid them altogether to protect themselves from potential harm.

Emotionally wounded individuals might also exhibit maladaptive behaviours, such as aggression, substance abuse, or self-harm, as a way to manage their pain or regain a sense of control. These behaviours, while serving as coping mechanisms, can further complicate their personal and social lives.

The impact on trust and worldview is significant. Trauma and abuse can shatter an individual's belief in a just, safe, and predictable world. This loss of a coherent worldview can lead to feelings of hopelessness, cynicism, and detachment from society.

Furthermore, emotional wounds can have a ripple effect on the individual's social and occupational functioning. They might struggle with concentration, decision-making, and maintaining regular employment. Social interactions can become challenging, leading to isolation and a further decline in mental health.

Healing from emotional wounds is a complex process that often requires professional intervention. Therapy can provide a safe space for individuals to process their experiences, develop healthy coping strategies, and rebuild their sense of self and trust in the world.

The impact of emotional wounds is profound and multifaceted, affecting individuals' mental health, relationships, behaviour, trust, and worldview. Understanding the depth and breadth of these effects is crucial for effective treatment and support, helping individuals to heal and regain control over their lives.

Differentiating Behaviours

Distinguishing behaviours resulting from emotional wounds from those indicative of psychiatric disorders is a complex yet crucial aspect of mental health diagnosis and treatment. It involves understanding the nuances between normal responses to traumatic experiences and behaviours that signify deeper, clinical mental health issues.

One key aspect in differentiating these is the context in which the behaviours occur. Behaviours stemming from emotional wounds are often directly related to traumatic experiences. For instance, a person may exhibit avoidance behaviours specifically in contexts reminiscent of their trauma. In contrast, psychiatric disorders generally manifest as a broader range of symptoms that are not necessarily tied to specific contexts or triggers. For example, generalized anxiety disorder presents as a pervasive and persistent worry not limited to specific situations or experiences.

The pattern and duration of behaviours also play a crucial role. Behaviours related to emotional wounds often follow a recognizable pattern linked to the trauma or abuse. These behaviours might emerge or intensify when the individual is reminded of their trauma. Psychiatric disorders, however, typically display a more consistent and persistent pattern that does not necessarily correlate with specific events or experiences.

Another important factor is the functionality of the individual. Behaviours due to emotional wounds, while distressing, might not significantly impair an individual's overall functioning in various life domains. Psychiatric disorders, however, often lead to substantial impairment in social, occupational, or other important areas of functioning.

The study of the relationship between trauma, emotional responses, and mental health disorders is complex. According to a study by Briere and Scott (2006), understanding the interplay between traumatic experiences and psychological symptoms is essential in differentiating trauma-related behaviours from psychiatric disorders. This understanding aids in providing appropriate treatment and interventions (Briere & Scott, 2006).

Additionally, a study by Cloitre, Stolbach, Herman, van der Kolk, Pynoos, Wang, and Petkova (2009) highlights the importance of considering the impact of cumulative trauma when assessing and treating emotional and behavioural symptoms. This perspective is crucial in distinguishing between responses to trauma and more pervasive psychiatric conditions (Cloitre et al., 2009).

Differentiating behaviours stemming from emotional wounds from psychiatric disorders requires a careful consideration of context, pattern, duration, and functionality. Understanding these distinctions is vital for mental health professionals in providing accurate diagnoses and effective treatment plans. It ensures that individuals receive the most appropriate care for their specific experiences and symptoms.

PTSD and the Brain

Post-Traumatic Stress Disorder (PTSD) significantly affects brain function and structure. Research has identified specific areas of the brain that are impacted by PTSD, leading to the symptoms experienced by those suffering from this disorder.

One of the key areas affected is the amygdala, known for its role in processing emotions, especially fear and anxiety. In individuals with PTSD, the amygdala can become overactive, leading to heightened responses to perceived threats and an increased state of fear and anxiety. This hyperactivity is often associated with the intrusive memories and heightened arousal symptoms of PTSD.

The hippocampus, involved in the formation and retrieval of memories, is also impacted. Studies have shown that individuals with PTSD may have a smaller hippocampus, which could affect the ability to distinguish between past and present experiences, contributing to flashbacks and intrusive memories. A study by Bremner et al. (1995) found that individuals with PTSD showed a significant reduction in hippocampal volume, which correlated with memory deficits (Bremner et al., 1995).

Another critical area is the prefrontal cortex, responsible for executive functions such as reasoning, problem-solving, and decision-making. Changes in this area may contribute to difficulties in concentration and decision-making, often reported in PTSD sufferers.

Neurobiological changes resulting from traumatic experiences also involve alterations in the brain's neurotransmitter systems, particularly those related to stress hormones like cortisol and norepinephrine. Dysregulation of these systems can lead to many PTSD symptoms, including hyperarousal and sleep disturbances.

PTSD leads to significant changes in the brain, particularly in the amygdala, hippocampus, and prefrontal cortex. Understanding these neurobiological changes is crucial for developing effective treatments for PTSD.

Evidence-Based Therapies for PTSD

Effective treatment of Post-Traumatic Stress Disorder (PTSD) requires a multifaceted approach tailored to the individual's experiences and symptoms. Several evidence-based therapies have been proven effective in treating PTSD.

Trauma-focused psychotherapies are among the most effective treatments for PTSD. These therapies include Cognitive Processing Therapy (CPT), Prolonged Exposure (PE), Exposure Therapy, Visual Therapy, Thought Developmental Practice (TDP), Grounding Techniques, Diaphragmic Breathing/Deep Breathing, and Trauma-Focused Cognitive Behavioural Therapy (TF-CBT). These therapies work by helping individuals process and make sense of their trauma, reducing the power of traumatic memories and associated symptoms.

Eye Movement Desensitization and Reprocessing (EMDR) is another effective therapy for PTSD. EMDR involves the patient/client recalling traumatic events while the therapist directs their eye movements. This process is thought to help in processing and integrating traumatic memories, thus reducing the symptoms of PTSD.

Medication, particularly Selective Serotonin Reuptake Inhibitors (SSRIs), has also been shown to be effective in treating some symptoms of PTSD, such as anxiety and depression. Medications are often used in conjunction with psychotherapy for the best results.

Tailoring therapy to individual experiences and symptoms is critical in PTSD treatment. For instance, individuals with severe avoidance symptoms might benefit more from prolonged exposure therapy, while those with distorted beliefs about their trauma might benefit from cognitive processing therapy.

A study by Bradley et al. (2005) reviewed various treatments for PTSD and found that trauma-focused cognitive-behavioural therapies had the strongest evidence for their efficacy. This research highlights the importance of specific, targeted therapeutic approaches for treating PTSD (Bradley et al., 2005).

Treating PTSD effectively involves a combination of trauma-focused psychotherapies, EMDR, and, in some cases, medication. The choice of treatment should be tailored to the individual's specific symptoms and experiences, ensuring the best possible outcome.

Coping Strategies for Emotional Wounds

Managing the effects of trauma and abuse requires a comprehensive approach that includes various coping strategies and techniques. These strategies are aimed at promoting emotional regulation, building resilience, and facilitating healing.

One key technique is mindfulness, which involves staying present and fully engaging with the here and now in a non-judgmental way. Mindfulness can help reduce the intensity of traumatic memories and alleviate stress and anxiety. Mindfulness-based stress reduction (MBSR) programs have shown effectiveness in reducing symptoms of PTSD and improving overall well-being (Kearney et al., 2013).

Journaling is another effective coping strategy. Writing about thoughts and feelings associated with traumatic experiences can provide a way to express emotions safely and process events. Research has demonstrated that expressive writing can lead to improvements in various psychological and physical health outcomes (Pennebaker & Seagal, 1999).

Developing a strong support system is crucial. Engaging with supportive family members, friends, or support groups can provide a sense of belonging and safety, essential for healing from emotional wounds.

Self-care practices, such as regular exercise, adequate sleep, and a balanced diet, can significantly improve mental health. These practices help in regulating mood, reducing anxiety, and improving overall physical health, which is often affected by trauma and stress.

Learning and practicing relaxation techniques, such as deep breathing, progressive muscle relaxation, or yoga, can help in managing symptoms of anxiety and hyperarousal often associated with trauma.

Professional therapy can be instrumental in coping with emotional wounds. Therapists can provide guidance on specific strategies tailored to individual needs and help navigate the complexities of healing from trauma and abuse.

The Importance of Closure

Closure is a critical concept in the healing process of emotional wounds. It involves coming to terms with traumatic events, making sense of them, and integrating them into one's life narrative.

Closure is essential because it allows individuals to process their experiences and emotions fully. Without closure, traumatic events can continue to exert a disruptive influence on an individual's life, leading to ongoing distress, anxiety, and other negative emotions.

One method of finding closure is through therapy, where individuals can explore and understand their experiences in a safe and supportive environment. Therapies like cognitive-behavioural therapy (CBT) and narrative therapy can be particularly helpful in this regard.

Another approach to achieving closure is through rituals or symbolic acts, which can help in acknowledging the impact of the trauma and symbolizing a move forward. This might include writing a letter (not necessarily to be sent) to express feelings related to the trauma or creating a piece of art to represent the journey of healing.

Self-reflection is also a key component in finding closure. This might involve re-evaluating personal values and beliefs that have been affected by the trauma and redefining one's identity in the context of the experiences.

Closure is not about forgetting the trauma or minimizing its impact. Rather, it is about integrating the experience into one's life in a way that allows for continued growth and development. It is a personal journey and can look different for each individual.

Achieving closure is a vital part of healing from emotional wounds. It involves processing and making sense of traumatic experiences, leading to a state where these events no longer exert a controlling influence on one's emotional well-being. Therapy, personal rituals, and self-reflection are key methods in facilitating this process.

Addressing SI/HI in Emotional Wounds

The significance of assessing risks for self-harm (SI) and suicidal ideation (HI) in individuals with emotional wounds cannot be overstated. Emotional trauma, often resulting from experiences such as abuse, neglect, or other forms of trauma, can significantly increase the risk of self-harm and suicidal thoughts or behaviours. It is essential for mental health professionals to be vigilant in assessing these risks as part of the therapeutic process.

Assessment of SI/HI should be an ongoing process in therapy and care management, especially for individuals known to have a history of trauma. Standard assessment tools and questionnaires can be used to gauge the severity and frequency of these thoughts or behaviours. Importantly, direct and open questions about self-harm and suicidal thoughts should be asked in a non-judgmental and supportive manner.

Recognizing warning signs is crucial. These may include increased withdrawal, changes in mood or behaviour, expressions of hopelessness or worthlessness, and direct or indirect talk about death or self-harm. Behavioural cues such as giving away possessions, sudden calmness after a period of depression, or increased substance use should also raise concerns.

When there is a risk of SI/HI, immediate action is necessary. This may involve developing a safety plan with the individual, which includes identifying triggers, coping strategies, and sources of support. Ensuring that the individual does not have access to means of self-harm or suicide (such as weapons or excessive medications) is also crucial.

Mental health professionals should collaborate with the individual to establish a crisis response plan. This plan should include contact information for emergency services, crisis hotlines, and supportive family members or friends. Regular follow-ups and check-ins can provide additional support and monitor the individual's state.

In cases of acute risk, hospitalization may be necessary to ensure the individual's safety. Inpatient treatment can provide intensive care and monitoring, as well as stabilization of the individual's mental state.

Long-term management of individuals at risk for SI/HI involves consistent and comprehensive mental health care. Support groups and community resources can provide additional layers of support, offering a sense of connection and shared experiences. Engaging family members or close friends in the care process can also be beneficial, as they can offer support and help monitor the individual's well-being.

Addressing the risk of self-harm and suicidal ideation in individuals with emotional wounds is a critical aspect of mental health care. Through vigilant assessment, crisis intervention, and ongoing support, mental health professionals can play a vital role in safeguarding the well-being of those at risk.

A Note on DBT

Dialectical Behaviour Therapy (DBT) is a comprehensive cognitive-behavioural treatment developed by Dr. Marsha Linehan, initially for individuals with borderline personality disorder (BPD) who struggle with suicidal ideation or self-harm behaviours. Over time, DBT has been adapted and found effective for a range of other mental health disorders, including those involving emotional regulation difficulties.

DBT combines standard cognitive-behavioural techniques for emotion regulation and reality-testing with concepts of distress tolerance, acceptance, and mindful awareness largely derived from Buddhist meditative practice. The core components of DBT include:

1. **Skills Training:** This is typically conducted in a group setting and focuses on teaching skills in four key areas: mindfulness, distress tolerance, emotion regulation, and interpersonal effectiveness.

2. **Individual Therapy:** These sessions focus on enhancing motivational aspects and applying DBT skills to specific challenges and events in the patient's/client's life.

3. **Phone Coaching:** This component provides clients with real-time support in applying DBT skills in challenging situations that occur in their daily lives.

4. **Consultation Team:** This is for therapists, designed to support DBT providers in their work with clients, promoting adherence to the treatment model and providing necessary support.

Numerous studies have demonstrated the efficacy of DBT in reducing suicidal behaviour and self-harm. A seminal study by Linehan et al. (1991) found that DBT was significantly more effective than treatment-as-usual in reducing parasuicidal behaviours in women with BPD. Furthermore, research indicates that DBT helps in reducing hospitalization rates and improving overall functioning (Linehan et al., 1991).

DBT's focus on skill-building, particularly in the areas of emotional regulation and distress tolerance, makes it especially effective for individuals struggling with intense emotional responses and impulsivity. The mindfulness component helps in cultivating a nonjudgmental awareness of the present moment, which is particularly beneficial for individuals who experience extreme emotional swings.

DBT has been adapted for various populations and settings, including adolescents, individuals with substance use disorders, eating disorders, and depression. Its principles have been effectively applied in both group and individual therapy settings.

DBT is a well-established and evidence-based therapy that is particularly effective for disorders related to emotion dysregulation, including BPD, PTSD, and depression. Its unique blend of cognitive-behavioural techniques with mindfulness principles offers a comprehensive approach to treatment that has shown significant positive outcomes in numerous studies.

Professional Knowledge on Emotional Wounds

For healthcare professionals, understanding emotional wounds, trauma, and abuse is crucial in providing effective care. These insights not only involve recognizing the symptoms and impacts of such experiences but also entail implementing best practices in empathetic, trauma-informed care.

Healthcare professionals must possess a deep understanding of emotional wounds, trauma, and abuse to provide effective and compassionate care. This knowledge encompasses various aspects, from recognizing symptoms to understanding the broader implications of these experiences.

Recognition of Symptoms

1. **Identifying Physical and Psychological Signs**: Professionals should be adept at recognizing both the physical and psychological signs of trauma and abuse. This includes symptoms such as anxiety, depression, unexplained physical ailments, and changes in behaviour or mood.

2. **Understanding Varied Presentations**: The manifestations of trauma can vary greatly among individuals. Some may display overt signs of distress, while others may appear withdrawn or numb.

3. **Recognizing Behavioural Changes**: Changes in behaviour, such as increased aggression, substance abuse, or withdrawal from social interactions, can be indicators of underlying trauma or abuse.

Impact of Trauma and Abuse

1. **Neurobiological Impact**: Trauma can lead to significant changes in brain regions such as the amygdala, hippocampus, and prefrontal cortex, affecting emotion regulation, memory, and cognitive processing.

2. **Emotional and Psychological Effects**: Understanding the emotional and psychological effects of trauma and abuse, including the development of PTSD, anxiety disorders, and depression, is crucial.

3. **Impact on Relationships and Functioning**: Trauma and abuse can profoundly affect a person's ability to form and maintain healthy relationships and can lead to difficulties in personal and professional life.

Complex Trauma

1. **Recognition of Prolonged and Repeated Trauma**: Complex trauma results from prolonged or repeated exposure to traumatic events, often of an interpersonal nature. This can lead to more severe psychological harm and complex symptomatology.

2. **Understanding Developmental Impact**: For individuals who experienced trauma in childhood, it's important to understand how these experiences can impact development and contribute to long-term emotional and psychological difficulties.

Spectrum of Abuse

1. **Identifying Different Forms**: Abuse can be physical, sexual, emotional, or psychological, and each form has its unique signs and symptoms. Professionals need to be aware of the nuances of each type.

2. **Interpersonal Dynamics**: Understanding the dynamics of abusive relationships, including the roles of power and control, is essential in identifying and addressing abuse.

3. **Cultural Considerations**: Recognizing how cultural factors can influence the perception and reporting of abuse is crucial in providing appropriate care.

Trauma-Informed Approach

1. **Implementing Trauma-Informed Practices**: This involves understanding the widespread impact of trauma and integrating this knowledge into policies, procedures, and practices.

2. **Screening for Trauma History**: Routine screening for a history of trauma and abuse can help in identifying those at risk and providing appropriate support and intervention.

3. **Providing Holistic Care**: Addressing the needs of trauma survivors requires a holistic approach that considers physical, emotional, social, and psychological aspects.

A comprehensive understanding of emotional wounds, trauma, and abuse is fundamental for healthcare professionals. Recognizing the signs and symptoms, understanding the impact on individuals, being aware of the complexities of trauma, and implementing a trauma-informed approach in care is important. Such knowledge is vital to support the healing and well-being of those affected by trauma and abuse.

Best Practices in Trauma-Informed Care

Trauma-informed care is an approach in mental health and social services that recognizes and responds to the effects of all types of trauma. It emphasizes physical, psychological, and emotional safety for both providers and survivors, creating opportunities for survivors to rebuild a sense of control and empowerment in their lives. Here are key best practices in implementing trauma-informed care:

1. Understanding the Prevalence and Impact of Trauma

Recognize that trauma is widespread and can affect individuals of any age, gender, or background. Understand how trauma impacts not just the mental and emotional health of individuals but also their physical health, relationships, and daily functioning.

2. Creating a Safe and Supportive Environment

Ensure that the care environment is physically and emotionally safe. This includes being sensitive to cues that might trigger distress in trauma survivors. Build trust through consistency, clear communication, and respectful interactions.

3. Adopting a Trauma-Informed Approach in All Interactions

Use a strengths-based approach that recognizes the resilience and coping abilities of the individual. Avoid re-traumatization by being aware of language, behaviours, and procedures that might inadvertently trigger trauma responses.

4. Empowering Survivors

Empower individuals by offering choices and control over their treatment whenever possible. Validate their experiences and feelings, reinforcing their right to respectful and compassionate care.

5. Integrating Cultural Competence

Acknowledge and respect cultural differences, understanding how culture impacts one's experience and response to trauma. Provide care that is respectful of and responsive to cultural, racial, ethnic, and gender identity.

6. Ensuring Collaborative Decision Making

Involve individuals in all aspects of their treatment planning and decision-making processes. Foster collaboration between various healthcare providers, the individual, and their support system.

7. Providing Comprehensive and Holistic Care

Address the multidimensional aspects of trauma, including its physical, emotional, psychological, and social impacts. Coordinate care among various providers and specialists to address all aspects of the individual's well-being.

8. Utilizing Evidence-Based and Trauma-Specific Interventions

Implement interventions that are specifically designed to address trauma and somatic experiencing. Stay informed about the latest research and best practices in trauma treatment.

9. Fostering Resilience and Recovery

Focus on building resilience and facilitating recovery, rather than merely treating symptoms. Help individuals identify and leverage their strengths and resources in the healing process.

10. Ongoing Training and Staff Support

Provide ongoing training to all staff members on trauma-informed care principles. Support staff through regular supervision, opportunities for reflection, and addressing secondary traumatic stress.

11. Advocacy and Community Outreach

Advocate for policies and practices that are trauma-informed at both the organizational and community level. Engage in community outreach to educate the public about trauma and its effects.

12. Evaluating and Improving Practices

Regularly evaluate the effectiveness of trauma-informed practices and make adjustments as necessary. Encourage feedback from individuals receiving services to continually improve care delivery.

Conclusion

Recognizing, understanding, and effectively managing emotional wounds are critical components of mental health care. This journey encompasses a comprehensive understanding of the nature of trauma, abuse, and their resultant psychological impacts, along with the implementation of empathetic, trauma-informed care practices. To summarize the key aspects:

1. **Recognition of Emotional Wounds**: It begins with the ability to identify the signs and symptoms of emotional trauma and abuse, understanding that these wounds are often deeper and more complex than they appear.

2. **Understanding Trauma and Abuse**: Acknowledging the various forms of trauma and abuse, and their profound impact on the brain, behaviour, and overall emotional well-being is crucial. This includes an appreciation of how past experiences can shape present responses and behaviours.

3. **Effective Management Strategies**: The adoption of evidence-based therapies and the importance of tailoring these treatments to individual needs, cannot be overstated. Additionally, coping strategies like mindfulness, self-care, and building support networks play a vital role in managing the effects of emotional wounds.

4. **Trauma-Informed Care**: Implementing a trauma-informed approach in care that emphasizes safety, empathy, patient/client-centeredness, and avoidance of re-traumatization is essential in fostering a healing environment.

5. **Holistic Approach**: Recognizing that emotional healing is a multifaceted process that may involve addressing various aspects of a person's life, including relationships, work, and personal beliefs.

6. **Continuous Learning and Advocacy**: The need for ongoing education for healthcare professionals in the latest findings in trauma research and treatment and advocating for policies and resources that support trauma survivors.

Healing from emotional wounds is a journey that requires compassion, understanding, and a multifaceted treatment approach. Healthcare professionals play a pivotal role in this process, not only as providers of care but also as advocates, educators, and supportive allies.

It's important to remember that recovery from emotional trauma is possible, and with the right support and interventions, individuals can regain their strength and resilience. Encouraging a compassionate approach to healing and recovery, one that respects the individual's experiences and fosters a sense of hope and empowerment, is essential in helping trauma survivors navigate their path to wellness.

Week 7

The Workbook

Week Seven

EMOTIONAL **WOUNDS**

As we concluded our insightful exploration of Addictions in Week Six, we brainstormed about the complexities of substance abuse and its far-reaching implications. We unravelled the nuanced differences between substance use and addiction, dissected the DSM-V criteria, and equipped ourselves with practical strategies for diagnosis, treatment, and coping. This comprehensive understanding lays a crucial foundation for our journey into Week Seven, where we shifted our focus to the realm of Emotional Wounds.

Emotional Wounds, often invisible yet profoundly impactful, have been the core of our exploration this week. We commence with a nuanced understanding of what constitutes emotional wounds, their genesis, and the spectrum that ranged from trauma to abuse. Our professional acumen has been further sharpened by distinguishing between trauma and abuse and understanding their distinct yet overlapping domains. As we have progressed, we meticulously dissected the DSM-V criteria for Post-Traumatic Stress Disorder (PTSD), a pivotal aspect of our week's study.

The week has been structured to enhance our proficiency in recognizing the signs and symptoms of trauma and abuse, understanding their intricate manifestations, and their profound impact on both individuals and their wider social circles. A crucial element of our learning has been the examination of the brain's response to PTSD, deepening our comprehension of its neurobiological underpinnings.

Our commitment to evidence-based practice steered us through an exploration of the most effective therapies for addressing emotional wounds. We have not only focus on treatment but also on empowering coping strategies that foster resilience and healing. This week's culmination has marked by a thorough understanding of the critical need for closure in emotional wounds and the essential professional knowledge required for effectively navigating this complex terrain.

Day 1: Understanding Emotional Wounds

1. **Reflective Exercise 1**: Describe your understanding of emotional wounds and their impact on mental health.

_____

_____

_____

_____

_____

_____

2. **Reflective Exercise 2**: Reflect on a case where emotional wounds were a significant factor in a patient s/client's condition.

_____

_____

_____

_____

_____

_____

3. **Guided Activity**: Research and summarize different types of emotional wounds and their psychological impacts.

_____

_____

_____

_____

_____

Day 2: Trauma and Abuse

1. **Reflective Exercise 1**: Discuss your understanding of trauma and abuse, and their impact on individuals.

_____

_____

_____

_____

_____

_____

2. **Reflective Exercise 2**: Reflect on a case involving trauma or abuse. What were the key challenges and learnings?

_____

_____

_____

_____

_____

_____

3. **Guided Activity**: Develop a brief overview of trauma and abuse, focusing on their psychological implications.

_____

_____

_____

_____

_____

Day 3: Trauma vs Abuse

1. **Reflective Exercise 1**: Reflect on the differences between trauma and abuse based on your experiences.

_____

_____

_____

_____

_____

_____

2. **Reflective Exercise 2**: Consider a case where distinguishing between trauma and abuse was challenging.

_____

_____

_____

_____

_____

_____

3. **Guided Activity**: Create a comparison chart outlining the key differences between trauma and abuse.

_____

_____

_____

_____

_____

_____

Day 4: Criteria for PTSD in DSM-V

1. **Reflective Exercise 1**: Compare the DSM-V criteria for PTSD with a real case you have encountered.

_____

_____

_____

_____

_____

_____

2. **Reflective Exercise 2**: Discuss the challenges of applying DSM-V criteria for PTSD across different patient/client demographics.

_____

_____

_____

_____

_____

_____

3. **Guided Activity**: Develop a checklist or guide based on DSM-V criteria for diagnosing PTSD.

_____

_____

_____

_____

_____

_____

Day 5: Signs and Symptoms of Trauma and Abuse

1. **Reflective Exercise 1**: Reflect on the common signs and symptoms of trauma, including PTSD, observed in your practice.

_____

_____

_____

_____

_____

_____

2. **Reflective Exercise 2**: Consider the signs and symptoms of abuse and their impact on individuals.

_____

_____

_____

_____

_____

_____

3. **Guided Activity**: Design an educational tool like an infographic illustrating the signs and symptoms of trauma and abuse.

_____

_____

_____

_____

_____

_____

Day 6: Effects of Emotional Wounds and PTSD on the Brain

1. **Reflective Exercise 1**: Discuss how emotional wounds, particularly PTSD, affect individuals and their relationships.

_____

_____

_____

_____

_____

_____

2. **Reflective Exercise 2**: Reflect on the parts of the brain affected by PTSD and their implications.

_____

_____

_____

_____

_____

_____

3. **Guided Activity**: Create a simple diagram or chart explaining the brain's changes due to PTSD.

_____

_____

_____

_____

_____

Day 7: Therapies, Coping Strategies, and Professional Knowledge for Emotional Wounds

1. **Reflective Exercise 1**: Share your experience with evidence-based therapies for emotional wounds, particularly PTSD.

2. **Reflective Exercise 2**: Reflect on effective coping strategies for managing emotional wounds.

3. **Guided Activity**: Prepare a brief presentation or educational material for colleagues highlighting the essential aspects of understanding and treating emotional wounds.

Week 8

PSYCHOSOCIAL **STRESSORS**

Psychosocial stressors are external pressures that can significantly impact an individual's psychological and social functioning. These stressors arise from one's interaction with elements of their environment, social settings, and personal life challenges. Contextual features refer to the specific conditions or surroundings in which these stressors occur, providing a background that shapes their impact and significance.

The concept of psychosocial stressors encompasses a broad range of experiences. These can include life events such as job loss, relationship difficulties, or bereavement, as well as ongoing challenges like chronic illness, financial instability, or social marginalization. Contextual features, on the other hand, might include an individual's support network, cultural background, or socioeconomic status, all of which play a role in how stressors are experienced and managed.

These stressors and features are significant in the field of mental health because they can contribute to the onset or exacerbation of various psychological conditions. For instance, chronic stressors have been linked to the development of depression and anxiety disorders. According to Monroe and Harkness (2005), the relationship between stressors and mental health is complex, with both the nature of the stressor and the individual's vulnerabilities and resources playing critical roles.

Furthermore, the impact of psychosocial stressors is not limited to mental health. They can also have significant physical health implications. Research has shown that chronic stress can contribute to a range of physical health problems, including heart disease, hypertension, and a weakened immune system (Cohen, Janicki-Deverts, & Miller, 2007). This connection underscores the importance of addressing psychosocial stressors in a holistic manner.

Causes of Psychosocial Stressors

Psychosocial stressors arise from various sources and their causes are often interrelated. Environmental factors such as living in a high-crime area or experiencing a natural disaster can be significant sources of stress. Social factors, including difficult relationships, workplace challenges, or social isolation, also contribute. Personal factors might include individual health issues, personal beliefs, or past traumatic experiences.

The causes of these stressors can be acute, such as in the case of a sudden job loss or the death of a loved one. However, they can also be chronic, such as ongoing financial difficulties or long-term caregiving responsibilities. The chronic nature of some stressors can lead to a cumulative effect, where the ongoing pressure progressively impacts an individual's well-being.

Research has shown that the perception and impact of stressors can vary greatly depending on individual factors such as personality, coping styles, and previous life experiences. For instance, some people may find certain workplace challenges stimulating and motivating, whereas others may perceive the same challenges as overwhelming and stressful.

Understanding the causes of psychosocial stressors is crucial in developing effective coping and intervention strategies. By recognizing the source of stress, individuals and professionals can better tailor their approach to managing these stressors effectively.

Evaluating Psychosocial Stressors

Evaluating psychosocial stressors involves assessing both the nature of the stressors and the individual's response to them. This assessment is critical in identifying the need for intervention and in formulating appropriate treatment plans.

Assessment tools and techniques used to evaluate psychosocial stressors include clinical interviews, self-report questionnaires, and standardized assessment instruments. These tools are designed to gather comprehensive information about the stressors, including their intensity, duration, and perceived impact on the individual.

A thorough evaluation will consider not only the stressors themselves but also the individual's resources and coping mechanisms. Factors such as social support, resilience, and past experiences with stress are all relevant in understanding how an individual is coping with current stressors.

Professional assessment of psychosocial stressors also involves understanding the contextual features that influence how these stressors are experienced. This includes consideration of cultural, socioeconomic, and environmental factors that may shape the individual's response to stress.

Evaluating psychosocial stressors is a complex process, requiring a nuanced understanding of both the objective nature of the stressors and the subjective experience of the individual. This process is essential in providing targeted and effective support to those dealing with significant psychosocial stress.

DSM-V Perspective on Psychosocial Stressors

The Diagnostic and Statistical Manual of Mental Disorders, Fifth Edition (DSM-V), provides a framework for understanding how psychosocial stressors impact mental health. According to the DSM-V, psychosocial stressors are significant in the development and exacerbation of mental disorders. These stressors are considered in the context of diagnostic criteria for various mental health conditions, acknowledging that they can be precipitating factors or exacerbate existing conditions.

The DSM-V categorizes psychosocial stressors into different types, including environmental, interpersonal, and occupational stressors. This categorization helps clinicians in understanding the multifaceted nature of stress and its diverse sources. The manual also emphasizes the importance of considering the severity and duration of stressors, as these aspects significantly influence their impact on mental health.

Moreover, the DSM-V introduces the concept of adjustment disorders, which are directly related to psychosocial stressors. Adjustment disorders are characterized by emotional or behavioural symptoms in response to an identifiable stressor, occurring within three months of the onset of the stressor. This category acknowledges that not all responses to stressors meet the criteria for more severe mental disorders but still require attention and treatment.

In the assessment of mental health conditions, the DSM-V also includes a consideration of the individual's coping capacity and resilience. This aspect recognizes that the same stressor can have different impacts on different individuals, depending on their coping strategies and support systems.

Signs and Symptoms of Psychosocial Stress

The signs and symptoms of psychosocial stress can manifest in various ways, affecting both mental and physical health. Common psychological symptoms include anxiety, depression, irritability, and feelings of overwhelm. These symptoms can lead to changes in mood, decreased motivation, and a general sense of unhappiness.

Physical symptoms of psychosocial stress are also prevalent. These can include headaches, muscle tension, fatigue, and sleep disturbances. Gastrointestinal problems such as stomach aches and changes in appetite are also common. These physical symptoms often exacerbate the individual's overall stress experience.

Behavioural changes are another indicator of psychosocial stress. This can include increased or decreased social interaction, changes in work or school performance, and altered eating or sleeping patterns. Substance use and abuse can also be a behavioural response to stress.

It is important to note that the experience of stress is subjective, and individuals may exhibit different signs and symptoms. The presence and severity of these symptoms can vary widely, depending on the individual's resilience, coping mechanisms, and social support.

Persistent or severe symptoms of stress may indicate the need for professional intervention. Early recognition and treatment of these symptoms can prevent the development of more serious mental health conditions.

Impact of Psychosocial Stressors

The impact of psychosocial stressors extends beyond immediate emotional and physical symptoms. Long-term exposure to stress can lead to a range of psychological and physiological conditions. Psychologically, chronic stress can contribute to the development of mental health disorders such as depression, anxiety, and post-traumatic stress disorder (PTSD).

From a physiological perspective, chronic stress has been associated with a range of health issues. These include cardiovascular diseases, obesity, diabetes, and gastrointestinal problems. The stress response, which involves the release of hormones such as cortisol and adrenaline, can have harmful effects on the body when activated over prolonged periods (Cohen et al., 2007).

Stress can also have a significant impact on cognitive functioning. It can impair concentration, decision-making, and memory. Chronic stress can lead to a state of mental fatigue, reducing an individual's ability to cope with daily challenges effectively.

The social impact of psychosocial stressors is also considerable. Stress can strain relationships, reduce social interaction, and lead to isolation. It can affect performance at work or school, potentially leading to job loss or academic difficulties.

The cumulative impact of these effects underscores the importance of addressing psychosocial stressors effectively. Interventions that target stress reduction, coping skill enhancement, and resilience building are essential in mitigating these impacts.

Evidence-Based Therapies for Psychosocial Stress

Evidence-based therapies for managing psychosocial stress focus on reducing the impact of stressors and enhancing coping mechanisms. Thought Developmental Practice (TDP) and other therapies is widely recognized as an effective treatment for stress-related disorders. The goal is to helps individuals identify and challenge their issues and develop healthier coping strategies. Studies have shown that CBT can effectively reduce symptoms of stress and improve overall well-being (Hofmann, Asnaani, Vonk, Sawyer, & Fang, 2012).

Another evidence-based approach is Mindfulness-Based Stress Reduction (MBSR). This therapy combines mindfulness meditation and yoga to help individuals focus on the present moment, reducing rumination and worry. Research indicates that MBSR can significantly reduce symptoms of stress and enhance quality of life (Khoury et al., 2015).

In addition to these therapies, other interventions like interpersonal therapy, problem-solving therapy, and psychodynamic therapy have shown effectiveness in managing psychosocial stress. These therapies focus on improving relationships, solving practical problems contributing to stress, and understanding underlying psychological patterns, respectively.

Pharmacotherapy, although not a first-line treatment for psychosocial stress, can be beneficial in some cases, especially when stress is contributing to or exacerbating other mental health conditions like depression or anxiety.

Group therapy and support groups are also valuable resources, providing individuals with a platform to share experiences, learn from others, and develop social support networks. These interventions can be particularly helpful in mitigating feelings of isolation and enhancing coping strategies.

Coping Strategies for Psychosocial Stress

Developing effective coping strategies for psychosocial stress is essential for maintaining mental and emotional well-being. These strategies help individuals manage and mitigate the impact of stressors in their daily lives. Here we explore a variety of approaches and techniques that can be employed to cope with psychosocial stress:

Building a Strong Social Support Network: Social support is a key factor in stress management. Engaging with friends, family, and community groups can provide emotional support, practical assistance, and a sense of belonging. Research highlights the buffering effect of social support on stress, with strong social ties linked to better mental health outcomes.

Practicing Self-Care: Self-care involves activities that promote physical, mental, and emotional well-being. This includes maintaining a balanced diet, getting regular exercise, ensuring adequate sleep, and engaging in hobbies and leisure activities. Physical exercise, in particular, is effective in reducing stress hormones like adrenaline and cortisol, and it stimulates the production of endorphins, the body's natural mood elevators.

Mindfulness and Relaxation Techniques: Mindfulness practices, such as meditation, deep breathing exercises, and yoga, help center the mind and reduce the impact of stressors. Relaxation techniques like progressive muscle relaxation and guided imagery can also be effective in managing stress, by promoting physical and mental relaxation.

Time Management and Prioritization: Effective time management involves organizing tasks, setting priorities, and establishing boundaries, which can reduce feelings of being overwhelmed. Techniques like breaking tasks into smaller steps and setting achievable goals can help manage work-related stress and improve productivity.

Cognitive Reframing: Cognitive reframing, a key component of Cognitive Behavioural Therapy, involves changing the way one perceives stressors. This shift in perspective can reduce the perceived threat or negativity of a situation. By recognizing and challenging negative thought patterns, individuals can develop a more positive and realistic outlook.

Engaging in Enjoyable Activities: Participating in activities that bring joy and fulfillment can serve as a distraction from stressors. This can include hobbies, sports, art, or any activity that provides a sense of accomplishment or pleasure. These activities can also provide opportunities for social interaction and personal growth.

Journaling and Expressive Writing: Writing about thoughts and feelings related to stress can provide a therapeutic outlet for emotional expression. Journaling helps in processing and making sense of stressful experiences, which can lead to insights and resolutions.

Seeking Professional Help: In cases where psychosocial stress is overwhelming or persistent, seeking professional help from a psychologist, counsellor, or therapist can be beneficial. Professional guidance can provide tailored strategies for stress management and address any underlying mental health conditions.

Developing Resilience: Building resilience involves developing the ability to adapt and bounce back from stress and adversity. This can be cultivated through practices like positive thinking, emotional regulation, and fostering a growth mindset.

Practicing Gratitude: Focusing on gratitude involves recognizing and appreciating the positive aspects of one's life. This practice can shift attention away from stressors and towards a more positive outlook. Keeping a gratitude journal or regularly reflecting on things one is thankful for can enhance overall well-being.

Balancing Work and Personal Life: Establishing a healthy work-life balance is crucial in managing stress. This might involve setting boundaries between work and personal time, delegating tasks, and taking regular breaks. Time off and vacations can also provide much-needed rest and recovery from work-related stress.

Each of these strategies can be tailored to fit individual needs and circumstances. The effectiveness of these coping mechanisms can vary from person to person, and what works for one individual may not work for another. It is important to explore different strategies and find the ones that best suit one's lifestyle and stressors.

Addressing SI/HI in the Context of Stress

Addressing suicidal ideation (SI) and homicidal ideation (HI) in the context of psychosocial stress is critical, as high levels of stress can increase the risk of self-harm and violence. Mental health professionals must be vigilant in assessing these risks, particularly in individuals presenting with significant stress.

Risk assessment for SI/HI should be an integral part of the evaluation process for individuals experiencing psychosocial stress. This includes asking direct questions about thoughts of self-harm or harming others, intent, and planning.

Interventions for individuals at risk of SI/HI typically involve crisis intervention strategies, such as safety planning, immediate mental health support, and, in some cases, hospitalization to ensure the safety of the individual and others.

Long-term treatment strategies for those at risk of SI/HI may include therapy to address underlying issues contributing to these thoughts, medication management, and ongoing risk assessment.

Coordination of care with other healthcare providers, family members, or social services may be necessary to provide comprehensive support and ensure safety.

Mental health professionals should also be trained in recognizing the warning signs of SI/HI, such as increased isolation, changes in mood, and expressions of hopelessness or rage.

Education and support for family members and caregivers of individuals at risk for SI/HI are also important. Providing them with resources, support, and guidance can be crucial in managing the situation effectively.

Professional Insights on Psychosocial Stressors

Healthcare professionals must have a nuanced understanding of psychosocial stressors. These stressors, arising from an individual's interaction with their social and physical environment, can significantly impact mental health. Stressors may include family dynamics, work-related stress, socio-economic challenges, or significant life changes. Recognizing the varied nature and sources of these stressors is the first step in effective intervention.

It's crucial for them to understand that these stressors are not just mere challenges; they can have profound and lasting impacts on an individual's mental and physical health. Professionals should be skilled in recognizing the signs and symptoms of stress, understanding its sources, and knowing how it can manifest differently in each individual.

Accurate identification and assessment of psychosocial stressors are crucial. Professionals should employ comprehensive assessment tools that consider the intensity, frequency, and impact of these stressors on an individual's life. This assessment should also explore the individual's perception and reaction to these stressors, as personal interpretation significantly affects their impact.

Professionals should be aware of the extensive research linking psychosocial stressors to both mental and physical health outcomes. Chronic stress has been associated with a range of conditions, including anxiety, depression, cardiovascular diseases, and weakened immune function. Understanding this connection is vital for holistic treatment planning.

Cultural competence and sensitivity to the individual's context are essential. Stressors and their impacts can vary significantly across different cultural, socio-economic, and environmental backgrounds. Professionals should tailor their approach to accommodate these differences, ensuring that care and advice are relevant and respectful of individual circumstances.

A multidisciplinary approach is often necessary to effectively manage psychosocial stressors. Collaboration with other healthcare professionals, social workers, and community resources can provide a more comprehensive support system. This approach ensures that all aspects of an individual's health and well-being are addressed.

Effective communication skills are paramount. This includes active listening, empathetic responding, and clear, non-judgmental communication. These skills help in building trust and rapport, which are critical for effective treatment and support. Professionals should be skilled in these therapies and stay updated on emerging treatment modalities.

In addition to treatment, healthcare professionals should focus on preventive measures and education. This includes teaching stress management techniques, promoting healthy lifestyle choices, and providing resources for additional support. Educating clients about the effects of stress and how to manage it can empower them to take proactive steps in their mental health care.

Healthcare providers should also pay attention to their own mental health. Working with individuals facing significant stressors can be emotionally taxing. Professionals should engage in self-care practices, seek supervision or consultation when needed, and be mindful of signs of burnout.

Professionals should advocate for policies and practices that reduce psychosocial stressors in communities. This could involve participating in public health initiatives, contributing to research, or advocating for policy changes that address the root causes of stress, such as poverty, inequality, or access to healthcare.

By incorporating these insights and approaches, healthcare professionals can effectively support individuals facing psychosocial stressors, contributing to improved mental health outcomes and overall well-being.

Conclusion

The recognition and management of psychosocial stressors are vital components of mental health care. Stress, if left unchecked, can lead to a variety of mental health disorders, including anxiety and depression, and can exacerbate existing conditions. Understanding the root causes of stress and how they impact individuals is the first step in effective management.

A proactive and informed approach to stress management can significantly improve individuals' quality of life. This involves not only treating the symptoms of stress but also addressing its underlying causes, whether they are personal, social, or systemic.

Encouraging individuals to develop healthy coping mechanisms, seek social support, and engage in self-care practices are integral parts of managing stress. For healthcare professionals, this means not only providing direct care but also educating individuals about stress and its effects.

Additional Resources

For further understanding and support regarding psychosocial stress, a variety of resources are available:

1. **Psychosocial Stress Research Programs**: Many universities and research institutions conduct studies on psychosocial stress. These can be valuable sources of the latest research findings and insights.

2. **Online Resources**: Websites such as the American Psychological Association (APA) and the National Institute of Mental Health (NIMH) offer detailed information on stress, its effects, and coping strategies.

3. **Professional Organizations and Support Groups**: Organizations like the National Alliance on Mental Illness (NAMI) provide support groups, educational materials, and advocacy for individuals dealing with stress and other mental health issues.

4. **Books and Publications**: There are numerous books and academic articles on the subject of stress and stress management. Notable works often include those by psychologists and researchers in the field.

5. **Mental Health Services and Stress Management Programs**: Local mental health services can provide counselling and therapy, while many community centers and hospitals offer stress management programs.

6. **Hotlines and Helplines**: For immediate assistance, national and local hotlines are available. These can be crucial resources for individuals experiencing acute stress or crisis situations.

By utilizing these resources, individuals and healthcare professionals can deepen their understanding of psychosocial stress and enhance their ability to manage it effectively.

Week 8

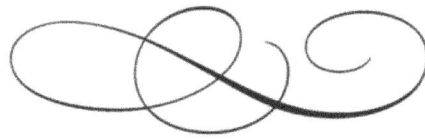

The Workbook

Week Eight

PSYCHOSOCIAL STRESSORS

In the previous week, we delved into the intricate landscape of emotional wounds, exploring the profound impact of trauma and abuse on the psyche. Our journey illuminated the complexities of identifying, understanding, and treating emotional wounds, notably PTSD, and the significance of therapeutic intervention in fostering healing and resilience.

This week, we shifted our focus to "Psychosocial Stressors." We unravelled the multifaceted nature of these stressors, examining their contextual features and the profound ways they influence mental health. Our exploration was a comprehensive understanding of what constitutes psychosocial stressors and extends into an in-depth analysis of their causes, evaluation methods, and the criteria outlined in the DSM-V. By identifying the common signs and symptoms, we have gained insight into how these stressors uniquely affect individuals and their interpersonal relationships.

The week's curriculum was designed not only to enhance professional knowledge but also to equip us with practical skills. We have delved into evidence-based therapies and coping strategies, tailoring our approach to effectively address the nuanced challenges posed by psychosocial stressors. Moreover, the importance of ruling out suicidal and homicidal ideation (SI/HI) in this context was underscored, emphasizing the critical need for comprehensive assessment and intervention.

As mental health professionals, our goal has been to navigate these complex waters with skill and empathy, understanding the far-reaching impact of psychosocial stressors. This week was an enlightening journey, enhancing our capabilities to provide informed, compassionate care to those grappling with these pervasive challenges.

Day 1: Understanding Psychosocial Stressors and Contextual Features

1. **Reflective Exercise 1**: Describe your understanding of psychosocial stressors and their impact on mental health.

_____

_____

_____

_____

_____

_____

_____

2. **Reflective Exercise 2**: Reflect on a case where psychosocial stressors played a significant role in a patient's/client's mental health.

_____

_____

_____

_____

_____

_____

_____

3. **Guided Activity**: Research and summarize different types of psychosocial stressors and their psychological impacts.

_____

_____

_____

_____

_____

_____

Day 2: Causes of Psychosocial Stressors

1. **Reflective Exercise 1**: Discuss your experiences with patients/clients where specific psychosocial stressors were identified as causal factors.

_____

_____

_____

_____

_____

_____

2. **Reflective Exercise 2**: Reflect on a case involving complex psychosocial stressors. What were the key challenges?

_____

_____

_____

_____

_____

_____

3. **Guided Activity**: Develop a list of common psychosocial stressors and their potential sources.

_____

_____

_____

_____

_____

Day 3: Evaluating Psychosocial Stressors

1. **Reflective Exercise 1**: Reflect on the process of evaluating psychosocial stressors in your practice.

_____

_____

_____

_____

_____

_____

2. **Reflective Exercise 2**: Consider a case where evaluation of psychosocial stressors was crucial for treatment planning.

_____

_____

_____

_____

_____

_____

3. **Guided Activity**: Create a guide or checklist for evaluating psychosocial stressors in a clinical setting.

_____

_____

_____

_____

_____

_____

Day 4: DSM-V on Psychosocial Stressors

1. **Reflective Exercise 1**: Compare your approach to psychosocial stressors with the DSM-V's perspective.

_____

_____

_____

_____

_____

_____

2. **Reflective Exercise 2**: Discuss the challenges and benefits of the DSM-V's approach to psychosocial stressors.

_____

_____

_____

_____

_____

_____

3. **Guided Activity**: Summarize the DSM-V's guidelines on psychosocial stressors and contextual features for mental health disorders.

_____

_____

_____

_____

_____

_____

Day 5: Signs and Symptoms of Psychosocial Stressors

1. **Reflective Exercise 1**: Reflect on the common signs and symptoms of psychosccial stressors observed in your practice.

_____

_____

_____

_____

_____

_____

2. **Reflective Exercise 2**: Consider a case where the symptoms of psychosocial stress were atypical.

_____

_____

_____

_____

_____

_____

3. **Guided Activity**: Design an educational tool like an infographic illustrating the signs and symptoms of psychosocial stress.

_____

_____

_____

_____

_____

Day 6: Impact of Psychosocial Stressors

1. **Reflective Exercise 1**: Discuss how psychosocial stressors affect individuals and their relationships.

_____

_____

_____

_____

_____

_____

2. **Reflective Exercise 2**: Reflect on a case where psychosocial stressors had a significant impact on an individual's life.

_____

_____

_____

_____

_____

_____

3. **Guided Activity**: Create a case study that illustrates the effects of psychosocial stressors on individual and interpersonal dynamics.

_____

_____

_____

_____

_____

_____

Day 7: Therapies, Coping Strategies, and Professional Knowledge for Psychosocial Stressors

1. **Reflective Exercise 1**: Share your experience with evidence-based therapies for managing psychosocial stressors.

_____

_____

_____

_____

_____

_____

2. **Reflective Exercise 2**: Reflect on effective coping strategies for managing psychosocial stressors.

_____

_____

_____

_____

_____

_____

3. **Guided Activity**: Prepare a brief presentation or educational material for colleagues highlighting the essential aspects of understanding and treating psychosocial stressors.

_____

_____

_____

_____

_____

Week 9

ASSESSMENT **TOOLS**

This chapter will explore various tools and techniques used for assessment, focusing on their application in different mental health contexts.

Mental Status Examination (MSE)

The Mental Status Examination (MSE) is a pivotal aspect of psychiatric assessment, serving as a crucial tool for clinicians in the evaluation of a patient's/client's mental state. It involves a comprehensive observation and analysis of a patient's/client's psychological functioning at a given point in time (Trzepacz & Baker, 1993). The MSE encompasses several key domains, each providing vital insights into various aspects of a patient's/client's mental health.

APPEARANCE AND BEHAVIOUR

- *Dress and grooming* (well groomed, clothing disheveled, etc).
- Dressed appropriately, clean, neat, unkempt, malodour, poor hygiene, offensive odour.
- *Posture and gait.*
- Typical, appropriate, slumped, rigid, tense, atypical, inappropriate, appropriate to interaction, anxiety, fear, no difficulties, steady, awkward, clumsy, staggered, shuffling.
- *Physical characteristics (apparent, vs chronologic age; weight, physical health).*
- AGE: - appears stated age, appears older than stated age, Appears younger than stated age.
- *Attitude towards interviewer.*
- Disinterested, cooperative, pleasant, bored, internally preoccupied, distractible, easily engaged, attentive, responsive, non-committal.

- *Facial expression.*
- Crying, screaming, tremulous, calm, cheerful, sad, anger, bizarre, inappropriate, depressed, hostile.
- *Eye contact, good, brief, fleeting, none.*
- *Motor activity.*
- Involuntary movements, psychomotor retardation, psychomotor agitation, atypical, peculiar, restless, fidgety, abnormal movements.
- *Specific mannerism (repetitive tics/grimaces; hair pulling etc).*
- MANNER:- cooperative, guarded, pleasant, suspicious, hostile, angry, evasive, friendly, inappropriately familiar, uncooperative, hostile, seductive, ingratiating.

SPEECH

- *Rate.*
- Pressured; rapid; appropriate, slowed, normal.
- *Pitch, volume and clarity.*
- Shouting, typical, appropriate, quiet, loud, soft, normal.
- *Specific abnormalities.*
- Spontaneously verbal, non-verbal, slurring of speech, mumbled, unintelligible.

EMOTIONS

- *Mood (given by client).*
- Appropriate to thought content, euphoria, elation, anger, hostility, fear, anxiety, depression, sadness, flat, elevated.
- *Affect.*
- Predominant affect, variability, intensity, appropriateness, flat, blunted, incongruent with mood, appropriate to content, inappropriate to content, constricted, despairing, embarrassed, depressed, sad, neutral, broad, liable, brighter, angry, fearful, happy.

THOUGHT PROCESS

- *Rate and flow of ideas.*
- *Associations.*
- *Other abnormalities.*
- Associations, coherent, concentration, incoherent, logical, illogical, organized, goal directed, circumstantial, tangential, loose, flight of ideas, rambling, word salad, clang associations, preservative, neologism, blocking, distractibility.

THOUGHT CONTENT

- Delusions, depersonalization/derealization, preoccupations.
- Loss of loved one, obsessions, compulsions, SI/HI (plan, intent, previous history), death wishes, depressive cognitions, ruminations, overvalued ideas, phobias, ideas of reference, paranoid ideation, magical ideation, magical ideations, religiosity, ideas of reference, ideas of influence, delusions of persecution, delusions of grandeur

PERCEPTION

- Illusions, (misperception or misinterpretation of an actual external sensory stimuli) Hallucinations, - (auditory, visual, olfactory, tactile, gustatory), depersonalization, (a subjective sense of being unreal, strange or unfamiliar) de'ja' vu, jamais vu, suspicious, derealization (a subjective sense that the environment is strange or unreal).

SENSORIUM AND INTELLECTUAL FUNCTIONS (Cognition)

- *Consciousness* – alert/drowsy/lethargic/delirious/comatose.
- *Orientation to Time, person, place.*
- *Concentration* – ability to focus and sustain attention over a period of time, mmse.
- *Memory (recall* – ability to immediate retention & recall of new info *Recent,*-ability to repeat after 3&5 minutes *remote*- ability to recount events from the distant past must be able to verify accuracy*).*
- Intact.
- *Judgment* (what would you do if….) – the process of forming an opinion or conclusion.
- Blames others, circumstances for problems, able to make decisions.
- *Insight* (awareness/understanding of illness – and the non-delusional understanding of it's cause or meaning).
- Good, poor, fair/limited.

Appearance: This facet of the MSE focuses on the patient's/client's observable physical characteristics, such as dress, grooming, hygiene, and physical health. The clinician observes and notes any peculiarities or neglect in appearance, as these can be indicative of the patient's/client's mental state and ability to care for themselves. For example, a well-kept appearance might suggest a certain level of functioning, while dishevelment could hint at neglect or a decline in mental health.

Behaviour: This domain assesses the patient's/client's actions, motor activity, and overall interaction with their environment. Behavioural observations include the patient's/client's level of cooperation, any unusual movements, and their response to stimuli. Key aspects include psychomotor agitation or retardation, which could indicate conditions ranging from anxiety disorders to depressive states.

Cognition: Cognitive assessment involves evaluating the patient's/client's orientation to time, place, and person, their attention span, concentration ability, memory (both immediate and long-term), and abstract thinking. This evaluation helps in identifying cognitive impairments, which are often observed in disorders such as dementia, delirium, or various neurocognitive disorders. Cognitive testing can include asking the patient/client to perform simple calculations, recall recent events, or interpret proverbs.

Thought Processes: This part of the MSE involves the assessment of the patient's/client's rate of speech, the continuity of speech, coherence, and the relevance of their thoughts. The clinician listens to how the patient/client speaks and expresses ideas, watching for disturbances in thought processes that might be evident in conditions such as schizophrenia, where patient's/client's might exhibit disorganized thinking, or in severe depression, where thought processes might be slowed.

Thought Content: This includes what the patient/client is actually thinking about, such as delusions, obsessions, phobias, and preoccupations. For instance, a patient/client with schizophrenia might have delusions of persecution, while a patient/client with obsessive-compulsive disorder might have persistent intrusive thoughts.

Perception: This involves the assessment of any hallucinations or illusions the patient/client may be experiencing. Hallucinations can occur in various modalities, including auditory, visual, olfactory, or tactile, and are important in diagnosing psychotic disorders.

Insight and Judgment: The clinician assesses the patient's/client's understanding of their current situation and condition. This includes whether they recognize they have a mental health issue and their ability to make sound decisions and judgments.

Mood and Affect: This aspect evaluates the patient's/client's prevailing emotional state and their external expression of emotion. Mood is the patient's/client's sustained emotional state, while affect is the outward expression of emotion, which could be congruent or incongruent with their stated mood.

Risk Assessment: A crucial part of the MSE is assessing the risk of harm to oneself or others. This includes evaluating suicidal ideation, plans, intent, and means, as well as any history of violence or aggression.

By systematically evaluating these aspects, the MSE provides a comprehensive view of the patient's/client's mental health, guiding diagnosis and treatment planning. It is a dynamic process, adapting to the evolving presentation of the patient/client, and forms the foundation for understanding the complex nature of psychiatric conditions.

Name: **DOB:**   **Date:**   **Time:**

IDENTIFYING MARKS	PERSONAL HISTORY	MEDICAL HISTORY
HISTORY OF PRESENTING ILLNESS		**PSYCHIATRIC HISTORY**
	FAMILY HISTORY	**RISK**
		SI ☐ HI ☐ Substance Abuse ☐ Self- care ☐ Violence ☐ Unemployed ☐ Death of love one ☐ Family History -SI ☐
MOOD		**MEDICATIONS**

NEUROVEGETATIVE SYMPTOMS		
		DOCTORS/TREATMENTS
	PROTECTIVE FACTORS	
	Religious beliefs: Overall good self esteem: Good problem solving skills: Employed: No recent losses: No psychiatric diagnosis. No previous attempts: Ability to "contract": Social Support:	
		HOSPITALIZATIONS
		©Harrison Mungal

The Role of Psychological Testing

Psychological testing is an integral component of mental health assessment and plays a critical role in diagnosing, treating, and managing various psychiatric conditions (Groth-Marnat, 2009). These tests are designed to provide objective and standardized information about a range of psychological functions, including emotional well-being, intellectual abilities, and behavioural functioning.

Importance of Psychological Testing

1. **Objective Assessment**: Psychological tests offer an objective means of assessing mental health symptoms and cognitive functioning. They provide standardized measures that help clinicians understand the severity and nature of a patient's/client's condition.
2. **Diagnostic Clarification**: These tests aid in confirming or ruling out specific mental health diagnoses. For example, neuropsychological tests can differentiate between depressive disorders and cognitive disorders like dementia.
3. **Treatment Planning**: Test results can inform the development of effective treatment plans. For instance, cognitive assessments can guide interventions for patients/client with learning disabilities or attention-deficit/hyperactivity disorder (ADHD).

4. **Progress Monitoring**: Regular psychological testing can be used to monitor a patient's/client's progress over the course of treatment, providing tangible evidence of changes in their mental health status.

Types of Psychological Tests

1. **Clinical Interviews**: Structured or semi-structured interviews are fundamental in psychological assessment. These interviews provide a comprehensive picture of the patient's/client's history, current symptoms, and how these symptoms impact their daily functioning.
2. **Personality Tests**: Tests like the Minnesota Multiphasic Personality Inventory (MMPI) or the Rorschach Inkblot Test assess aspects of personality and can identify traits associated with various psychological disorders.
3. **Neuropsychological Tests**: These assess cognitive functioning and are essential in diagnosing conditions that affect cognitive abilities, such as Alzheimer's disease or after a traumatic brain injury.
4. **Behavioural Assessments**: Observational tools and behaviour checklists help in understanding behaviours in specific contexts, particularly useful in diagnosing conditions like ADHD or autism spectrum disorders.
5. **Projective Tests**: Techniques like the Thematic Apperception Test (TAT) use ambiguous stimuli to elicit responses that reveal aspects of an individual's personality, underlying conflicts, and emotional functioning.
6. **Self-Report Inventories**: These involve standardized questionnaires like the Beck Depression Inventory, which provide a self-reported measure of symptom severity in conditions like depression and anxiety.

Challenges and Considerations

1. **Cultural Sensitivity**: It is crucial to consider the cultural and social context of the patient/client when administering and interpreting psychological tests to avoid biases.
2. **Test Selection and Administration**: Choosing the right test for the specific diagnostic question and ensuring it is administered correctly is vital for reliable results.
3. **Interpretation**: The interpretation of test results requires skill and experience. Clinicians must integrate test findings with clinical observations and patient/client history to form a comprehensive understanding of the patient's/client's condition.
4. **Ethical Considerations**: Maintaining confidentiality and using tests ethically is paramount. The results must be used to benefit the patient/client and inform their care.

Psychological testing, when used effectively, is a powerful tool in the mental health field. It complements clinical evaluation and helps in forming a more complete picture of an individual's mental health, guiding more targeted and effective interventions.

Testing for Mood Disorders and Anxiety Disorders

In the realm of mental health, accurately diagnosing mood and anxiety disorders is crucial. This is where specialized testing and assessment tools play a pivotal role. These tools are designed to measure symptom severity, aid in diagnosis, and guide treatment decisions for disorders such as Major Depressive Disorder (MDD), Bipolar Disorder, and various anxiety disorders.

Mood Disorders: Mood disorders encompass a range of conditions, including MDD and Bipolar Disorder. For MDD, the Hamilton Depression Rating Scale (HDRS) and the Beck Depression Inventory (BDI) are commonly used. The HDRS assesses the severity of depressive symptoms in individuals diagnosed with MDD, covering areas such as mood, guilt feelings, suicidal ideation, insomnia, and weight loss. It provides a quantifiable measure of depression, which is invaluable for both diagnosing the condition and monitoring the effectiveness of treatment.

Bipolar Disorder, characterized by alternating episodes of mania and depression, requires a different assessment approach. The Mood Disorder Questionnaire (MDQ) is a useful tool for screening for Bipolar Disorder. It asks patients/clients about their history of manic or hypomanic episodes, providing critical information for differential diagnosis.

Anxiety Disorders: Anxiety disorders, including Generalized Anxiety Disorder (GAD), Panic Disorder, and various phobias, have their own set of assessment tools. The Hamilton Anxiety Rating Scale (HARS) is widely used for evaluating the severity of anxiety symptoms. It assesses both psychic anxiety, which refers to mental agitation and psychological distress, and somatic anxiety, which relates to physical complaints linked to anxiety.

For disorders like GAD, the GAD-7 is a brief measure that patients/clients can complete. It assesses the frequency of symptoms associated with generalized anxiety over the past two weeks. Similarly, for Panic Disorder, tools like the Panic and Agoraphobia Scale (PAS) can be used to evaluate the severity of panic symptoms and associated agoraphobia.

Special Considerations in Testing: When utilizing these assessment tools, it's important to consider the patient's/client's overall context, including their history, current life circumstances, and other comorbid conditions. The interpretation of these scales should be done by qualified professionals who can contextualize the results within the broader clinical picture.

Guiding Treatment: These assessment tools are not only valuable in diagnosing mood and anxiety disorders but are also critical in guiding treatment. For instance, the severity of symptoms as measured by these scales can inform decisions about medication, the need for psychotherapy, and other interventions. Regular use of these tools can also help in monitoring the effectiveness of treatment over time, allowing for adjustments as needed.

Cultural Sensitivity: It is also crucial to approach these assessments with cultural sensitivity. The expression of symptoms and the interpretation of questions can vary significantly across different cultural contexts. Clinicians must be aware of these nuances and adjust their approach accordingly.

By employing these specialized assessment tools, clinicians can gain a deeper understanding of the patient's/client's symptoms, leading to more accurate diagnoses and tailored treatment plans. These tools are an integral part of the process, guiding clinicians through the complex landscape of mood and anxiety disorders.

Assessing Psychosis and Addictions

Assessment of psychosis typically involves evaluating symptoms like hallucinations, delusions, disorganized thinking, and negative symptoms such as apathy or lack of emotion. Tools such as the Positive and Negative Syndrome Scale (PANSS) are widely used for this purpose. The PANSS provides a comprehensive measurement of the positive symptoms, negative symptoms, and general psychopathology associated with schizophrenia and other psychotic disorders.

In the realm of addictions, assessment focuses on the extent of substance use and its impact on the individual's life. The Addiction Severity Index (ASI) is a commonly used tool in this area. It assesses multiple domains affected by addiction, including medical status, employment, drug use, alcohol use, legal status, family/social status, and psychiatric status (McLellan et al., 1992). This multidimensional approach is crucial as it provides a comprehensive view of the individual's challenges and needs, guiding effective treatment planning.

Trauma and Abuse Assessment

Assessing trauma and abuse involves understanding the impact of traumatic events and abusive experiences on an individual's mental health. The Clinician-Administered PTSD Scale (CAPS) is considered the "gold standard" in PTSD assessment. CAPS provides a detailed and reliable assessment of the presence and severity of PTSD symptoms in accordance with DSM-5 criteria (Weathers, Blake, Schnurr, Kaloupek, Marx, & Keane, 2013).

For assessing the impact of abuse, particularly in cases of childhood abuse, tools like the Childhood Trauma Questionnaire (CTQ) are often employed. The CTQ is a self-report instrument that quantitatively measures the severity of emotional, physical, and sexual abuse (Bernstein et al., 2003). It is instrumental in identifying past abuse experiences that may be contributing to current psychological distress.

These assessment tools are vital for accurately diagnosing and understanding the full extent of an individual's trauma and abuse experiences, enabling targeted and effective therapeutic interventions.

Professional Knowledge on Assessment Tools

Healthcare professionals must possess a comprehensive understanding of the various assessment tools available for diagnosing and managing mental health conditions. Familiarity with these tools enables professionals to accurately identify specific mental health disorders, assess their severity, and monitor treatment progress. The effective use of assessment tools requires a blend of theoretical knowledge and practical skills, ensuring that practitioners can interpret results within the context of each patient's/client's unique situation.

For mood disorders, professionals should be skilled in using tools like the Beck Depression Inventory or the Hamilton Depression Rating Scale, understanding their application in both clinical and research settings. Similarly, for anxiety disorders, the familiarity with the Hamilton Anxiety Rating Scale or the State-Trait Anxiety Inventory is crucial for accurate diagnosis and treatment monitoring.

When assessing psychosis, practitioners need to be adept at using tools like the Positive and Negative Syndrome Scale (PANSS) to differentiate between various types of psychotic symptoms and to gauge their impact on the patient's/client's functioning. In the realm of addictions, knowledge of the Addiction Severity Index (ASI) or the Alcohol Use Disorders Identification Test (AUDIT) is essential for a holistic assessment of the individual's substance use and its ramifications.

For trauma and abuse, tools such as the Clinician-Administered PTSD Scale (CAPS) and the Childhood Trauma Questionnaire (CTQ) are vital. Professionals should be able to employ these tools not just for diagnostic purposes but also to understand the broader impact of trauma and abuse on an individual's life.

Additionally, the ability to conduct a comprehensive Mental Status Examination (MSE) is fundamental for all mental health professionals. The MSE provides crucial insights into the patient's/client's current state of mind and is often the first step in the psychiatric assessment process.

Incorporating these tools into practice requires ongoing education and training. Mental health professionals should stay updated with the latest developments in assessment techniques and continuously refine their skills through professional development opportunities. Understanding the cultural and contextual factors that may influence assessment outcomes is also vital in ensuring an accurate and comprehensive evaluation.

Furthermore, ethical considerations, including respecting patient/client confidentiality and ensuring informed consent, are paramount in the administration of these assessment tools. Professionals should be aware of the potential impact of these assessments on patients/client and handle the process with sensitivity and care.

A thorough knowledge and skillful application of mental health assessment tools are indispensable for professionals in the field. This expertise not only aids in accurate diagnosis and effective treatment planning but also contributes to the broader understanding of mental health disorders and their management.

Conclusion

The utilization of assessment tools in mental health is a critical aspect of providing comprehensive care to individuals experiencing mental health issues. These tools offer invaluable insights into the patient's/client's mental state, aiding in the accurate diagnosis and effective management of various mental health conditions.

The importance of these tools extends beyond diagnosis. They play a crucial role in treatment planning, helping professionals tailor interventions to meet the specific needs of their patients/client. By regularly employing these tools, mental health professionals can also monitor the progress of their patients/clients over time, making necessary adjustments to treatment plans as needed.

Moreover, the integration of these assessment tools into regular mental health care practice enhances the overall quality of care provided to patients/clients. It allows for a more targeted approach to treatment, increasing the likelihood of positive outcomes. The objective data gathered from these tools also contribute to a better understanding of mental health disorders on a broader scale, informing research and policy development.

Assessment tools are indispensable in the field of mental health. Their judicious application by skilled professionals not only benefits individual patients/clients but also advances our collective understanding of mental health. As the field continues to evolve, the ongoing development and refinement of these tools will remain a key component in the effective management and treatment of mental health disorders.

Additional Resources

For further exploration and understanding of mental health assessment tools, there are several resources available:

1. **Professional Journals:** Journals such as the "Journal of Clinical Psychiatry" or "Psychological Assessment" often publish articles on the latest developments in assessment tools and techniques.
2. **Online Databases:** Databases like PubMed and PsycINFO provide access to a wide range of research articles and studies on mental health assessment.
3. **Training Workshops and Seminars:** Many professional organizations offer workshops and seminars on the use of assessment tools in mental health. These can be valuable opportunities for hands-on learning and skill development.
4. **Textbooks:** Texts such as "Handbook of Psychological Assessment" by Groth-Marnat offer comprehensive overviews of various assessment tools and their application in mental health.
5. **Websites:** Organizations such as the American Psychological Association (APA) and the National Institute of Mental Health (NIMH) provide online resources and guidelines on mental health assessment.

6. **Continuing Education Courses:** Many universities and professional bodies offer courses focused on assessment in mental health, which can be beneficial for practitioners looking to enhance their knowledge and skills.

Week 9

The Workbook

Week Nine

ASSESSMENT TOOLS

Building on the insights from Week Eight, where we explored the multifaceted impact of psychosocial stressors, Week Nine transitions into a critical component of mental health care: the realm of assessment tools. This week, we delve into the art and science of effectively evaluating mental health conditions, grounding our approach in proven methodologies and the latest psychological research.

Our focus this week has been to unravel the complexities of various assessment tools, understanding their pivotal role in diagnosing and managing a range of mental health issues. From the nuanced intricacies of the Mental Status Examination to the specificities of psychological testing for mood disorders, anxiety, psychosis, and addictions, we aimed at equipping professionals with a comprehensive understanding of these essential instruments.

As we traversed this week, we have examined the essential elements required for a thorough Mental Status Examination, underscore the indispensable nature of psychological testing, and discerned the most effective assessment strategies for mood disorders, anxiety, psychosis, addictions, as well as traumas and abuse. This exploration was not just about understanding the tools themselves but also about appreciating their relevance in the broader context of mental health care.

Week Nine has been designed to enhance your diagnostic acumen, offering insights into the selection and application of appropriate assessment tools. This knowledge is vital in tailoring treatment plans that address the unique needs of each individual, ultimately contributing to more effective and empathetic mental health care.

Day 1: Mental Status Examination (MSE)

1. **Reflective Exercise 1**: Consider what information is crucial for an effective Mental Status Examination and why.

_____

_____

_____

_____

_____

_____

2. **Reflective Exercise 2**: Reflect on a case where the MSE provided key insights into a patient's/client's condition. Put an MSE together using sample data intake cheat sheet.

_____

_____

_____

_____

_____

_____

3. **Guided Activity**: Create a comprehensive checklist or template for conducting a Mental Status Examination.

_____

_____

_____

_____

_____

_____

Day 2: Importance of Psychological Testing

1. **Reflective Exercise 1**: Discuss the role and importance of psychological testing in mental health assessment.

_____

_____

_____

_____

_____

_____

2. **Reflective Exercise 2**: Reflect on a case where psychological testing significantly impacted diagnosis and treatment.

_____

_____

_____

_____

_____

_____

3. **Guided Activity**: Research and summarize the various types of psychological tests used in mental health and their purposes.

_____

_____

_____

_____

_____

_____

Day 3: Testing for Mood Disorders

1. **Reflective Exercise 1**: Identify the types of testing most effective for diagnosing mood disorders and their rationale.

_____

_____

_____

_____

_____

_____

2. **Reflective Exercise 2**: Consider a case where testing for a mood disorder was particularly revealing or challenging.

_____

_____

_____

_____

_____

_____

3. **Guided Activity**: Develop a guide on the most commonly used assessment tools for mood disorders, including their applications and limitations.

_____

_____

_____

_____

_____

_____

Day 4: Testing for Anxiety Disorders, Psychosis, and Addictions

1. **Reflective Exercise 1**: Discuss the assessment tools you find most effective for anxiety disorders, psychosis, and addictions.

_____

_____

_____

_____

_____

_____

2. **Reflective Exercise 2**: Reflect on a challenging case involving anxiety, psychosis, or addiction and the role of testing in it.

_____

_____

_____

_____

_____

_____

3. **Guided Activity**: Create a comparison chart of various assessment tools used for anxiety disorders, psychosis, and addictions.

_____

_____

_____

_____

_____

Day 5: Testing for Traumas and Abuse

1. **Reflective Exercise 1**: Identify which assessment tools are most effective for identifying traumas and abuse.

_____

_____

_____

_____

_____

_____

2. **Reflective Exercise 2**: Reflect on a case where trauma or abuse was identified through specific assessment tools.

_____

_____

_____

_____

_____

_____

3. **Guided Activity**: Compile a list of recommended assessment tools for traumas and abuse, noting their specific applications.

_____

_____

_____

_____

_____

Day 6: Understanding Assessment Tools

1. **Reflective Exercise 1**: Discuss the challenges and ethical considerations in using various assessment tools.

_____

_____

_____

_____

_____

_____

2. **Reflective Exercise 2**: Reflect on how assessment tools have evolved in your practice and their impact.

_____

_____

_____

_____

_____

_____

3. **Guided Activity**: Research the latest developments in psychological assessment tools and their potential future directions.

_____

_____

_____

_____

_____

_____

Day 7: Professional Knowledge about Assessment Tools

1. **Reflective Exercise 1**: Consider the key things every professional should know about assessment tools in mental health.

_____

_____

_____

_____

_____

_____

2. **Reflective Exercise 2**: Reflect on a situation where your knowledge of assessment tools significantly impacted patient/client care.

_____

_____

_____

_____

_____

_____

3. **Guided Activity**: Prepare a brief educational presentation or material for colleagues on the essential aspects of psychological assessment tools.

_____

_____

_____

_____

_____

_____

Week 10

MOTIVATIONAL INTERVIEWING
TECHNIQUES

"Motivational Interviewing Techniques (MIT)," a crucial skill set for engaging clients and patients/clients effectively in clinical settings. This chapter will provide guidance on preparing for clinical assessments, conducting interviews, and building rapport.

Preparing for a Clinical Assessment

The preparation for a clinical assessment is a meticulous process that sets the stage for effective therapeutic interaction. It involves a comprehensive review of the client's history, including a thorough examination of their previous medical records, therapy notes, and any psychological evaluations. This preliminary review is crucial as it informs the clinician about the client's past interventions, responses to treatment, and any persistent or emerging patterns in their behaviour or symptoms.

In addition to reviewing historical data, the clinician must establish clear objectives for the assessment These objectives should be tailored to the client's present concerns and symptoms. They guide the clinician in focusing on relevant areas during the assessment, ensuring that all significant aspects of the client's condition are explored.

The setting in which the assessment takes place is also of paramount importance. The clinician should ensure that the environment is comfortable, private, and conducive to open communication (Michaels, 2006). This includes considerations of physical comfort, privacy, and an atmosphere free from distractions. Creating an environment that feels safe and non-judgmental is vital for fostering trust and rapport, which are essential for a successful clinical assessment.

Another key aspect of preparation is the clinician's mental and emotional readiness. The clinician must approach the assessment with an open mind, free from biases or preconceived notions about the client. This unbiased stance enables the clinician to effectively engage with the client, understanding their unique experiences and perspectives.

Essential Information in Assessments

The core of a clinical assessment involves gathering essential information that forms the foundation for diagnosis and treatment planning. This includes a detailed exploration of the client's current mental health symptoms, their intensity, duration, and the impact on the client's daily functioning. Understanding the current symptoms in depth allows the clinician to gauge the severity of the mental health condition and its implications on the client's life.

A comprehensive assessment also delves into the client's mental health history. This includes any prior diagnoses, treatments received, and the outcomes of those treatments. Such historical data provide valuable insights into the client's mental health journey and are crucial in informing current treatment approaches.

Substance use history is another vital aspect of the assessment. The clinician must explore any past or present use of substances, including alcohol, prescription medications, and illicit drugs. This information is important because substance use can significantly impact mental health, either as a co-occurring disorder or as a complicating factor in the treatment of existing mental health conditions.

The client's physical health should also be considered, as physical ailments can have profound effects on mental well-being. The clinician should inquire about any chronic conditions, recent illnesses, or medications that the client is taking. This holistic approach ensures that all factors affecting the client's mental health are considered in the treatment plan.

Family history of mental health conditions is another crucial piece of information. Genetic predispositions can play a significant role in the development of certain mental health conditions. Understanding the family history helps the clinician to identify potential risks and informs decisions about interventions and monitoring.

Rapid Assessment and Decision Making

In emergency situations where quick decision-making is critical, such as determining the need for hospitalization or apprehension, clinicians are required to rapidly assess the client's mental state. This process involves a swift yet comprehensive evaluation of the client's risk of harm to themselves or others, the severity of their current symptoms, and their overall ability to care for themselves.

In such high-pressure scenarios, clinicians often rely on standardized assessment tools like the Brief Psychiatric Rating Scale advocated by Overall & Gorham (1962). This scale provides a rapid and structured method for evaluating psychiatric symptoms such as depression, anxiety, hallucinations, and unusual behaviour. The scale's concise format allows clinicians to quickly ascertain the severity of symptoms and make informed decisions about immediate care needs.

When making these rapid assessments, clinicians must balance the urgency of the situation with the ethical imperative to understand the client's condition comprehensively. They need to swiftly gather key information about the client's current mental state, potential risks, and available support systems. This information is crucial in making ethical and effective decisions regarding the client's immediate care needs, such as hospitalization or other interventions.

The ability to make accurate and timely decisions in such scenarios is a skill that comes with experience and training. Clinicians must be adept at quickly synthesizing information, recognizing warning signs, and prioritizing the client's safety and well-being. This skill set is crucial in ensuring that clients receive the appropriate level of care promptly, especially in situations where delays could lead to harm.

Introduction to Motivational Interviewing Techniques

Motivational Interviewing (MI) is a client-centered counselling approach designed to facilitate and engage intrinsic motivation within the client in order to change behaviour. It is a goal-oriented, therapeutic style that respects the autonomy of the client and helps them explore and resolve their ambivalence about change. Developed by Miller and Rollnick, MI focuses on the motivational processes within the individual that facilitate change, emphasizing an atmosphere of acceptance and compassion. The primary purpose of MI is to encourage clients to articulate and explore their reasons for change in their own words and to strengthen their own motivation and commitment to change (Miller & Rollnick, 2013).

MI is particularly effective in dealing with addictions and other behavioural issues where ambivalence or resistance to change is a significant challenge. It has been widely applied in various settings, including substance abuse treatment, healthcare, and mental health, demonstrating its versatility and effectiveness. The underlying principle of MI is that directive, client-centered counselling can promote behavioural change by helping clients to explore and resolve ambivalence.

Implementing Motivational Interviewing

Implementing MI involves a set of specific techniques, collectively known as OARS: Open-ended questions, Affirmations, Reflective listening, and Summarizing. These techniques are designed to facilitate a conversation that is guided by the client's own motivation and values.

- **Open-ended questions** are used to encourage clients to think and reflect, giving them the opportunity to express their thoughts and feelings in an open and safe environment. These questions are designed to elicit more than a simple yes or no response and encourage a deeper exploration of the client's perspectives and experiences.

- **Affirmations** are statements that recognize the client's strengths and efforts. They serve to validate the client's experiences and feelings, building their confidence and self-efficacy. Affirmations should be genuine and specific to be effective.
- **Reflective listening** is a key aspect of MI, where the clinician listens actively to the client's statements and then reflects them back. This technique helps clients hear their own thoughts and feelings echoed back to them, often providing clarity and further insight into their own motivations and concerns.
- **Summarizing** involves the clinician summarizing the key points of what the client has shared. This technique helps to consolidate the information and ensures that the clinician and client are on the same page. Summarizing also reinforces the client's statements, highlighting their readiness for change.

The successful implementation of MI requires the clinician to adopt a non-judgmental, empathetic, and supportive stance. This approach helps to create a safe and trusting environment where clients feel comfortable discussing sensitive issues and exploring their ambivalence towards change.

Retrieving Information Through MI

Retrieving information using MI techniques involves a delicate balance of guiding the conversation while allowing the client to lead the direction and depth of the discussion. The clinician's role is to facilitate the client's exploration of their own motivations and barriers to change.

The use of open-ended questions is central to this process. These questions encourage the client to open up and share more about their experiences and feelings. For example, asking a client, "What brought you here today?" can elicit more detailed and personal responses than closed questions that require a yes or no answer.

Reflective listening is another critical technique for information retrieval in MI. It involves the clinician listening attentively to the client and then reflecting back what they have heard. This not only demonstrates that the clinician is listening and understands the client's perspective but also encourages the client to continue sharing and exploring their thoughts and feelings. For example, if a client expresses frustration about their lack of progress, the clinician might reflect, "It sounds like you're really disappointed with where things are right now."

These techniques, when used skillfully, create a dialogue that is client-centered and focused on exploring the client's own reasons for change. The clinician's role is not to direct the client, but rather to facilitate a conversation that helps the client uncover their own motivations and barriers to change. This approach respects the client's autonomy and acknowledges their capacity for self-directed change, making MI a powerful tool in the therapeutic process.

Types of Questions to Ask in Motivational Interviewing

The effectiveness of Motivational Interviewing largely hinges on the types of questions asked by the clinician. These questions are designed to encourage clients to express themselves freely and explore their thoughts and feelings. Open-ended questions are foundational in MI as they invite expansive responses and encourage clients to delve deeper into their experiences. For instance, instead of asking, "Do you feel stressed at work?" (a closed question), a more effective MI approach would be, "Can you tell me about your experiences at work?" This open-ended inquiry allows clients to explore and articulate their feelings and perspectives in depth.

Apart from open-ended questions, reflective and probing questions are also essential in MI. Reflective questions serve to mirror the clients' statements, enabling them to hear their own thoughts and feelings, which often provides new insights. Probing questions, on the other hand, are used to delve deeper into specific areas that the client has mentioned, helping to uncover underlying issues or motivations.

The clinician must be adept at using these various types of questions judiciously to maintain the flow of conversation and ensure that the client feels heard and understood. The goal is to create a dialogue that empowers the client to explore their own motivations and barriers to change in a supportive and non-judgmental environment.

Maintaining Flow in Questioning

Maintaining a natural and productive flow in questioning is a skill that is central to effective MI. It involves a delicate balance of guiding the conversation while allowing it to evolve organically based on the client's responses. To achieve this, clinicians must be adept at listening and responding in a way that encourages the client to continue sharing their thoughts and feelings. This might involve using transitional phrases, maintaining appropriate pacing, and revisiting important points to ensure a comprehensive understanding.

Navigating the conversation requires sensitivity to the client's verbal and non-verbal cues. The clinician should be able to gauge when to probe deeper and when to give the client space to reflect. The aim is to create a conversational rhythm that feels natural and engaging, encouraging the client to open up and explore their experiences in depth.

Building and Maintaining Rapport

Building and maintaining rapport with clients is an indispensable aspect of MI. This process begins with the clinician demonstrating genuine empathy, respect, and interest in the client's experiences. Establishing rapport involves not just what is said, but also how it is said. Non-verbal communication, such as maintaining appropriate eye contact, nodding, and adopting an open body posture, plays a significant role in establishing a connection with the client.

Throughout the therapeutic relationship, it is vital for the clinician to consistently demonstrate understanding and acceptance. This includes being attentive to the client's feelings and perspectives, acknowledging their struggles without judgment, and validating their experiences. Consistent empathy and understanding are crucial in maintaining rapport and creating a safe space where the client feels valued and understood.

Professional Insights on Motivational Interviewing

For professionals utilizing Motivational Interviewing, it is essential to understand that MI is more than just a set of techniques; it is an approach that embodies a particular philosophy about the nature of change and the therapeutic relationship. It requires clinicians to adopt a collaborative stance, viewing the client as the expert in their own life and respecting their autonomy and capacity for self-directed change.

Professionals need to be skilled in balancing directive and reflective approaches, adapting their style to align with the client's readiness for change. This requires sensitivity, patience, and the ability to listen actively and respond empathetically. Training and ongoing practice in MI are crucial for professionals to hone these skills and effectively incorporate MI into their therapeutic repertoire.

Incorporating MI into clinical practice involves a commitment to client-centered care, where the client's values, preferences, and strengths are at the forefront of the therapeutic process. It challenges clinicians to move away from a prescriptive approach, instead fostering a therapeutic environment that encourages clients to explore and resolve their ambivalence about change. This approach has been shown to be effective across a range of behavioural issues and settings, making it a valuable tool in the arsenal of mental health professionals.

Conclusion

In conclusion, focusing on Motivational Interviewing Techniques (MIT), has provided an extensive exploration of this client-centered, empathetic, and effective approach to counselling. We delved into the intricacies of preparing for a clinical assessment, highlighting the importance of comprehensive understanding, environment setting, and establishing clear objectives. The discussion emphasized the necessity of gathering key information during assessments, covering current symptoms, mental health history, substance use, physical health, and family history.

Week 10

The Workbook

Week Ten

MOTIVATIONAL INTERVIEWING
TECHNIQUES

In the preceding week, we delved deeply into the realm of psychosocial stressors, exploring their multifaceted nature, the impact they have on mental health, and the array of strategies to address them effectively. The insights gained from this exploration are not only crucial for understanding the complexities of mental health but also lay a strong foundation for our next topic: Motivational Interviewing Techniques (MIT).

As we embarked Week Ten, our focus shifted to a crucial skill set in the mental health professional's toolkit: Motivational Interviewing Techniques. This week, we unravelled the nuanced art of conducting effective clinical assessments, emphasizing the vital role of MIT in facilitating client engagement, enhancing the accuracy of our assessments, and optimizing therapeutic outcomes.

We started by addressing the preparation phase for a clinical assessment, recognizing that thorough preparation is the bedrock of any successful client interaction. Building upon this, we explored the essential information that must be gathered during an assessment, ensuring that no critical aspect of the client's mental health is overlooked.

A pivotal skill we aimed to refine in the ability to make rapid yet informed decisions in crisis situations, a capability that is often called upon in mental health settings. The ability to assess an individual and decide on the need for immediate intervention or hospitalization within a limited timeframe is a testament to a clinician's expertise and adaptability.

Central to this week's exploration was a comprehensive understanding of Motivational Interviewing Techniques. MIT is not just a method but an approach that embodies empathy, collaboration, and respect for the client's autonomy. We dissected the components of MIT, discuss its implementation, and reflected on how these techniques could transform the dynamics of client interactions.

Furthermore, we discussed the art of effective questioning and information retrieval, a skill that is pivotal in uncovering the underlying factors contributing to a client's mental health status. The maintenance of a seamless flow in questioning and the ability to build and sustain rapport with clients was an additional focal points that enhanced our proficiency in conducting assessments.

Day 1: Preparing for a Clinical Assessment

1. **Reflective Exercise 1**: Discuss the key steps and considerations in preparing for a clinical assessment.

_____

_____

_____

_____

_____

_____

2. **Reflective Exercise 2**: Reflect on a clinical assessment preparation that was particularly effective or challenging.

_____

_____

_____

_____

_____

_____

3. **Guided Activity**: Create a checklist or guide for preparing for a clinical assessment, covering all necessary steps.

_____

_____

_____

_____

_____

_____

Day 2: Essential Information in Assessment

1. **Reflective Exercise 1**: Identify the essential information that must be covered in assessing someone and why.

_____

_____

_____

_____

_____

_____

2. **Reflective Exercise 2**: Consider a case where crucial information was missed during assessment. What was the impact?

_____

_____

_____

_____

_____

_____

3. **Guided Activity**: Develop a template or form ensuring all critical information is covered in an assessment.

_____
_____
_____
_____
_____
_____

Day 3: Quick Assessment and Decision Making

1. **Reflective Exercise 1**: Reflect on how to assess an individual quickly and decide on apprehension or hospitalization.

_____
_____
_____
_____
_____
_____

2. **Reflective Exercise 2**: Recall a situation where you had to make a quick assessment decision. What were the key factors?

_____
_____
_____
_____
_____
_____

3. **Guided Activity**: Create a flowchart or decision tree for making quick assessment decisions in crisis situations.

_____

_____

_____

_____

_____

_____

Day 4: Understanding and Implementing Motivational Interviewing Techniques

1. **Reflective Exercise 1**: Discuss your understanding of Motivational Interviewing Techniques and their benefits.

_____

_____

_____

_____

_____

_____

2. **Reflective Exercise 2**: Reflect on a case where implementing MIT altered the course of a client's treatment or outcome.

_____

_____

_____

_____

_____

3. **Guided Activity**: Practice MIT with a colleague or through role-play and record observations and insights.

_____

_____

_____

_____

_____

_____

Day 5: Effective Information Retrieval

1. **Reflective Exercise 1**: Identify strategies for effectively retrieving information during clinical assessments.

_____

_____

_____

_____

_____

2. **Reflective Exercise 2**: Reflect on a situation where effective information retrieval led to a significant insight or breakthrough.

_____

_____

_____

_____

3. **Guided Activity**: Develop a list of open-ended questions that can facilitate better information retrieval.

_____

_____

_____

_____

_____

_____

Day 6: Questioning Techniques and Maintaining Flow

1. **Reflective Exercise 1**: Discuss the types of questions that are most effective in clinical assessments and why.

_____

_____

_____

_____

_____

_____

2. **Reflective Exercise 2**: Reflect on how to maintain a flow in asking questions without overwhelming or leading the patient/client.

_____

_____

_____

_____

3. **Guided Activity**: Role-play a client interview focusing on smooth transitions between different types of questions.

_____

_____

_____

_____

_____

_____

Day 7: Rapport Building and Professional Knowledge about MIT

1. **Reflective Exercise 1**: Share techniques for maintaining rapport with a patient/client during clinical assessments.

_____

_____

_____

_____

_____

_____

2. **Reflective Exercise 2**: Reflect on a situation where rapport building significantly impacted a clinical assessment.

_____

_____

_____

_____

_____

_____

3. **Guided Activity**: Prepare a brief educational presentation or material for colleagues on the essential aspects of MIT and rapport building in clinical assessments.

_____

_____

_____

_____

_____

Week 11

MENTAL HEALTH PROFESSIONAL
REPORT

"Mental Health Professional Report Writing," an essential skill for documenting and communicating clinical findings and treatment plans. This chapter will guide participants through the process of creating effective and comprehensive mental health reports.

Mental health clinical reports are essential documents that provide a comprehensive overview of a patient's/client's mental health status. These reports serve multiple purposes, including aiding in diagnosis, guiding treatment plans, and communicating vital information to other healthcare professionals. A well-structured clinical report is a critical tool in mental health care, as it consolidates patient/client information into a format that is accessible and useful for ongoing treatment and care coordination (American Psychiatric Association, 2013).

Components of a Mental Health Clinical Report

A thorough mental health clinical report must include several key components to ensure that it provides a complete picture of the patient's/client's mental health:

1. **Patient/Client Identification and Demographic Information**: This includes basic information such as the patient's/client's name, age, gender, and contact details.

2. **Reason for Referral and Source of Referral**: Clearly stating why the patient/client was referred for assessment and who made the referral is crucial for understanding the context of the report.

3. **Clinical History and Background Information**: This encompasses the patient's/client's psychological history, including previous diagnoses, treatments, and family mental health history, which is vital for a comprehensive assessment (Kaplan & Sadock, 2015).

4. **Assessment Findings**: This should detail the results of clinical evaluations, including observations and any standardized test results.

5. **Diagnosis or Clinical Impressions**: Based on the assessment, this section provides the clinician's professional interpretation of the patient's/client's condition.

6. **Treatment Recommendations and Plan**: Here, the report outlines suggested treatment approaches and goals, tailored to the patient's/client's specific needs.

7. **Prognosis and Disposition Outcomes**: This section gives an informed prediction about the likely course and outcome of the patient's/client's condition.

8. **Confidentiality and Ethical Considerations**: The report must address how patient/client confidentiality and ethical standards are upheld.

The creation of a mental health clinical report requires meticulous attention to detail and a comprehensive understanding of the patient's/client's condition and context. It is a fundamental component in effective mental health care and treatment planning.

Writing a Mental Health/Psychological Report

When writing a mental health or psychological report, it is important to maintain a structure that is clear and comprehensive. The report should begin with an introduction that outlines the purpose of the assessment and the methods used.

This is followed by a detailed presentation of the findings, which should include both quantitative data, such as test scores, and qualitative observations. The language used in the report should be professional and free of jargon to ensure that it is accessible to all readers, including those who may not have a background in mental health. It is crucial to present the information in a manner that is unbiased and based solely on the evidence gathered during the assessment.

The report should also include a section on diagnosis, where the clinician provides their professional opinion based on the DSM-V criteria or other relevant diagnostic tools. This diagnosis should be supported by evidence from the assessment findings. The treatment recommendations section should outline the proposed plan for addressing the identified issues, including specific therapies, medications, or other interventions. These recommendations should be based on the latest research and best practices in the field. The prognosis section should give an overview of the expected outcomes of the proposed treatment plan, including any potential challenges or areas of concern. Clinicians, Therapists, Counsellors and other professionals should not be giving a formal diagnosis to a patient/client unless they are a registered Physician or Psychologist, however their report should give the reader the impression as to the possible diagnosis.

Finally, the report should conclude with a summary that reiterates the key findings and recommendations, providing a clear and concise overview of the patient's/client's mental health status. Throughout the report, it is essential to maintain a focus on the patient's/client's wellbeing and to ensure that all information is presented in a manner that respects their privacy and dignity.

Professional Considerations in Report Writing

When writing a mental health clinical report, professionals need to be aware of several key considerations. Firstly, it is essential to adhere to ethical guidelines, including maintaining patient/client confidentiality and obtaining informed consent for any assessments or treatments. The report should be written with an awareness of the legal implications of the findings, especially if the report is to be used in a legal context.

Clinicians must also be mindful of the cultural and social context of the patient/client, ensuring that the report is sensitive to these factors. It is important to use evidence-based practices when conducting assessments and making recommendations, referencing current research and guidelines in the field.

The report should be tailored to its intended audience, whether that be other healthcare professionals, insurance companies, or legal representatives, using language and terminology that is appropriate for that audience. Accuracy is paramount in report writing, with all information needing to be double-checked for correctness.

The report should also be comprehensive, covering all relevant aspects of the patient's/client's mental health, including addictions, suicide/self-harm, hospitalizations, medication use, and family psychological history. Timeliness is another important factor, with reports needing to be completed and submitted in a timely manner to ensure that they are useful in the patient's/client's ongoing care. Finally, clinicians should engage in ongoing professional development to ensure that their report writing skills remain up-to-date with the latest standards and practices in the field.

Sample report for a GP, Psychiatrist and or other professional health care workers.

PRESENTATION

The patient/client is a 34-year-old Caucasian female who presented for therapy today seeking support for her feelings of "dizziness" and anxiety. She was diagnosed with anxiety in 2003. The patient/client appeared fearful and teary-eyed. She sought support from you.

CHIEF COMPLAINT

The patient/client reported that she came seeking support because she has been feeling dizzy, "faintish," and has difficulty breathing since the start of this weekend. She expressed fearfulness as she is unsure of the cause. Although she initially considered a thyroid issue, she ruled out all possible medical causes.

PARTICIPATING EVENTS

The patient/client explained that she began experiencing difficulty breathing since last Saturday while at her trailer up north with her husband and two children. She sought medical attention at Collingwood Hospital, where she was diagnosed with hyperventilation and discharged without medication. She was advised to seek psychotherapy support. Today, she returned with similar symptoms and believes it may be more medically related than anxiety. She mentioned feeling a "choking sensation" around her neck, possibly related to her thyroid condition.

COMMENTS

The patient/client denied experiencing any neurovegetative symptoms of anxiety, such as changes in eating habits or sleeping patterns, except for disruptive sleep last night.

PSYCHIATRIC HISTORY

The patient/client was formally diagnosed with anxiety in 2003 and was prescribed Paxil and Citalopram. She denied any history of psychiatric hospitalization and currently receives support from her GP and Narcotics Anonymous.

MEDICAL HISTORY

No medical history reported.

SUBSTANCE ABUSE

The patient/client reported past cocaine, marijuana, and alcohol use for over a year and entered a recovery program in 2005. She has been abstinent from substance use for over six years.

SUICIDE HISTORY

None reported.

PSYCHOSOCIAL HISTORY

The patient is a 34-year-old Caucasian female happily married for over 15 years with two children aged 13 and 15 years. She currently works full-time at CML Health Care. No further information provided.

CRIMINAL HISTORY

None reported

IMPRESSIONS/FORMULATION/PROBLEM LIST

The patient/client presented today reporting feelings of dizziness and faintness. She has had a fulfilling summer with her family and enjoys her job without financial concerns. Despite no apparent stressors related to anxiety, she expressed concerns about her thyroid. She denies self-harm or suicidal ideations, and there are no safety concerns. The cause of her symptoms leading to therapy remains unknown. Further ongoing therapy support is recommended.

CONSULT WITH PSYCHIATRIST

No consultation with a psychiatrist was deemed necessary as the patient/client's current situation appears to be more situational.

DISPOSITION/RECOMMENDATION

It is recommended that the patient/client continue with ongoing therapy support. Additionally, she may benefit from a medical check-up, including blood work, to further investigate her symptoms.

Conclusion

In conclusion, mental health clinical report writing is a complex task that requires a high level of skill and expertise. The report must be clear, comprehensive, and accurate, providing a detailed overview of the patient's/client's mental health status and needs. It should be based on a thorough assessment and adhere to the latest research and ethical guidelines. The report plays a crucial role in the patient's/client's treatment and care, informing decisions made by healthcare professionals and other stakeholders. As such, it is a vital component of the mental health care process, and one that requires careful attention and professionalism from clinicians.

Week 11

The Workbook

Week Eleven

MENTAL HEALTH PROFESSIONAL
REPORT

In the preceding week of our comprehensive mental health program, we delved deeply into the nuanced techniques of Motivational Interviewing (MIT). Our journey through the complexities of MIT underscored its pivotal role in clinical assessments, enhancing our understanding of patient/client engagement and communication strategies. The week was a profound exploration of the art and science of extracting valuable information through a patient/client-centered approach, reinforcing the idea that successful clinical outcomes are often rooted in effective communication. We learned how to craft questions that unearth crucial insights, maintain a steady flow in our dialogues, and, most importantly, build and sustain rapport with our clients. This knowledge is not just a cornerstone of clinical excellence but a testament to our commitment to understanding and empathizing with our patient's/client's experiences.

As we transitioned into Week Eleven, our focus shifted to another essential skill set in the realm of mental health care; the art of crafting a Mental Health Professional Report. This week, we have embarked on a meticulous exploration of what constitutes a mental health clinical report, unraveling its complexities and understanding its critical role in patient/client care. The mental health clinical report is not merely a document; it is a comprehensive narrative that encapsulates the patient's/client's journey, presenting a holistic view of their mental health status. It serves multiple purposes: it is a tool for communication among healthcare professionals, a record for future reference, and, significantly, a roadmap that guides the course of treatment and patient/client care.

Our exploration began by deciphering the fundamental elements that make up a mental health clinical report. This understanding is crucial as it lays the groundwork for creating reports that are not only informative but also resonate with clarity and purpose. We explored the essential components that must be included in such a report – from patient/client history and current presentation to the assessments conducted and the interpretations drawn from them. Each element of the report serves a unique function, contributing to a comprehensive understanding of the patient's/client's condition.

Following this foundational understanding, we were engaged in the practical aspects of writing a mental health or psychological report. This exercise transcended beyond the mere act of writing; it shed light of how to encapsulate complex clinical information into a coherent, concise, and ethically sound document. We addressed the challenges of maintaining objectivity while weaving in the subjective experiences of our patients/clients, striking a balance between detailed descriptions and the necessity of brevity.

Clarity and conciseness in report writing are skills that we honed, recognizing that these attributes are paramount in ensuring that the reports we produce are not only readable but also actionable. The ability to distill complex clinical data and observations into clear, concise language is a skill that enhances the utility of our reports, making them valuable tools for all stakeholders involved in patient/client care.

Ethical considerations in report writing have been a focal point of our learning this week. We delved into the ethical responsibilities that underpin our documentation processes, ensuring that our reports uphold the highest standards of professional integrity. This included respecting patient/client confidentiality, accurately representing clinical findings, and avoiding biases that may colour our interpretations.

Integration of data and observations has been another critical area of focus. We explored the art of synthesizing diverse pieces of information – from clinical assessments and test results to patient/client narratives and behavioural observations. This synthesis is pivotal in creating a report that is not just a collection of data points but a cohesive narrative that provides a clear understanding of the patient's/client's mental health status.

Finally, turned our attention to our professional development in the domain of report writing. Reflecting on our own experiences and identifying areas for growth, we set actionable goals to enhance our skills in clinical report writing. This self-reflective process is not just about improving our ability to write reports; it's about committing to ongoing professional development and excellence in our practice.

Day 1: Understanding Mental Health Clinical Reports

1. **Reflective Exercise 1**: Discuss your understanding of what a mental health clinical report is and its purpose.

_____

_____

_____

_____

_____

2. **Reflective Exercise 2**: Reflect on how a well-prepared clinical report has impacted patient/client care or treatment outcomes.

_____

_____

_____

_____

_____

3. **Guided Activity**: Research different formats and styles of mental health clinical reports for various settings.

_____

_____

_____

_____

_____

_____

Day 2: Essential Components of a Clinical Report

1. **Reflective Exercise 1**: Identify and discuss the essential components that must be included in a mental health clinical report.

_____

_____

_____

_____

_____

_____

2. **Reflective Exercise 2**: Consider a clinical report you have written or read. Reflect on what was particularly effective or lacking.

_____

_____

_____

_____

_____

_____

3. **Guided Activity**: Create a checklist or template that includes all necessary elements of a mental health clinical report.

_____

_____

_____

_____

_____

_____

Day 3: Writing a Mental Health/Psychological Report

1. **Reflective Exercise 1**: Discuss the process and best practices for writing a mental health or psychological report.

_____

_____

_____

_____

_____

_____

2. **Reflective Exercise 2**: Reflect on a challenging experience you had while writing a clinical report. What did you learn?

_____

_____

_____

_____

_____

_____

3. **Guided Activity**: Write a mock psychological report based on a hypothetical case, incorporating best practices.

_____

_____

_____

_____

_____

_____

Day 4: Clarity and Conciseness in Report Writing

1. **Reflective Exercise 1**: Explore the importance of clarity and conciseness in mental health report writing.

_____

_____

_____

_____

_____

2. **Reflective Exercise 2**: Analyze a past report you have written or encountered, assessing its clarity and conciseness.

_____

_____

_____

_____

_____

3. **Guided Activity**: Practice rewriting a section of a report to improve its clarity and conciseness.

_____

_____

_____

_____

_____

Day 5: Ethical Considerations in Report Writing

1. **Reflective Exercise 1**: Discuss the ethical considerations and responsibilities involved in writing a mental health report.

_____

_____

_____

_____

_____

_____

2. **Reflective Exercise 2**: Reflect on a situation where ethical considerations significantly influenced a clinical report.

_____

_____

_____

_____

_____

_____

3. **Guided Activity**: Review a sample report and identify any potential ethical issues or areas for improvement.

_____

_____

_____

_____

_____

_____

Day 6: Integrating Data and Observations

1. **Reflective Exercise 1**: Explore the importance of integrating various data and observations in a clinical report.

_____

_____

_____

_____

_____

_____

2. **Reflective Exercise 2**: Reflect on how the integration of different types of data (e.g., test results, observations) can impact a report's effectiveness.

_____

_____

_____

_____

_____

_____

3. **Guided Activity**: Analyze a case study and practice integrating diverse types of data into a coherent report. Use sample report for a GP, Psychiatrist and or other professional health care workers.

_____

_____

_____

_____

_____

_____

Day 7: Professional Development in Report Writing

1. **Reflective Exercise 1**: Discuss what mental health professionals need to know about report writing and its role in professional development.

2. **Reflective Exercise 2**: Reflect on your personal growth areas in report writing and how you plan to address them.

3. **Guided Activity**: Develop a personal action plan or set goals for enhancing your skills in clinical report writing.

Week 12

QUESTIONS *AND* ANSWERS

"Questions and Answers," is designed as an interactive and informative session that addresses a variety of important and often complex topics in the field of mental health. The focus is on clarifying key legal, ethical, and practical aspects of mental health care and treatment.

Confidentiality and Its Limits in Mental Health Care

In the realm of mental health care, patient/client confidentiality is a cornerstone of professional practice, ensuring trust and openness in the therapeutic relationship. However, there are specific circumstances under Canadian law where confidentiality may be legally and ethically breached. According to the Canadian Psychological Association (CPA), confidentiality can be broken when there is an imminent risk of harm to the patient/client or others, when abuse of a vulnerable individual (such as a child or elder) is suspected, or when legal requirements, such as court orders, mandate disclosure. These exceptions are critical for ensuring safety and adherence to legal obligations while maintaining the integrity of the therapeutic relationship as much as possible.

Comparing PHIPA and HIPAA

The Personal Health Information Protection Act (PHIPA) in Canada and the Health Insurance Portability and Accountability Act (HIPAA) in the United States both aim to protect patients'/clients' health information, but they differ in scope and application. PHIPA, as outlined by the Ontario Ministry of Health, governs how personal health information is managed within the province of Ontario, emphasizing patient/client consent and the principle of least information for use in healthcare. In contrast, HIPAA, a federal law in the U.S., sets standards for the protection of health information across the country, focusing on the privacy and security of medical records and other personal health information. While both acts share the goal of protecting personal health information, their implementation and jurisdictional scope differ, reflecting the specific legal and healthcare environments of Canada and the U.S.

Health Care Forms in Mental Health

In mental health care, various forms are utilized to facilitate and document patient/client care and treatment, particularly in involuntary treatment scenarios. For instance, in Ontario, Form 1 under the Mental Health Act authorizes a physician to conduct a psychiatric assessment of an individual for up to 72 hours if there are reasonable grounds to believe the person poses a risk to themselves or others.

Form 2, on the other hand, is a court order from the Justice of The Peace or a Judge for a psychiatric examination when someone believes another person is exhibiting signs of a mental disorder that could result in harm.

A Form 3 (*Certificate of Involuntary Admission*) under the Ontario Mental Health Act is completed when a patient/client meets the criteria for involuntary admission. The expiry date on the Form 3 is always 13 days later (or "two weeks minus a day"), not 14 days, as the day the form was filled is included. A Form 3 permits only the physical detention of an individual; it does not authorize physicians to administer treatment without the patient's/client's consent. Emergency treatment is permitted only in cases of significant risk for self-harm, harm to others, or the inability to care for oneself. Therefore, if there is no emergency and a patient/client declines treatment, physicians must respect the patient's/client's wishes, even if the patient/client is under a Form 3. A patient/client may be placed on a Form 3 but later found to be capable. If determined capable by the consent and capacity board, a patient/client retains the right to refuse treatment. In such cases, only a finding of incapacity under the Health Care Consent Act (HCCA) would allow physicians to treat the patient/client. For instance, a patient/client with schizophrenia may be placed under a Form 3 due to the risk of serious physical impairment but still possess the capacity to refuse antipsychotic medication. Notably, a physician cannot sign both a Form 1 and a Form 3 for the same patient/client; a separate assessment by a different physician is required to determine involuntary admission, providing the patient/client with a second opinion assessment.

Finally, a Form 4 (*Certificate of Renewal*) under the Ontario Mental Health Act is issued when a patient/client continues to meet the criteria for involuntary admission after a Form 3 expires. The first Form 4 lasts one month (add one month, minus a day) The second Form 4 lasts two months (add two months, minus a day) The third Form 4 lasts three months (add three months, minus a day) Rights advice must be provided, along with a Form 30 each time, and the patient/client can appeal each time. The initial certificate of involuntary admission, or Form 3, is legally limited to a two-week duration; the initial certificate of renewal, or Form 4, is limited to an additional one month; the second certificate of renewal is limited to an additional two months; and the third certificate of renewal is limited to an additional three months. Following the third certificate of renewal, if the patient/client still meets the criteria for involuntary admission, the patient/client will then become subject to a certificate of continuation or Form 4A. A first and any subsequent certificate of continuation is also valid for a period of three months.

These forms, governed by provincial laws, are essential for ensuring the safety and rights of individuals with mental health issues, while also providing a legal framework for mental health professionals to administer necessary care.

Criteria for Apprehension under Section 17 of the MHA

Under Section 17 of the Mental Health Act (MHA) in Canada, specific criteria must be met for the apprehension and involuntary admission of an individual into a mental health facility. These criteria are designed to ensure that involuntary admission is used only when necessary and with due regard for the individual's rights and safety. The key criteria include:

1. **Reasonable Cause:** There must be reasonable cause to believe that the individual is suffering from a mental disorder that seriously impairs their ability to react appropriately to their environment or to associate with others.
2. **Risk of Harm:** The individual must pose a substantial risk of harm to themselves or others, or be at risk of serious physical impairment.
3. **Necessity for Treatment:** The condition of the individual is such that they require treatment in a mental health facility and cannot be admitted voluntarily. Patient/Client may be breaching their Community Treatment Order (CTO).
4. **Lack of Suitability for Less Restrictive Means:** There are no less restrictive ways to provide the necessary treatment or care.

It's important for healthcare professionals to understand and apply these criteria carefully, respecting legal obligations and patient/client rights. Involuntary admission is a significant intervention, and it's crucial to balance the need for treatment with respect for individual autonomy.

Patient/Client Rights on Forms

Patients/Clients placed under various mental health forms, such as Form 1 (Application for Psychiatric Assessment) or Form 3 (Certificate of Involuntary Admission), have specific rights under Canadian law. These rights include:

1. **Right to Information:** Patients/Client have the right to be informed about the reasons for their admission, the duration of the form, and their legal rights, including the right to legal counsel.
2. **Right to Appeal:** Patients/Client have the right to challenge their involuntary admission through a Review Board or court.
3. **Right to Treatment:** Patients/Client have the right to receive appropriate care and treatment for their mental health condition.
4. **Right to Privacy and Dignity:** The treatment must be carried out with respect for the patient's/client's privacy and dignity.

Healthcare professionals must ensure these rights are upheld and communicated clearly to the patient/client. Understanding and respecting these rights is fundamental to ethical and effective mental health care.

Right to Refuse Medications

In Canada, patients/clients have the right to refuse medication as part of their healthcare. This right is underpinned by the principles of consent and autonomy in medical treatment. Key aspects include:

1. **Informed Consent:** Patients/Clients must be provided with all relevant information about the proposed medication, including its benefits, risks, and alternatives, to make an informed decision.
2. **Competence:** Patients/Clients must be deemed competent to make decisions about their treatment. If a patient/client is found to be incompetent, decisions about medication may be made by a substitute decision-maker.
3. **Exceptional Circumstances:** In certain situations, such as emergencies or under specific legal provisions like those outlined in the MHA, medication may be administered without consent.

The right to refuse medication is a critical component of patient/client-centered care. Healthcare professionals need to navigate this right with sensitivity and respect, ensuring that patients/clients are fully informed, and their decisions are respected.

Multiaxial System of Diagnosis in DSM-V

The transition in the Diagnostic and Statistical Manual of Mental Disorders from the multiaxial system in previous editions to its current format in DSM-V represents a pivotal change in the approach to mental health diagnosis. This evolution signifies a shift towards a more integrated perspective, where mental health conditions are considered in conjunction with overall physical health, emphasizing the interplay between psychological and physiological factors.

The significance of this change lies in its potential to facilitate a more comprehensive understanding of an individual's health status, providing a broader context for mental health conditions within the general spectrum of health and illness.

The study by Regier, Kuhl, and Kupfer (2013) in the American Journal of Psychiatry provides an insightful exploration into the reasoning and implications behind these modifications in the DSM-V. It highlights the aim of aligning the manual more closely with the International Classification of Diseases (ICD), thereby enhancing the uniformity and coherence of mental health diagnoses across various healthcare settings.

Formulating a Crisis or Action Plan

The development of a crisis or action plan is a critical element in mental health care, particularly for individuals at risk of a crisis. This process, which necessitates a collaborative effort between the patient/client and the mental health professional, involves identifying potential triggers, warning signs, and effective coping strategies that the patient/client can employ in times of distress. The plan should be personalized, taking into account the unique circumstances and needs of the patient/client. It serves as a roadmap for both the patient/client and healthcare providers, outlining clear steps to be taken in the event of a crisis, thereby potentially averting emergency situations.

A key aspect of this planning process is its emphasis on patient/client empowerment and self-management. Stanley and Brown's (2012) research in the Journal of Psychiatric Practice emphasizes the efficacy of such proactive planning in reducing the risk of suicide and enhancing patient/client safety. Their work underscores the importance of involving patients/clients in their own care, thereby improving the likelihood of successful intervention during critical periods.

The Importance of Psychoeducation

Psychoeducation is a cornerstone in the treatment and management of mental health conditions. It entails providing patients/clients and their families with comprehensive information about mental disorders, treatment options, coping mechanisms, and strategies for managing daily challenges.

This educational approach is instrumental in demystifying mental health conditions, reducing stigma, and fostering a supportive environment for recovery. By equipping patients/clients with knowledge about their conditions, psychoeducation enhances their ability to participate actively in their treatment process, leading to improved adherence to treatment plans and overall better outcomes.

The impact of psychoeducation is not just limited to patient/client empowerment; it also extends to family members and caregivers, providing them with the tools and understanding necessary to support their loved ones effectively. Xia, Merinder, and Belgamwar's (2011) study in the Journal of Clinical Psychiatry illustrates the positive outcomes associated with psychoeducation in the context of schizophrenia, highlighting its role in reducing relapse rates and improving the quality of life for patients/clients.

Conclusion

This session has provided a comprehensive overview of essential aspects of mental health care, ranging from the nuanced changes in the DSM-V to the critical role of crisis action plans and psychoeducation.

The adaptations in the DSM-V reflect an evolving understanding of mental health, emphasizing a more integrated approach to diagnosis and treatment. The formulation of crisis action plans is fundamental in pre-emptive care, empowering patients/clients and ensuring their safety.

Furthermore, psychoeducation emerges as a pivotal tool in enhancing patient/client and caregiver understanding, promoting active involvement in treatment, and facilitating better outcomes. As mental health professionals, it is imperative to stay informed and adapt to new methodologies and research findings, such as those discussed in the aforementioned studies, to provide the highest standard of care to our patients/clients.

Week 12

The Workbook

Week Twelve

QUESTIONS *AND* ANSWERS

Welcome to the final week of our comprehensive program, a pivotal week that navigates the intricate realm of mental health through a series of crucial questions and answers. This week has been dedicated to unraveling some of the most pressing queries and dilemmas faced by mental health professionals. Our journey this week delved deep into the ethical, legal, and practical aspects of mental health care, ensuring a thorough understanding and skillful handling of various situations that arise in professional practice.

As mental health professionals, we are often at the crossroads of making critical decisions, balancing ethical considerations, legal mandates, and the well-being of our clients. This week, we confronted these challenges head-on, dissecting complex scenarios and providing clear, concise, and practical answers. Each day was structured to address key questions, fostering a robust understanding and equipping you with the tools to navigate the often murky waters of mental health practice.

We explored the boundaries of confidentiality, a cornerstone of therapeutic relationships. Understanding when and how these boundaries can be ethically and legally traversed is crucial for effective and responsible practice. Our discussions and activities were designed to crystallize the principles that guide these decisions, ensuring that the sanctity of client trust is upheld while also adhering to legal obligations and ethical mandates.

Comparative analysis forms were an essential part of this week, particularly in understanding the nuances between Canada's PHIPA and the US's HIPAA. This comparison not only highlights international differences in handling patient/client information but also underscored the importance of being cognizant of these variations, especially in an increasingly interconnected world.

Day 1: Confidentiality in Mental Health

1. **Reflective Exercise 1**: Discuss situations where patient/client confidentiality can be ethically or legally broken.

_____

_____

_____

_____

_____

_____

2. **Reflective Exercise 2**: Reflect on a case where confidentiality was a key concern. How was it handled?

_____

_____

_____

_____

_____

_____

3. **Guided Activity**: Research and summarize the legal and ethical guidelines on confidentiality in mental health.

_____

_____

_____

_____

_____

Day 2: Comparing PHIPA and HIPAA

1. **Reflective Exercise 1**: Explore the key differences between Canada's PHIPA and the US's HIPAA.

_____

_____

_____

_____

_____

_____

2. **Reflective Exercise 2**: Reflect on how understanding these differences is important for international practice or collaboration.

_____

_____

_____

_____

_____

_____

3. **Guided Activity**: Create a comparison chart highlighting the main differences between PHIPA and HIPAA.

_____

_____

_____

_____

_____

_____

Day 3: Understanding Health Care Forms

1. **Reflective Exercise 1**: Discuss the different health care forms (e.g., forms 1, 2, 4) and their purposes.

_____

_____

_____

_____

_____

_____

2. **Reflective Exercise 2**: Reflect on a situation where you had to use one of these forms. What were the challenges?

_____

_____

_____

_____

_____

_____

3. **Guided Activity**: Develop summaries or fact sheets explaining the use and implications of these different forms.

_____

_____

_____

_____

_____

_____

Day 4: Criteria for Apprehension under Section 17 of the MHA

1. **Reflective Exercise 1**: Discuss the criteria for apprehension under Section 17 of the Mental Health Act.

_____

_____

_____

_____

_____

_____

2. **Reflective Exercise 2**: Reflect on a case where Section 17 was invoked. What did you learn from this experience?

_____

_____

_____

_____

_____

_____

3. **Guided Activity**: Create a scenario-based exercise to practice applying the criteria of Section 17.

_____

_____

_____

_____

_____

_____

Day 5: Patient/Client Rights on a Form

1. **Reflective Exercise 1**: Explore the rights of patients/clients when they are placed on a mental health form.

_____

_____

_____

_____

_____

_____

2. **Reflective Exercise 2**: Reflect on how you ensure patient/client rights are respected and communicated when using these forms.

_____

_____

_____

_____

_____

_____

3. **Guided Activity**: Prepare an informational guide for patients/clients about their rights when placed on a mental health form.

_____

_____

_____

_____

_____

_____

Day 6: Patient's/Client's Right to Refuse Medication

1. **Reflective Exercise 1**: Discuss the implications of a patient's/client's right to refuse medications in mental health care.

_____

_____

_____

_____

_____

_____

2. **Reflective Exercise 2**: Reflect on a situation where a patient/client refused medication. How was it handled?

_____

_____

_____

_____

_____

_____

3. **Guided Activity**: Develop a policy or guideline for handling medication refusal in a mental health setting.

_____

_____

_____

_____

_____

_____

Day 7: Crisis Plan, Psychoeducation, and DSM-V

1. **Reflective Exercise 1**: Explore the multiaxial system of diagnosis in the DSM-V and its practical implications.

_____

_____

_____

_____

_____

_____

2. **Reflective Exercise 2**: Discuss how to formulate an effective crisis or action plan for a patient/client.

_____

_____

_____

_____

_____

_____

3. **Reflective Exercise 3**: Reflect on the importance of psychoeducation in mental health treatment.

_____

_____

_____

_____

_____

_____

4. **Guided Activity**: Create a sample crisis plan for a hypothetical patient/client and a psychoeducational tool to accompany it.

_____

_____

_____

_____

_____

_____

CONCLUSION

As we reach the conclusion of this workbook, it's essential to reflect on the journey we've undertaken together. Over the past twelve weeks, we've explored a wide range of topics in mental health, each critical to understanding the complex tapestry of human psychology and wellbeing. Our journey began with the fundamental distinctions between mental health and mental illnesses, setting the groundwork for deeper explorations.

We delved into specific mental health conditions like anxiety and mood disorders, discussing their characteristics, impacts, and treatment approaches. By doing so, we aimed to demystify these conditions, fostering a better understanding and compassion for those who experience them. Our exploration then extended to the realms of psychosis and personality disorders, where we unravelled the intricate details of these challenging conditions.

In addressing addictions, we confronted a pervasive issue that affects individuals and societies globally. Our discussion was not just about the mechanics of addiction but also about empathetic approaches to treatment and recovery. The segment on emotional wounds and trauma shed light on the profound impacts of life experiences on mental health, emphasizing the importance of healing and support.

Turning our attention to psychosocial stressors, we recognized the significant role of environmental and social factors in mental health. This understanding is crucial in developing resilience and coping strategies in the face of life's challenges. The week dedicated to assessment tools highlighted the importance of accurate and ethical evaluation methods in mental health care, providing a foundation for effective treatment.

In our discussion on motivational interviewing techniques, we equipped you with skills to engage clients in a meaningful and transformative way. This approach underscores the importance of empathy and active listening in mental health practice. Our exploration of mental health professional report writing emphasized the significance of clear, concise, and accurate documentation, a skill vital for all mental health practitioners.

Finally, our last week focused on addressing various questions and providing clarifications, ensuring that you have a well-rounded understanding of the vast field of mental health. This cumulative knowledge equips you not only with theoretical insights but also with practical tools to make a difference in your own life and in the lives of others.

As you move forward, remember that mental health is a continuous journey, both personally and professionally. The learning doesn't stop with the closing of this workbook. In fact, this is just the beginning. You are encouraged to keep exploring, questioning, and learning. Stay updated with the latest research and developments in the field. Attend workshops, join professional networks, and engage in ongoing education to enhance your understanding and skills.

Moreover, apply the knowledge you've gained here in your everyday life. Whether you're a mental health professional, a student, or someone interested in personal growth, the insights from this workbook can guide your interactions and self-awareness. Be an advocate for mental health in your community. Share what you've learned, offer support to those in need, and contribute to building a more informed and compassionate society.

Remember, mental health is not just the absence of illness but a state of overall wellbeing. It's about finding balance, building resilience, and nurturing connections. Take care of yourself, both physically and mentally. Practice self-care, seek support when needed, and extend that same compassion to others.

Lastly, we'd like to express our gratitude for your commitment and effort throughout this workbook. Your engagement and willingness to learn are commendable. We hope this workbook has been a valuable resource, providing you with insights and tools to navigate the complex world of mental health.

Remember, every step you take in understanding and addressing mental health issues makes a difference. Keep learning, keep growing, and keep making an impact.

REFERENCES

Addington, J., Cadenhead, K. S., Cannon, T. D., Cornblatt, B., McGlashan, T. H., Perkins, D. O. & Woods, S. W. (2007). North American Prodrome Longitudinal Study: A collaborative multisite approach to prodromal schizophrenia research. Schizophrenia Bulletin, 33(3), 665-672. doi:10.1093/schbul/sbl075

American Psychiatric Association. (2013). Diagnostic and statistical manual of mental disorders (5th ed.). Arlington, VA: American Psychiatric Publishing.

Bandelow, B., & Michaelis, S. (2015). Epidemiology of anxiety disorders in the 21st century. Dialogues in Clinical Neuroscience, 17(3), 327–335.

Belmaker, R. H., & Agam, G. (2008). Major depressive disorder. New England Journal of Medicine, 358(1), 55-68. https://doi.org/10.1056/NEJMra073096

Bernstein, D. P., Stein, J. A., Newcomb, M. D., Walker, E., Pogge, D., Ahluvalia, T. & Zule, W. (2003). Development and validation of a brief screening version of the Childhood Trauma Questionnaire. Child Abuse & Neglect, 27(2), 169-190.

Bertolote, J., & McGorry, P. (2005). Early intervention and recovery for young people with early psychosis: consensus statement. The British Journal of Psychiatry Supplement, 48, s116-s119.

Briere, J., & Scott, C. (2006). Principles of trauma therapy: A guide to symptoms, evaluation, and treatment. Sage Publications.

Bradley, R., Greene, J., Russ, E., Dutra, L., & Westen, D. (2005). A multidimensional meta-analysis of psychotherapy for PTSD. American Journal of Psychiatry, 162(2), 214-227.

Bremner, J. D., Randall, P., Scott, T. M., Capelli, S., Delaney, R., McCarthy, G., & Charney, D. S. (1995). MRI-based measurement of hippocampal volume in patients with combat-related posttraumatic stress disorder. American Journal of Psychiatry, 152(7), 973-981.

Burns, T., Catty, J., Dash, M., Roberts, C., Lockwood, A., & Marshall, M. (2007). Use of intensive case management to reduce time in hospital in people with severe mental illness: systematic review and meta-regression. BMJ, 335(7615), 336.

Canadian Mental Health Association. (2021). Fast Facts about Mental Illness. Retrieved from https://cmha.ca/fast-facts-about-mental-illness

Carpenter, J. K., Andrews, L. A., Witcraft, S. M., Powers, M. B., Smits, J. A., & Hofmann, S. G. (2018). Cognitive Behavioral Therapy for Anxiety and Related Disorders: A

Meta-Analysis of Randomized Placebo-Controlled Trials. Depression and Anxiety, 35(6), 502–514. DOI: 10.1002/da.22728.

Cloitre, M., Stolbach, B. C., Herman, J. L., van der Kolk, B., Pynoos, R., Wang, J., & Petkova, E. (2009). A developmental approach to complex PTSD: Childhood and adult cumulative trauma as predictors of symptom complexity. Journal of Traumatic Stress, 22(5), 399-408.

Cohen, S., Janicki-Deverts, D., & Miller, G. E. (2007). Psychological stress and disease. JAMA, 298(14), 1685-1687. https://doi.org/10.1001/jama.298.14.1685

Cowen, P. J., & Browning, M. (2015). What has serotonin to do with depression? World Psychiatry, 14(2), 158–160. https://doi.org/10.1002/wps.20229

Correll, C. U., Galling, B., Pawar, A., Krivko, A., Bonetto, C., Ruggeri, M., ... & Nielsen, J. (2016). Comparison of Early Intervention Services vs Treatment as Usual for Early-Phase Psychosis: A Systematic Review, Meta-analysis, and Meta-regression. JAMA Psychiatry, 73(6), 555-565. doi:10.1001/jamapsychiatry.2016.0091

Craske, M. G., Stein, M. B., Eley, T. C., Milad, M. R., Holmes, A., Rapee, R. M., & Wittchen, H.-U. (2017). Anxiety disorders. Nature Reviews Disease Primers, 3, 17024. DOI:10.1038/nrdp.2017.24.
Goldman, D., Oroszi, G., & Ducci, F. (2005). The genetics of addictions: uncovering the genes. Nature Reviews Genetics, 6(7), 521-532. doi:10.1038/nrg1635

Groth-Marnat, G. (2009). Handbook of Psychological Assessment. Wiley.

Hofmann, S. G., Asnaani, A., Vonk, I. J., Sawyer, A. T., & Fang, A. (2012). The Efficacy of Cognitive Behavioral Therapy: A Review of Meta-analyses. Cognitive Therapy and Research, 36(5), 427–440. DOI: 10.1007/s10608-012-9476-1.

Kalivas, P. W., & Volkow, N. D. (2005). The neural basis of addiction: A pathology of motivation and choice. The American Journal of Psychiatry, 162(8), 1403-1413. doi:10.1176/appi.ajp.162.8.1403

Kaplan, H. I., & Sadock, B. J. (2015). Kaplan and Sadock's synopsis of psychiatry: Behavioral sciences/clinical psychiatry (11th ed.). Philadelphia: Wolters Kluwer.

Kearney, D. J., McDermott, K., Malte, C., Martinez, M., & Simpson, T. L. (2013). Association of participation in a mindfulness program with measures of PTSD, depression and quality of life in a veteran sample. Journal of Clinical Psychology, 69(1), 101-116.

Kelly, J. F., Magill, M., & Stout, R. L. (2009). How do people recover from alcohol dependence? A systematic review of the research on mechanisms of behavior change in Alcoholics Anonymous. Addiction Research & Theory, 17(3), 236-259. doi:10.1080/16066350902770433

Khoury, B., Sharma, M., Rush, S. E., & Fournier, C. (2015). Mindfulness-based stress reduction for healthy individuals: A meta-analysis. Journal of Psychosomatic Research, 78(6), 519-528. https://doi.org/10.1016/j.jpsychores.2015.03.009

Lebow, H. I. (2021, July 2). How does PTSD affect the brain? the physical effects of trauma. Psych Central. Retrieved March 27, 2023, from https://psychcentral.com/ptsd/the-

science-behind-ptsd-symptoms-how-trauma-changes-the-
brain?slot_pos=article_1&utm_source=Sailthru+Email&utm_medium=Email&utm_campa
ign=weekly&utm_content=2023-01-
25&apid=&rvid=a61d340305c0c28b12afbde3d63c30d3d9ae4dc9399ad609dd609e81b511
9a9e   combat-related   PTSD.
sciencedirect.com/science/article/pii/S2213158218301190

Leucht, S , Cipriani, A., Spineli, L., Mavridis, D., Orey, D., Richter, F. & Davis, J. M. (2013).
    Comparative efficacy and tolerability of 15 antipsychotic drugs in schizophrenia: a
    multiple-treatments meta-analysis. The Lancet, 382(9896), 951-962.

Levy, K. N. (2005). The implications of attachment theory and research for understanding
    borderline personality disorder. Development and Psychopathology, 17(4), 959-
    986.

Linehan, M. M., Armstrong, H. E., Suarez, A., Allmon, D., & Heard, H. L. (1991). Cognitive-
    behavioral treatment of chronically parasuicidal borderline patients. Archives of
    General Psychiatry, 48(12), 1060-1064.

Linehan, M. M. (1993). Cognitive-behavioral treatment of borderline personality disorder.
    Guilford Press.

Linszen, D. H., Dingemans, P. M., & Lenoir, M. E. (1994). Cannabis abuse and the course of
    recent-onset schizophrenic disorders. Archives of General Psychiatry, 51(4), 273-
    279. doi:10.1001/archpsyc.1994.03950040017002

Lüscher, C., & Malenka, R. C. (2011). Drug-evoked synaptic plasticity in addiction: from
    molecular changes to circuit remodeling. Neuron, 69(4), 650-663.
    doi:10.1016/j.neuron.2011.02.017

Maron, E., & Nutt, D. (2017). Biological markers of generalized anxiety disorder. Dialogues
    in Clinical Neuroscience, 19(2), 147–158.

McHugh, R. K., Hearon, B. A., & Otto, M. W. (2010). Cognitive-behavioral therapy for
    substance use disorders. The Psychiatric Clinics of North America, 33(3), 511-525.
    doi:10.1016/j.psc.2010.04.012

McLellan, A. T., Kushner, H., Metzger, D., Peters, R., Smith, I., Grissom, G. & Argeriou, M.
    (1992). The fifth edition of the Addiction Severity Index. Journal of Substance
    Abuse Treatment, 9(3), 199-213.

Michaels M. H. (2006). Ethical considerations in writing psychological assessment
    reports. Journal of clinical psychology, 62(1), 47–58.
    https://doi.org/10.1002/jclp.20199

Miller, W. R., & Rollnick, S. (2013). Motivational interviewing: Helping people change (3rd
    ed.). Guilford Press.

Monroe, S. M., & Harkness, K. L. (2005). Life stress, the "kindling" hypothesis, and the
    recurrence of depression: Considerations from a life stress perspective.
    Psychological Review, 112(2), 417-445. https://doi.org/10.1037/0033-
    295X.112.2.417

National Institute on Drug Abuse. (2020). Drugs, brains, and behavior: The science of addiction. Retrieved from https://www.drugabuse.gov/publications/drugs-brains-behavior-science-addiction

Overall, J. E., & Gorham, D. R. (1962). The Brief Psychiatric Rating Scale. Psychological Reports, 10(3), 799-812. doi:10.2466/pr0.1962.10.3.799

Pennebaker, J. W., & Seagal, J. D. (1999). Forming a story: The health benefits of narrative. Journal of Clinical Psychology, 55(10), 1243-1254.

Pharoah, F., Mari, J., Rathbone, J., & Wong, W. (2010). Family intervention for schizophrenia. Cochrane Database of Systematic Reviews, (12).

Public Health Agency of Canada. (2016). The Chief Public Health Officer's Report on the State of Public Health in Canada 2016: A Focus on Family Violence in Canada.

Regier, D. A., Kuhl, E. A., & Kupfer, D. J. (2013). The DSM-5: Classification and criteria changes. American Journal of Psychiatry, 170(6), 593-602.

Remes, O., Brayne, C., van der Linde, R., & Lafortune, L. (2016). A systematic review of reviews on the prevalence of anxiety disorders in adult populations. Brain and Behavior, 6(7), e00497. DOI: 10.1002/brb3.497.

Ronningstam, E. (2005). Identifying and understanding the narcissistic personality. Oxford University Press

Stanley, B., & Brown, G. K. (2012). Safety planning intervention: A brief intervention to mitigate suicide risk. Journal of Psychiatric Practice, 18(2), 113-121

Substance Abuse and Mental Health Services Administration. (2020). Medication-Assisted Treatment (MAT). Retrieved from https://www.samhsa.gov/medication-assisted-treatment

Sullivan, P. F., Neale, M. C., & Kendler, K. S. (2000). Genetic epidemiology of major depression: Review and meta-analysis. The American Journal of Psychiatry, 157(10), 1552-1562.

Tandon, R., Nasrallah, H. A., & Keshavan, M. S. (2008). Schizophrenia, "just the facts" 4. Clinical features and conceptualization. Schizophrenia Research, 102(1-3), 1-18.

Torgersen, S., Lygren, S., Oien, P. A., Skre, I., Onstad, S., Edvardsen, J., & Kringlen, E. (2000). A twin study of personality disorders. Comprehensive Psychiatry, 41(6), 416-425.

Trzepacz, P. T., & Baker, R. W. (1993). The psychiatric mental status examination. Oxford University Press.

Volkow, N. D., Koob, G. F., & McLellan, A. T. (2016). Neurobiologic advances from the brain disease model of addiction. The New England Journal of Medicine, 374(4), 363-371. doi:10.1056/NEJMra1511480

Volkow, N. D., Frieden, T. R., Hyde, P. S., & Cha, S. S. (2014). Medication-assisted therapies — Tackling the opioid-overdose epidemic. The New England Journal of Medicine, 370(22), 2063-2066. doi:10.1056/NEJMp1402780

Volkow, N. D., Frieden, T. R., Hyde, P. S., & Cha, S. S. (2014). Medication-assisted therapies — Tackling the opioid-overdose epidemic. The New England Journal of Medicine, 370(22), 2063-2066. doi:10.1056/NEJMp1402780

Volkow, N. D., Wang, G. J., Fowler, J. S., & Tomasi, D. (2012). Addiction circuitry in the human brain. Annual Review of Pharmacology and Toxicology, 52, 321-336. doi:10.1146/annurev-pharmtox-010611-134625

Weathers, F. W., Blake, D. D., Schnurr, P. P., Kaloupek, D. G., Marx, B. P., & Keane, T. M. (2013). The Clinician-Administered PTSD Scale for DSM-5 (CAPS-5). Interview available from the National Center for PTSD at www.ptsd.va.gov.

World Health Organization. (2018). Mental health: strengthening our response.

Wykes, T., Steel, C., Everitt, B., & Tarrier, N. (2008). Cognitive behavior therapy for schizophrenia: effect sizes, clinical models, and methodological rigor. Schizophrenia Bulletin, 34(3), 523-537.

Xia, J., Merinder, L. B., & Belgamwar, M. R. (2011). Psychoeducation for schizophrenia. Cochrane Database of Systematic Reviews, (6), CD002831Stein, M. B., & Stein, D. J. (2008). Social anxiety disorder. The Lancet, 371(9618), 1115-1125. DOI:10.1016/S0140-6736(08)60488-2.

Zimmerman, M., & Spitzer, R. L. (2012). Diagnosis in the assessment of depressive disorder: The use of rating scales and structured interviews. Journal of Clinical Psychiatry, 73(9), e19. DOI:10.4088/JCP.11075tx7c